# Quentin Tarantino
# and Philosophy

# Popular Culture and Philosophy®
## Series Editor: George A. Reisch

Popular Culture and Philosophy®

# Quentin Tarantino and Philosophy

*How to Philosophize with a Pair of Pliers and a Blowtorch*

Edited by

RICHARD GREENE

and

K. SILEM MOHAMMAD

OPEN COURT
Chicago and La Salle, Illinois

*Volume 29 in the series, Popular Culture and Philosophy*®, edited by George A. Reisch

**To order books from Open Court, call 1-800-815-2280, or visit our website at www.opencourtbooks.com**.

Open Court Publishing Company is a division of Carus Publishing Company.

**Library of Congress Cataloging-in-Publication Data**

Quentin Tarantino and philosophy : how to philosophize with a pair of pliers and a blowtorch / edited by Richard Greene and K. Silem Mohammad.

    p. cm. — (Popular culture and philosophy ; v. 29)
    Summary: "A collection of essays that addresses philosophical aspects of the films of Quentin Tarantino, focusing on topics in ethics, aesthetics, metaphysics, language, and cultural identity"— Provided by publisher.
    Includes bibliographical references and index.
    ISBN-13: 978-0-8126-9634-9 (trade paper : alk. paper)
    ISBN-10: 0-8126-9634-4 (trade paper : alk. paper)
    1. Tarantino, Quentin—Criticism and interpretation. I. Greene, Richard, 1961- II. Mohammad, K. Silem.
PN1998.3.T358Q46 2007
791.4302'33092—dc22

                                                        2007035105

*For Dan, Lisa, Lori, and Wade*

# Contents

# Acknowledgments

Working on this project has been a pleasure, in no small part because of the many fine folks who have assisted us along the way. In particular a debt of gratitude is owed to George Reisch and David Ramsay Steele at Open Court, the contributors to this volume (each of whom agreed to produce top-notch work at a highly accelerated pace), and our respective academic departments at Southern Oregon University and Weber State University (Terry Thiel has been particularly supportive). Finally, we'd like to thank those students, friends, and colleagues with whom we've had fruitful and rewarding conversations on various aspects of Tarantino's work in relation to philosophical themes.

# Let's Go to Woik

Quentin Tarantino makes the most aggressively reflexive films in contemporary mainstream cinema. From dialogue about Madonna, Lee Marvin, and the Fantastic Four in 1992's *Reservoir Dogs*, to the Seventies retro pastiche of 2007's *Death Proof*, Tarantino's movies are obsessed with pointing self-consciously to their own knowledge of the position they occupy among the disposable (but infinitely recyclable) entertainments of American pop culture.

Are movies like *Pulp Fiction* and *Kill Bill* themselves disposable, or do they rise above the cultural products to which they refer? Are these movies truly thoughtful, or are they merely elaborate superficial gestures that generate the illusion of theoretical depth through a canny wink? Does Tarantino have a philosophy? Has he ever even read any?

Although Tarantino has a quick and often wicked intellect, his favored genres—the gangster flick, the martial arts epic, the "B" car-chase movie—are ones whose familiar conventions emphasize action over contemplation. One of his pet strategies is to undermine these conventions by indulging in extended sequences of dialogue about topics external to the plot: topics as trivial as fast food and as ponderous as divine will.

Even in the latter case, however, the terms in which "heavy" issues are discussed are often borrowed from mass media representations. The contract killer Jules in *Pulp Fiction* announces his intentions of renouncing worldly pursuits to "walk the earth, like Caine in *Kung Fu*"; the Asian philosophy in *Kill Bill* is no more intensive than what anyone could absorb from watching a few Bruce Lee films. Although an acknowledgment of the conspicuous talkiness of Tarantino's scripts may be key to philosophical readings such as the ones gathered in this volume, whatever significant insights there are to be gleaned from such readings will most likely not come out of straightforward interpretations of "content."

This is not to say that Tarantino is unconcerned with questions relevant to traditional philosophical practice. Three particular fascinations recur throughout the body of his work:

- the irony of ethical standards in criminal society (and perhaps contemporary capitalism in general);

- the difficulty of sorting out received information from direct experience; and

- the slippery role of language as a determinant of identity and value.

At different points in *Pulp Fiction*, hit man Vincent Vega pontificates on the immorality of damaging another man's car (in the middle of scoring some heroin from his dealer), acknowledges that the gossip he's repeating is "not a fact" but "just what I heard," and gives an elaborate account of the different names given to fast-food hamburgers in France. Taken by themselves, these are amusing bits of colorful dialogue; perceived as a pattern throughout fifteen years' worth of films, they begin to suggest that Tarantino has some interesting philosophical preoccupations.

Nonetheless, much of Tarantino's appeal to intelligent viewers has less to do with any positive beliefs or values evidenced in the films than with their exemplifying a larger trend in pop culture towards texts (movies, music, books, images) that flaunt their knowing enmeshment in and dependence on a multi-layered network of other texts. Part of what makes these films interesting to look at is the way they themselves "look at" prior films, sometimes through explicit repetitions (for example, the visual quoting in *Pulp Fiction* of set design from John Boorman's 1967 *Point Blank*). This play of surfaces renders any literal-minded consideration of, say, criminal ethics in Tarantino's work problematic: the commentor must deal not only with what the characters think, say, and do, but with the way in which they recall similar characters who have thought and said and done it all before. This presents a formidable challenge to the writers in Quentin Tarantino and Philosophy, a challenge they take on from various angles and with different intellectual modes of attack.

Enough preambling; "Let's go to woik," as Joe Cabot would say. Sit back and enjoy the ride, confident in the knowledge that despite the sudden eruptions of random and bloody violence that happen without warning in Tarantino's world, you are safe with this volume's gang of thinkers behind the wheel—unless your name happens to be Marvin.

# PART I

## "Everybody Be Cool, This Is a Robbery"

### Aesthetics, Pop, Style

# 1

# Tarantino's Films: What Are They About and What Can We Learn from Them?

BRUCE RUSSELL

In the *Symposium* (line 221e), Alcibiades says of Socrates that he couches his arguments in the most mundane terms, talking of pack asses, blacksmiths, shoemakers, tanners, and the like, and "he always seems to be saying the same old thing in just the same old way." On the surface this seems mistaken since Socrates talked about piety, justice, courage and a host of different issues including the "Why be moral?" question. But we could see all of Socrates's inquiries directed toward just one question: "How should we live?"

## What Are Tarantino's Films About?

In an interview in 2004, Quentin Tarantino said: "I'm kind of making the same movie again and again and again." On the surface this seems mistaken since his films are about a jewelry heist gone bad (*Reservoir Dogs*), the lives of two "low-rent hitmen" and their boss (*Pulp Fiction*), a woman's clever plot to take money from a dealer in illegal arms (*Jackie Brown*), and a woman's revenge against her ex-lover (*Kill Bill*). What do these films have in common?

The first and most obvious thing is that in all the films something goes awry in the life of some cruel, brutal, and violent man due to the intentional actions, or negligence, of other people. In *Reservoir Dogs* the jewelry heist goes bad because an undercover cop has tipped off the police. In *Pulp Fiction*, some young criminals have failed to pay off their debt to a crime boss, and later a prizefighter double-crosses him. In *Jackie Brown*, two

3

employees of the arms dealer Ordell Robbie (Samuel L. Jackson) are caught by the police in illegal activities, which makes the gunrunner fear that they will testify against him in order to go free or receive a reduced sentence. In *Kill Bill*, the girlfriend (Uma Thurman) of Bill (David Carradine), the leader of a group of paid assassins, tries to start a new life away from him by marrying the owner of a small-town used record store, which makes Bill very angry.

The second thing that these films have in common is that brutal and violent behavior ensues as a result of what goes awry in the lives of the violent men. As Bill says at the end of *Kill Bill Volume 2*, "I'm a killer. I'm a murdering bastard, you know that, and there are consequences to breaking the heart of a murdering bastard." Once the rage of these violent and brutal men is unleashed, people suffer terribly, innocents and non-innocents alike. Often the actions of these men ultimately result in their own deaths, but not always. Jules Winnfield (Samuel L. Jackson) and his boss, Marsellus Wallace (Ving Rhames), do not die in *Pulp Fiction*, and neither does Mr. Pink (Steve Buscemi) in *Reservoir Dogs*, though he is arrested. What happens to the good (or at least, better) people in the films is often a matter of luck, both good and bad, and the cruel intentions of the angry, evil men. Butch Coolidge (Bruce Willis) is lucky that one of the hitmen out to get him is on the toilet when he returns to his apartment to retrieve a treasured watch. The undercover cop Mr. Orange (Tim Roth) in *Reservoir Dogs* is unlucky that the woman from whom he tries to commandeer a car carries a handgun in her glove compartment and uses it to shoot him in the stomach. Jackie Brown (Pam Grier) is lucky that Ordell's associate, Louis Gara (Robert De Niro), is not more curious as to why bail bondsman Max Cherry (Robert Forster), who knows Jackie, is at the dress shop with her when a money pick-up is to take place. She is also lucky that Louis kills Melanie (Bridget Fonda), Ordell's girlfriend, because that prevents her from telling Ordell what she knows about the pick-up.

Finally, what is common to all the Tarantino films is that there are glimpses of compassion and morality among the tough, cruel, and immoral people that populate them. Mr. White (Harvey Keitel) takes pity on Mr. Orange when Orange is shot. He holds Orange's hand, and encourages and comforts him, as he drives toward the warehouse where he is to rendezvous with the others involved in the heist. When they arrive, Mr. White holds Orange in his arms, again comforts and encourages him, and assures him that he is not going to die. After a night out on the town with Marsellus's girlfriend Mia (Uma Thurman), Vincent Vega (John Travolta), one of the "low-rent hitmen" in *Pulp Fiction*, tells himself in her bathroom that he must have just one drink and then go home because he is facing a moral test involving loyalty and "being loyal is important." In that same film Jules Winnfield spares the couple who try to rob the restaurant, and its patrons, in the coffee shop where he is having breakfast with Vincent Vega. In *Kill Bill Volume 1*, Bill tells Elle Driver (Daryl Hannah) not to kill "The Bride" (Uma Thurman) because to "sneak into her room in the night like a filthy rat and kill her in her sleep" would "lower us." In that same film The Bride and Vernita Green (Vivica A. Fox) postpone their fight to the death when Vernita's daughter comes home from school so the daughter won't be traumatized. In addition, he clearly loves his daughter and is very gentle with her.

The "good guys" also sometimes show great courage and a strong moral sense in Tarantino's films. In *Pulp Fiction*, Butch goes back to save Marsellus, the crime boss who is trying to kill him, from some perverts who want to rape and torture him. Butch does this because he thinks it is the right thing to do and even though he thereby puts himself back at risk. In *Reservoir Dogs* the cop that Mr. Blonde (Michael Madsen) has captured refuses to disclose that Mr. Orange is the undercover cop that tipped off the police, even under severe torture and when facing the prospect of immolation. So within a sea of brutality and immorality, Tarantino still depicts some people, both good and bad, acting admirably and displaying admirable human emotions.

### Is There Anything About Human Nature We Can Learn From Tarantino's Films?

Can we learn anything about what real people are like by watching Tarantino's films? We might learn that Quentin Tarantino thinks that cruel and evil people eventually get their comeuppance (even Marsellus gets raped and beaten, though not killed, and Mr. Pink gets arrested) unless they have had a change of heart (like Jules Winnfield in *Pulp Fiction* and Beatrix Kiddo in *Kill Bill*). Even that is doubtful, however, for there is no reason to think that the message a series of films delivers reflects what the writer and filmmaker thinks about real-life people. He might just be offering a point of view that he does not share.

Further, even if Tarantino did hold that view about real people, would his films help to establish its truth? Noel Carroll argues that no one could justify the view that humans are taller than monkeys through a fictional film that shows them to be taller.[1] So how could a fictional film justify the view that it is usually not in the long-term self-interest for bad people to act badly? Such a film might remind us of something that we have forgotten, or that is not at the forefront of our minds, that would support such a view. Perhaps it reminds us of statistics we have read that support the idea that the "bad guys" often get caught by the authorities, or suffer at the hands of other "bad guys." But just as likely, it will remind us of instances that we have read of in the newspaper about some bad guy getting his comeuppance, and that sort of anecdotal evidence will not support the view that crime doesn't pay. Such evidence does not include cases where the bad guys get away with their heinous crimes and so does not constitute a representative sample.

Perhaps Tarantino's films can impart some practical advice: think twice before you engage in cruel and brutal behavior, for it may not pay in the end; the suffering you ultimately experience, or your loss of life, will outweigh whatever satisfaction revenge, and the feeling that justice has been served, might afford you. But even here, how good that advice is depends on the probability in the real world that you will be caught, or feel remorse for, your evil deeds. That all the bad guys in Tarantino's films pay in some way for their evil deeds is not evidence that all, or even most, of the bad guys in real life do the same.

## What of Philosophical Relevance Is there in Tarantino's Films?

But is there some philosophical point that Tarantino's films make or question that they raise? As I've argued elsewhere, a film without explicit philosophical argumentation cannot justify

---

[1] Noel Carroll, "Introduction to Part VIII: Film and Knowledge," in Noel Carroll and Jinhee Choi,eds., *Philosophy of Film and Motion Pictures* (Malden: Blackwell, 2006), p. 381.

some general philosophical proposition.[2] Examples can serve as counterexamples to philosophical theses, but they cannot by themselves establish such theses. A film of some philosophical dialogue could establish some general philosophical theses, but, of course, it would contain explicit argumentation. And fictional films can raise philosophical questions, as, say, *The Matrix* does, but this is different from justifying some general philosophical proposition. These general points apply, of course, to Tarantino's films, which, I will argue, raise philosophical questions about miracles and morality.

In *Pulp Fiction*, there is what might pass for a philosophical conversation between Vincent Vega and Jules Winnfield about the nature and justification of a miracle. One of the young men from whom Jules and Vincent come to collect steps out of a bathroom and fires six shots at them from a "hand cannon," at point-blank range, without hitting either of them. Jules thinks that their not being hit was a result of "divine intervention"; Vincent, that it was "luck." Later at a restaurant Vincent and Jules discuss what happened earlier that day. When Jules asks Vincent what a miracle is, he responds, "When God makes the impossible possible, but this morning I don't think qualifies."

Generally, philosophers think of a miracle as a violation of a law of nature, like the law of gravity, by a divine being. So a miracle would involve God's making something *actual* that is physically, though not logically, impossible. There is no contradiction in the idea of water's turning into wine, unlike in the idea of a circle's being square, but its turning into wine is contrary to the laws of chemistry. So if some divine being really turned water into wine, or brought someone who was really dead back to life, that would be a miracle.

The question of whether it's reasonable to believe a miracle has occurred will be the question of whether it is reasonable to believe that an event has been caused by a divine being that is contrary to what is really a law of nature, not to what is just thought to be such a law. Even if Vincent and Jules agree on the definition of a miracle, they do not agree on whether what

---

[2] Bruce Russell, "The Philosophical Limits of Film," *Film and Philosophy* (Special Edition on Woody Allen, 2000), pp. 163–67; reprinted in *Philosophy of Film and Motion Pictures*, pp. 387–390. Also see my article, "There Can Be Little Philosophy in Fictional Film," forthcoming in *Film and Philosophy*.

happened to them was a miracle. Vincent thinks it was just a "freak occurrence." Jules thinks it was a miracle, but does not seem interested in addressing the question of whether it is *reasonable to believe* that it was or was not. In the restaurant he says to Vincent,

> You're judging this shit the wrong way. I mean, it could be God stopped the fucking bullets or he changed Coke to Pepsi, he found my fucking car keys. You don't judge shit like this based on merit. Now whether or not what we experienced was an according-to-Hoyle miracle is insignificant. What is significant is that I felt the touch of God. God got involved.

Jules thinks he has had a religious experience, and he is not interested in judging what happened on its "merit," that is, on the evidence. So the discussion in *Pulp Fiction* of the nature of a miracle, and whether it can be reasonable to believe one has occurred, is brief and insufficient to justify some view about the nature of miracles and whether a belief in them can be reasonable. For instance, it does not seem that a miracle must be caused by God. Couldn't the Devil, if he exists, do something evil that violates a law of nature (such as make a roof tile fall off and kill a person who walks below), and wouldn't that be a miracle? And, contra Hume (at least when evidence is restricted to testimony), could it ever be rational to believe that a miracle has occurred, and so rational for someone in Jules's position to believe that their not getting shot was a miracle? Or is Vincent justified in thinking they were just lucky not to be shot? *Pulp Fiction* raises these questions but does nothing to answer them.

The other interesting philosophical question it raises concerns what it is to have a morality, even if it is not a sound or correct one. Vincent seems to have a morality, one that prizes loyalty and that contains a view of punishment that permits throwing someone off a fourth-floor balcony because he has massaged your wife's feet and killing someone who has keyed your car.

There are various views about what it is for a person to have a morality, and on all of them Vincent has one. John Stuart Mill said the following about wrongness:

> We do not call anything wrong unless we mean to imply that a person ought to be punished in some way or other for doing it—if not

by law, by the opinion of his fellow creatures; if not by opinion, by the reproaches of his own conscience.[3]

More recently Allan Gibbard has modified Mill's account and come up with the following account of blameworthiness:

> To say a person is to blame for doing something is to say that it is rational for him to feel guilty for having done it, and for others to be angry with him for having done it.[4]

For Gibbard, to say a person does wrong is, roughly, to say he would be to blame for doing the action if he did not have a legitimate excuse stemming from his psychological state. So, for instance, because of my grief I may be blameless in speaking rudely to someone who has offered condolences for my loss, even though what I did was wrong because it would be rational for me to feel guilty, and for others to be angry with me, for having spoken rudely if I were in a normal state of mind (p. 44). Not only grief, but ignorance, anger, depression, extreme hunger, or extreme fatigue can sometimes excuse. In general, it is sometimes thought that compulsion and some types of ignorance are what can excuse.

Gibbard's account of wrongness differs from Mill's in that he thinks that it does not follow that we think an act wrong if we think legal sanctions should be imposed on its performance. His example involves illegal parking where we might think a fine should be imposed, but we needn't think such parking is morally wrong (p. 41).

Suppose that to have a morality is to be disposed to make moral judgments, that is, to make moral judgments if the appropriate circumstances arise. Then on Gibbard's account of morality, Vincent will have a morality just in case he is disposed to judge that the person who performs some act should feel guilty, and others should be angry with him, if that person acts in a certain way, say, massaging someone's feet without her husband's permission or keying someone's car, and he has no excuse

---

[3] John Stuart Mill, *Utilitarianism*, Chapter 5, paragraph 14, second edition (Indianapolis: Hackett, 2001).
[4] Alan Gibbard, *Wise Choices, Apt Feelings* (Cambridge, Massachusetts: Harvard University Press), pp. 42, 45.

stemming from his state of mind. Though Vincent never explicitly says anything that implies certain people should feel guilty
and others should be angry with them for what they have done,
his endorsing his boss's throwing someone off the balcony and
the killing of people who key other people's cars strongly suggests that he would judge that certain agents should feel guilty
about, and others be angry with, what they have done. So, on
the Mill-Gibbard account of judgments of moral wrongness, it is
reasonable to think that Vincent has a morality since it is reasonable to think he is disposed to make what, on those
accounts, are moral judgments.

There is another important account of what it is to make a
moral judgment, and derivatively, of what it is to have a morality. R.M. Hare was a well-known twentieth-century philosopher
who argued that moral judgments are universal prescriptions.
They are universal because we must judge exactly similar cases
in the same way. If I judge some action good or obligatory
because it has certain features, say, it involves keeping a
promise and helps relieve terrible suffering, then I must judge
any act just like that in the same way. But non-moral, descrip-
tive judgments also have this feature. If I judge some object to
be a cube or red, then I must judge any object just like those to
be a cube and red. When I judge that someone ought to do
something, however, I am recommending its performance, and
committing myself to condemning its non-performance and to
my acting that way in similar circumstances. In short, I am not
attributing a property to an action when I say it ought to be
done, but prescribing its performance. Similarly, when I say
some action is wrong I am not describing it, but proscribing its
performance, or prescribing its non-performance. Because
morality requires us to prescribe similarly in *all* similar cases,
Hare calls his view *universal* prescriptivism. So on this view
moral judgments are universal prescriptions.

On Hare's account of the nature of moral judgments, Vincent
makes moral judgments. Surely, Vincent would condemn anyone who massaged the feet of another man's wife without that
man's permission and anyone who keyed someone else's car,
not just the particular man who massaged the feet of his boss's
wife nor the one who keyed Vincent's car. So when Vincent
judges that what those particular men did was wrong, on Hare's
view he is making moral judgments. Again, to have a morality

is to be disposed to make moral judgments. So given Hare's account of moral judgments, Vincent has a morality. So on both Hare's and the Mill-Gibbard accounts of moral judgments, it seems that Vincent makes moral judgments and has a morality.

There's a third approach to what it is to make a moral judgment exemplified in the writings of David Hume. Hume writes:

> When a man denominates another his *enemy*, his *rival*, his *antagonist*, his *adversary*, he is understood to speak the language of self-love, and to express sentiments peculiar to himself and arising from his particular circumstances and situation. But when he bestows on any man the epithets of *vicious* or *odious* or *depraved*, he then speaks another language, and expresses sentiments in which he expects all his audience to concur with him. He must here, therefore, depart from his private and particular situation and must choose a point of view common to him with others; he must move some universal principle of the human frame and touch a string to which all mankind have an accord and symphony.[5]

For Hume, a person makes a moral judgment if and only if that person judges from an impartial standpoint on the basis of sentiments that he *expects* everyone to share. We do not have enough evidence in *Pulp Fiction* to tell whether Vincent adopts the relevant impartial standpoint, but his arguing with his friend Jules about whether his boss should have thrown someone off a balcony at least shows that he "expresses sentiments in which he *expects* . . . his audience to concur with him."

Still, even if Vincent has a morality, it does not follow that it is a sound or correct one. Whether it is would require a good argument for some account of what a sound or correct morality is and an application of that account to Vincent's own morality. No such argument, or even discussion of what makes a morality sound or correct, is to be found in any of Tarantino's films. So while his films raise interesting philosophical questions about what it is to have a morality, and a correct one, and what the nature of a miracle is, and whether it is possible for us to ever rationally believe one has occurred, they do not actually discuss these issues in any depth.

---

[5] David Hume, *Enquiry Concerning the Principles of Morals* in *Hume's Moral and Political Philosophy* (New York: Hafner, 1948), p. 252.

Like most fictional films, Tarantino's at most raise philosophical questions and so can do a useful job, even if they do not provide support for any philosophical position.

# 2
# Stuntman Mike, Simulation, and Sadism in *Death Proof*

AARON C. ANDERSON

Quentin Tarantino's *Death Proof* (2007): four female characters, four cruel deaths, four short sequences. Several rapid close-ups of the girls rocking out to a radio song, a quick point-of-view shot from the front seat of the girls's car. Stuntman Mike (Kurt Russell) pulls his headlights on. Slow motion as the vehicles collide. Slow motion as the bodies of Mike's victims tear apart in repeated collisions of metal, rubber, bone, flesh. In an instant, the human body forcibly joins with technology and pleasure fuses with pain.

*Death Proof* hinges on its two major car crash sequences. The first crash, repeated four times, marks a distinct shift in genre, setting, and cast. You could easily argue that *Death Proof* fuses two very different films, the first part of the film being largely a horror movie and the last part an action movie. Tarantino frontloads the structure of this film with combinations of horror with action, reality with fiction, pleasure with pain, and references with nonreferences.

The U.S. theatrical cut of *Death Proof* opens with a disclaimer from "The Management": "The following film may contain one or more missing film REELS. Sorry for the inconvenience." From the beginning, with this sort-of-comical warning, Tarantino draws attention to his film's status *as a film*, as a constructed work of fiction, and as a "simulation." Nowhere is this film's status as a fictional piece more obvious than in the countless references to other films that Tarantino plugs into *Death Proof*. Ultimately, however, Tarantino really references himself and his mental film library while constantly

13

drawing attention to what the French theorist Jean Baudrillard calls "hyperreality."

In *Death Proof*'s case, hyperreality is sometimes an unclear mixture of images with reality and sometimes an unclear mixture of images with each other. For example, Tarantino continually references his influences, such as *Vanishing Point* (1971) and *Dirty Mary, Crazy Larry* (1974), both in dialogue and in image. These references to 1970s action flicks go on to become more "authentic" than Tarantino's "original" work in *Death Proof*. Tarantino uses the camera to interpret and moderate reality, but at the same time, he uses it erase history by reducing it to movie and TV references.

## Rewriting the History of Cinema

From the opening stroll through Jungle Julia (Sydney Poitier)'s apartment (a character whose alliterative name throws back to *Vanishing Point*'s disk jockey Super Soul) to the pursuit of the "fuck-me-swingin'-balls-out" white 1970 Dodge Challenger (also of *Vanishing Point* fame), Tarantino's characters constantly explore images, simulations of cinematic history, and simulations of these simulations. In *Death Proof*, references and images become a form of "simulation" that somehow makes the "real" more "real" or authentic. Through the mixing of human bodies with machines and, by extension, the mixing of pleasure with pain, Tarantino repeatedly emphasizes the fact that simulation is at work in *Death Proof*. By combining human bodies with machines, Tarantino opens the door to the combination of the real with the artificial or simulated.

*Death Proof*, in many ways, is an attempt to rewrite cinematic history. Tarantino largely does away with the more grand "history" of Baudrillard. For instance, while the posters for *Death Proof* as well as Robert Rodriguez's *Planet Terror* (the other half of *Grindhouse*, the two-in-one "double feature" of which *Death Proof* is the second part) might throw back to the exploitation posters covering the grindhouses of Times Square in the 1960s and 1970s, the contents of *Death Proof* and *Planet Terror* are stripped of all traces of the historic and economic eras that produced the films that they reference. Tarantino seems to be the first to do away with this larger history as he freely mixes cell phones and text messaging, markers of the present, with pristine muscle cars, markers of the past.

The multi-million dollar collaboration of *Grindhouse* quickly erases the actual economic structure that dictated the tiny budgets of much grindhouse fare (although depending on your understanding of "exploitation cinema," you could still define Tarantino and Rodriguez as "exploiters" of their own niche markets). Similarly, in the contemporary production of *Death Proof* there is no space for the quickly disappearing open-road speed-freak freedom of the early 1970s that you find in *Vanishing Point*. The original historical and cinematic context can't help but be lost.

*Death Proof* throws away memory in favor of the speed of the muscle car. Moving away from memory like this is actually part of *Death Proof*'s structure: with the movement of the story from Texas to Tennessee, Tarantino practically erases the entire first half of the film, with the exception of a few passing references and the character that links them together, Stuntman Mike.

## Hyperreality and Simulation

Baudrillard, in *Simulacra and Simulation* (1999) and *America* (1994), argues that the United States, and Hollywood productions in particular, are evidence of an all-pervading "hyperreality."[1] It is in hyperreality that there is "no more fiction or reality," only a blurring of the two.[2] Hyperreality and simulation, in turn, connect directly to the hyper-speed of capital's circulation: everything moves, everything sells, everything disappears.

According to Baudrillard, "America is neither dream nor reality" (1999, p. 3). Instead, it is hyperreality through and through. The U.S. and American cultural productions must be understood "as fiction" (p. 29). And *Death Proof* always seems ready to embrace its position as fiction whether it's through countless references to other films or fictions or the self-imposed cult status of the film.

The characters of the second part of the film are in fact, simulations. As actresses playing stuntpersons (Kim [Tracie

---

[1] Jean Baudrillard, *America* (London: Verso, 1999), p. 28.
[2] Baudrillard, *Simulacra and Simulation* (Ann Arbor: University of Michigan Press, 1994), p. 118.

Thorns] and Zoë [Zoë Bell]), and actresses playing a make-up girl and an actress (Abernathy [Rosario Dawson] and Lee [Mary Elizabeth Winstead]), they create simulations in their fictional work. They also constantly draw attention to their occupations verbally, be it as stuntperson, make-up artist, or actress. Meanwhile, when the action shifts from the stuntperson's game of "Ship's Mast" to the actual violence on the part of Stuntman Mike, Stuntman Mike still *simulates* violence. The action consists at base of stuntpersons acting out car chases from their favorite movies.

What Baudrillard calls "the era of simulation," others more loosely dub "postmodernity." Theorists now, according to Baudrillard, must primarily concern themselves with the "question of substituting the signs of the real for the real" itself (1994, p. 2). Images and markers of reality take the place of what anyone might actually consider "reality." Simulation is essentially a representation. It is a representation, however, that bears no link to what it claims to represent (p. 6). You might think of the filmic references packed into *Death Proof*: to what extent do these references actually throw back to their originals and to what extent do they simply exist as references (that reference nothing)?

Baudrillard outlines four distinct stages of simulation. In the first stage, the image "reflects" a "profound reality." In the second, the image blurs or obscures a profound reality. In the third, the image disguises the nonexistence of a profound reality, and in the fourth, the image bears absolutely no relation to any reality at all. The fourth stage sees the simulation become a *simulacrum*, a simulation or duplicate without an original. Finally, the real begins to mimic the simulation of real images of the real become more real than the real itself (p. 6).

Baudrillard writes that simulation is a repetition of an original object or image. However, this repetition is somehow more authentic, more "real" than the real (1999, p. 41). Tarantino's car chases, in many ways, are perfect simulations, as they appear more genuine to the viewer than the car chases in, say, *Dirty Mary, Crazy Larry, Vanishing Point*, or *Gone in 60 Seconds* (1974). The challenge for us as viewers of *Death Proof* is to determine where simulation stops and the simulacrum starts. You can dig deeper and deeper but eventually certain images and objects that appear to be references are pure simulacra.

Could you simply call this originality? Perhaps. But there's something else. It's originality with a façade of references and referentiality. In this way, Tarantino seems to write his own cinematic history from his own cinematic library. After seeing *Death Proof*, you can't help but look differently at the female characters in Russ Meyer's *Faster, Pussycat! Kill! Kill!* (1965). Tarantino replaces that film's original historical context and meaning with his own.

Similarly, the car chase that closes *Death Proof* is a hip-hop style sampling of *Dirty Mary, Crazy Larry*'s and *Vanishing Point*'s chase scenes. It even includes similar automobile makes. Tarantino's car chase ultimately holds this referential significance and so might be characteristic of the third stage of simulation. However, the simulacrum emerges as Tarantino begins to self-consciously reference a sort of mythic exploitation film. Here Tarantino simulates a simulation thus producing a simulacrum.

## Freedom, Horror, and the Road

The road in Baudrillard functions in many of the same ways as Tarantino's road, specifically in the closing car chase and crash in *Death Proof*. The road is a way to move quickly, as quickly as possible, and to forget. It is a way to traverse the referential desert of simulated and anonymous Tennessee (a bucolic landscape harking back to the car chases of *Dirty Mary, Crazy Larry*), or the semi-rural road networks surrounding Austin, Texas (p. 5).

Similarly, in *Death Proof*, Tarantino's stuntpersons Kim and Zoë find America in the road, in the uninhibited circulation of driving, in the unqualified *free*dom of the *free*ways. This is a freedom to traverse as much space as one wishes at the moment of one's choosing. Baudrillard observes the ability and willingness to move quickly and a parallel willingness to forget in the U.S. According to Baudrillard, Americans shake themselves free of "historical centrality" (p. 81). As postmodern Americans embark on their daily commutes, they think about only the present *now*.

Baudrillard argues that "the only truly profound pleasure" these days is "that of keeping on the move" (p. 53). Tarantino takes this pleasure one step further as he presents the audience with the mythology of the all-powerful Detroit muscle car. With these powerful machines, Tarantino gives Kim and Zoë the practically *unlimited* speed and power of the 1970 *Vanishing Point* Challenger and gives Stuntman Mike the parallel power of the souped-up Nova and Charger. Here the apparatus of movement and speed, the automobile, becomes both a means to pleasure and a means to pain as the drivers of cars repeatedly collide, bang each other up, scrape stock paint jobs, and spin out. This is one of several moments in which pleasure and pain seem to coincide in *Death Proof.*

Bound up in the endless circulation of goods and peoples, Baudrillard also spots a bizarre interrelatedness and impersonality in American culture. In the U.S., "everything connects, without any two pairs of eyes ever meeting" (p. 60). Perhaps this is where the thrill and horror comes from in the interaction between Mike and his would-be victims: Mike's first victims, speeding along a deserted country road, are literally in the dark up until the moments of their deaths. The eyes of the victims (Jungle Julia, Butterfly [Vanessa Ferlito], Lanna-Frank [Monica Staggs], and Shanna [Jordan Ladd]) and the victimizer (Stuntman Mike) can't meet until Mike pulls on his headlights. Even then, it is unclear if their eyes meet Mike's eyes or meet the technological extensions of his eyes, his headlights. Their deaths, along with the repeated event of headlights flashing on, replay multiple times, from multiple angles, and in slow motion. Only in the most sadistic (or perhaps sadomasochistic) act can eyes meet, can the impersonality of the road become personal. That is, with the exception of Butterfly, whose eyes, immediately before impact, deliberately close rather than open.

## Getting Off on Car Crashes

While *Death Proof* fuses simulation with reality and technology with the body, it also fuses sadism with a peculiar form of masochism through the character of Stuntman Mike. Mike's first car crash is a deliberate act of violence (in which he drives his car head-on into his victims' car); the machine becomes an extension of his murdering body. It also becomes a death chamber and death-proof chamber at same time as the crash kills one victim in Mike's car while he remains largely unharmed. This scene enacts a pairing of technology with the sadistic body. However, there is also some sort of risk to Mike and it may therefore be a genuine sadomasochistic scene.

The French philosopher Gilles Deleuze, in *Masochism* (1989), argues that a "meeting of violence and sexuality" is characteristic of both sadism, a condition characterized by a desire to inflict pain, and masochism, a condition characterized by a desire to be humiliated and to have pain inflicted.[3] Stuntman Mike might possess both of these conditions as he desires to inflict pain and gains sexual stimulation from actually experiencing pain.

According to Deleuze, sadism does not necessarily imply masochism nor does masochism necessarily imply sadism (p. 43). Stuntman Mike, however, confuses these separate entities and becomes a true sadomasochist: as Mike obtains a certain pleasure in doing, a pleasure in inflicting pain, when he collides with the car carrying Jungle Julia, Butterfly, Lanna-Frank, and Shanna, he obtains another sort of pleasure from his own injuries (a broken nose, a broken collarbone, and a shattered left index finger). Mike arrives at this pain willingly, even seeking it out as part of his sexual pleasure, and it is therefore a fusion of sadistic and masochistic pleasure (p. 38). Additionally, Mike seems almost completely to confuse technology and body as his car becomes the only way for him to gain sexual pleasure and inflict pain.

However, at the end of the second part of *Death Proof,* the sadisms of Kim, Zoë, and Abernathy turn Mike's sadomasochism on its head. Tarantino, in *Death Proof*'s somewhat abrupt climax, invites the audience to participate in these female characters' sadisms. After Kim shoots Mike in the arm he hurriedly speeds away. Down the road he screeches to a halt, wails in pain, pours alcohol on his wound, then wails in pain again, weeping "Oh why!?" Tarantino encourages the audience to laugh, to become sadists themselves.

Immediately before the final confrontation, as the girls chase Mike, Kim quite clearly becomes a sadist, and a masculine sadist at that. She also mixes technology with the body in her approach to Stuntman Mike as the rear-end of Mike's car metaphorically becomes his "ass" and Kim promises to "bust a

---

[3] Gilles Deleuze, "Coldness and Cruelty," In *Masochism* (Cambridge, Massachusetts: Zone, 1989), p. 17.

nut up in this bitch right now," being as she is "the horniest motherfucker on the road." This sexualized dialogue meanwhile simulates the hypersexual car and body dialogue toward the end of *Dirty Mary, Crazy Larry.*

## Freeze-Frame Ending

Looking back, the repeated images of car crashes are absolutely central to the structure of *Death Proof* as well as to the structures of the films that *Death Proof* pays homage to, especially *Vanishing Point.* Stuntman Mike's violent and sadistic body forces a collision between the nonviolent bodies of Jungle Julia, Butterfly, Lanna-Frank, and Shanna, and the disinterested metal of their car and Mike's death-proof car in the first car crash. Later, the final car crash finds Mike's car, an extension of his murdering body, beaten and half-destroyed by his would-be victims. Here Kim, Zoë, and Abernathy prove themselves bigger sadists than the professional sadist, Stuntman Mike. Ultimately, Mike's sadism itself might be a sort of simulation of the violence in the films he claims to have acted in.

With its postmodern sampling of 1960s and 1970s exploitation cinema, Tarantino's *Death Proof* journeys through terrain mapped by Baudrillard as it veers from simulation to simulacrum and from pleasure to pain, combining all elements in a decidedly postmodern way. Ultimately, the performance of the simulacrum, a negative effect of postmodernity according to Baudrillard, might be Tarantino's greatest contribution to the cinema. In the end such simulacra, through Tarantino, emerge as new forms of cinematic innovation.[4]

---

[4] Many thanks to K. Silem Mohammad and Justine Lopez for their comments on earlier drafts of this chapter and to Alain J.-J. Cohen for his guidance through Baudrillard and Deleuze. All mistakes, however, are my own.

# 3

# Unleashing Nietzsche on the Tragic Infrastructure of Tarantino's *Reservoir Dogs*

TRAVIS ANDERSON

> **MR. BLONDE:** Are you gonna bark all day, little doggie? Or are you gonna bite?
>
> —Quentin Tarantino, *Reservoir Dogs*

> Oh, wretched ephemeral race, children of chance and misery, why do you compel me to tell you what it would be most expedient for you not to hear? What is best of all is utterly beyond your reach: not to be born, not to *be*, to be *nothing*. But the second best for you is—to die soon.
>
> —Friedrich Nietzsche, *The Birth of Tragedy*

Separated by almost a century, the unconventional German philosopher Friedrich Nietzsche (1844–1890) and the American independent filmmaker Quentin Tarantino (1963– ) have more in common than their famous renegade spirit. They are also two thinkers who share a deep aesthetic understanding of their respective passions: writing, music and ancient Greek culture in Nietzsche's case; movie-making, music, and American popular culture in Tarantino's. In addition, they each brought their first major work to full fruition when only twenty-eight years old, and in the process they both took a real bite out of conventional wisdom about art.

But these two mongrel artists have something else in common as well, something far less obvious: Greek tragedy. In Tarantino's case, the violent, conflicted protagonists of *Reservoir Dogs*, his first film, together with its musical infrastructure and dramatically spectacular scenes, all bear a striking resemblance

21

to the heroes, music, and spectacle of classical tragedies. In Nietzsche's case, the unorthodox analysis of *The Birth of Tragedy*, Nietzsche's first book, explains the murky machinations and psychological importance of Greek tragedies with unmatched bravado and profundity. Unlike Aristotle, whose influential though relatively pedantic study of Greek drama provided us with the universally imitated structure of classic Hollywood narratives, Nietzsche's lively and provocative analysis found in tragedy the key to an understanding of art in general. And that key unlocks in Tarantino's film a textbook example of the artistic paradigm articulated in Nietzsche's book. In fact, the correlation between these two works is almost uncanny. Thus, a Nietzschean interpretation of *Reservoir Dogs* can not only help explain the otherwise puzzling dissonance between the beauty and horror, comedy and violence, and music and story characteristic of Tarantino films to date; it can also provide us with more than mere Beggin' Strips® for philosophical thought about all cinematic art.

Tarantino looks to be the Nietzsche of our day, a genius upstart right out of the gate. But Nietzsche's ideas have proved resilient and profound beyond anyone's expectations. Might the same be said of Tarantino 100 years from now? Will his films possess the same artistic influence and philosophical staying power as Nietzsche's books? Is his art of blood and banter just matinee Kibbles 'n' Bits®, or is there some philosophical meat to it?

## Nietzsche and Tarantino: Life Outside the Pack

Nietzsche wrote prodigiously even as a child. By the time he was twenty-four he had composed at least nine lengthy autobiographical sketches, numerous historical and philosophical essays, and a staggering count of poems, letters and diaries. While his childhood friends played as a way to escape life's seriousness, precocious young Friedrich played in order to produce material about which he could later write.[1] While *The Birth of Tragedy* was his first book-length publication, it was several years in the making and integrated ideas developed in at least

---

[1] Rüdiger Safranski, *Nietzsche: A Philosophical Biography* (New York: Norton, 2002), pp. 25–27, 353–57.

three prior essays ("Greek Music Drama," "Socrates and Tragedy," and "The Dionysian Worldview"). Nietzsche himself later wrote the most incisive criticism of this early work and judged it "ponderous," "image-mad," and "disdainful of proof."[2] Yet, Nietzsche's mature ideas remain thoroughly indebted to its radical insights about art, pessimism and morality, and Nietzsche's own appraisal of *The Birth of Tragedy* in his last published book reaffirms and reiterates its "decisive innovations,"[3] despite the fact that he later rejects all metaphysical responses to pessimism, even the semi-transparent metaphysics he attributed to Greek tragedy.

In a nutshell, *The Birth of Tragedy* employs examples from Greek history and art to argue that all vital artistic inventions are the products of two dialectically opposed powers locked in creative conflict. Nietzsche called these two powers the Dionysian and the Apollonian, after the two Greek Gods that he believed were their most direct artistic embodiments. According to Nietzsche, any noteworthy creative endeavor is essentially an expression of one or the other of these two primordial forces, or a mixture of them both.

The title of Nietzsche's book derives from his imaginative claim that Hellenic tragedy originated with a Dionysian chorus and developed into an Apollonian dream-like spectacle which preserved and expressed these two natural impulses in a perfectly balanced and historically unique way. *The Birth of Tragedy* was famously described in 1912 as "a work of profound imaginative insight, which left the scholarship of a generation toiling in the rear."[4] But when it was first published in 1872 its general reception was much less appreciative.

Most readers were probably baffled by the book; respected critics were openly hostile towards it. In large measure, this unfavorable reaction was the consequence of Nietzsche's highly personal and poetic writing style, which disoriented readers accustomed to the rigid scholarly methods of nineteenth-century philology and philosophy. Then again, it also reflected the biting resentment of jealous peers who were antagonized by

---

[2] Friedrich Nietzsche, "Attempt at Self-Criticism," *Basic Writings of Nietzsche* (New York: Modern Library, 1968; hereafter BW), p. 19.

[3] Friedrich Nietzsche, *Ecce Homo*, in BW, p. 727.

[4] F.M. Cornford, *From Religion to Philosophy*, as quoted in BW, p. 8.

Nietzsche's accelerated advancement in academic circles and his choice to answer that good fortune with a flamboyant criticism of intellectualism instead of a conventional scholarly treatise.[5] The book sealed his reputation as a speculative eccentric and effectively stalled his career. But with equal decisiveness, it heralded a bright new philosophical light—at least for those who had eyes to see.

Little Q, as Quentin Tarantino's mother reportedly called him as a child, developed a youthful passion for writing stories and screenplays and for watching movies that was almost as intense as Nietzsche's creative passion. Quentin spent much of his childhood scripting and staging elaborate games, recitations and plays (including annual Mother's Day dramas in which he repeatedly, but always apologetically, killed off his mother).[6] He saw John Boorman's *Deliverance* when he was only nine years old and it seems to have marked an important milestone in his life; not only was it one of innumerable films he saw as a child, and later as a video-store employee and action-movie aficionado, it solidified in him a lasting appreciation for the emotional power of the cinematic experience, as one of his many biographers has observed: "he loved the visceral effect movies had on him, even when he didn't understand what was really going on" (Bernard, p. 13).

*Reservoir Dogs* famously begins in a restaurant with a bunch of loquacious crooks comically deliberating over the subtext of early Madonna lyrics and the social merits of obligatory tipping. After their meal, the crime boss, his managerial son, and six operatives who make up the unlikely job crew, jauntily approach their cars as the cheery, melodic '70s hit "Little Green Bag" plays on the radio. The slo-mo shot that ends this amiable

---

[5] Three years earlier Nietzsche had been awarded a chair at the University of Basel at the recommendation of a respected scholar, and a year later he was promoted to full professor—all without his having ever written a dissertation for his PhD, which was awarded to him in *consequence* of his appointment, not prior to it. As his most influential English translator pointed out, "Nietzsche's appointment to a chair at twenty-four was a sensation in professional circles, and it was to be expected that in his first book he would try to show the world of classical philology that his meteoric rise had been justified" (Walter Kaufmann, "Introduction," in BW, p. 5).

[6] Jami Bernard, *Quentin Tarantino: The Man and His Movies* (New York: Harper, 1995), p. 12.

scene, an image of six happy thieves walking together in identical black suits, white shirts and skinny black ties, has become the signature image of the film. But it is the disturbing and incongruent violence that immediately follows this scene that has become the primary trait of Tarantino's signature style: before the credits have finished rolling, and while the same infectious music is still blaring away, the film abruptly transports us to the bloodsoaked backseat of a getaway car, where one of the eight criminals is now writhing in agony while his partner dispenses maternal comfort from behind the wheel. The rest of the movie (including the musically choreographed torture and threatened immolation of a captive policeman), bleeds out in a rendezvous warehouse amid brutal confrontations, profane accusations, and brilliant back-story digressions.

As with Nietzsche's unconventional book, Tarantino's unconventional movie left critics wondering what had hit them—or bit them, as the case may be.

## Is *Reservoir Dogs* a Comedic Heist Film? That Dog Don't Hunt

The first question any serious viewer is prompted to ask of *Reservoir Dogs* is what kind of movie *is* this exactly, and why was it such a sensation? A month after the film premiered at Sundance in January of 1992, producer Richard Gladstein described it as "a very, very, very, *very*, violent comedy." At the time, Tarantino himself described it in much the same way: "It's a heist film, about a bunch of guys who get together to pull a robbery and everything that can go wrong, goes wrong. . . . It all leads to violence and blood, but it ends up being black, gallows humor."[7]

Well . . . not exactly. There is, to be sure, plenty of wry humor in *Reservoir Dogs*. And some very funny scenes and dialogue are cleverly juxtaposed to the movie's raw violence. But is that enough to make the film itself a comedy (even a black, violent comedy)? Think of John Cusack in *Grosse Pointe Blank*. Now there's a violent comedy. And despite its bloody wall-to-

---

[7] David Fox, "Let's See. Whose Calls Won't I Return Today," *Quentin Tarantino: Interviews*, edited by Gerald Peary (Jackson: University Press of Mississippi, 1998; hereafter QTI), p. 4.

wall violence, *that* film isn't anywhere near as disturbing as *this* film. On the other hand, *Reservoir Dogs* isn't an action movie either. Nor is it a straightforward crime drama. In fact, the closest we come to seeing anything of the actual crime is a flashback of Steve Buscemi's Mr. Pink racing down a crowded sidewalk with three pistolero cops dogging his tail. Ironically, the same moments of unconventional humor and self-parody which render Tarantino's film oddly but indeterminately comedic, also problematize any attempt to categorize it in other established genres.

One of the more interesting Tarantino conversations I've read was one with Robert Zemeckis for the *Los Angeles Times* in which the two filmmakers mused over where *Forrest Gump* and *Pulp Fiction* (which competed against each other in 1994 for the Best Picture Oscar®) should be shelved in a video store:

**QT:** (*to Zemeckis*) OK. Now if you owned a video store, what section would you put *Forrest Gump* in?

**RZ:** You know what, I can't answer that. I don't know. Comedy? Drama? Adventure? They should have a video store section that's unclassifiable movies.

**QT:** I was thinking, if I was working at the video store, I would imagine my boss would put it in the drama section, and I'd be making fun of him for doing that, saying, "People might look for it in the drama section, but you should make a *stand* and put it in the comedy section!"

For any video store owners out there, when *Pulp Fiction* comes out, I want it in the comedy section! If I come in and *Pulp Fiction* is in the drama section, that'll be the last time I go into *your* closed-minded video store!

**RZ:** Well, would you put *Pulp Fiction* in the action section?

**QT:** There's not that much action in it!

**RZ:** See, but you know, you can understand why they would put it there—

**QT:** Oh, I can totally see.

**RZ:** —because they would think it's like a caper movie.

**QT:** See, one of the things that I think about both of the two movies is the fact that, whether you like them or not—and both of our movies are movies you either embrace or you put at arm's length—when you saw them, you saw a *movie.* You've had a night at the movies; you've gone this

way and that way and up and down. And it wasn't just
one little tone that we're working to get right. . . .[8]

Tarantino seems here to have a real appreciation for the fact that
a question like "where would you shelve it?" isn't just an amusing exercise, but a way to begin discriminating between token
art and the real deal, which captures something of the moral
ambiguity and emotional variety true to life itself. As interesting
as this discussion is, however, it doesn't tell us how we should
categorize *Reservoir Dogs*.

Even if they didn't entirely understand it, experienced critics
and film enthusiasts who saw *Reservoir Dogs* somewhere along
the '92 festival circuit seemed to appreciate its strange blend of
sing-along music, black humor and violent bloodletting, at least
on some level. But until the DVD market revived it, the film's
violence almost beat it into cinematic oblivion: when it opened
in the U.S. theatrically later in the year, whatever comedy and
craft the film could boast was for most viewers overpowered by
the film's paralyzing brutality. Ella Taylor's October 16th 1992
review for the *LA Weekly* provides us with a representative
response. She began with lavish praise for both the film and its
novice director, praise that was attuned to the very questions
about style and genre that we're wrestling with:

> The fact is that torture and all, *Reservoir Dogs*, opening in Los
> Angeles next week, is one of the most poised, craftily constructed,
> and disturbing movies to come out this year. It's a fond genre
> movie that's forever chortling up its sleeve at the puerile idiocy of
> the genre: a heist caper without a heist, an action movie that's
> hopelessly in love with talk, a poem to the sexiness of storytelling,
> and a slice of precocious wisdom about life. All this from a first-
> time filmmaker whose training consists of six years behind the
> counter of a Manhattan Beach video store, a stint at the Sundance
> Institute Director's Workshop, and a lot of acting classes.[9]

Taylor said she was pleasantly surprised by the movie's unpre-
dictable but expertly realized swings in mood and tone. She

---

[8] Chris Willman, "Celluloid Heroes," in QTI, p. 146.
[9] Ella Taylor, "Quentin Tarantino's *Reservoir Dogs* and the Thrill of Excess," in
QTI, p. 41.

accordingly described *Reservoir Dogs* as a romp, "a brave, cocky, enormously self-satisfied adventure in film as manipulation . . . flipping us from laughs to sympathy to horror and back again" (Taylor, p. 42). She was also charmed by the original and compelling characters. But in the end, Taylor strongly criticized the film for its merciless excesses:

> When it pushes to extremes, it becomes an exercise in spurious, sadistic manipulation. At his most self-consciously "cinematic," Tarantino is all callow mastery, and nowhere more so than in his favorite scene in which [Michael] Madsen, dancing around to the tune of "Stuck in the Middle With You," gets creative with a razor and a fairly crucial part of a cop's anatomy [his ear]. "I sucker-punched you," says Tarantino, all but jumping up and down with glee. "You're supposed to laugh until I stop you laughing." The torture scene is pure gratuity, without mercy for the viewer. "The cinema isn't intruding in that scene. You are stuck there, and the cinema isn't going to help you out. Every minute for that cop is a minute for you." He's wrong; the cinema *is* intruding. That scene is pure set piece; it may even be pure art. That's what scares me. (p. 46)

While Taylor later reasoned (somewhat unconvincingly) that perhaps what was really at issue in her dispute with Tarantino was not violence *per se*, but artistic style and personal sensibility, she remained infuriated by the torture scene, which she thought masked the horror of real violence by depicting it with a "cool, giggly insouciance" (pp. 47–48).

But like many critics, in condemning Tarantino's film Taylor relies too little on careful exegesis of the artwork and too much on casual commentary by the artist (much of which—in this case, at least—reveals more about Tarantino's naïve and forthright pleasure in simple, unguarded conversation than about the workings and meanings of the film itself). Quentin Tarantino, especially in his more substantial and artistic works to date, deals with violence in a much more ambiguous, nuanced, and yes, *philosophical* way than do any of the other gratuitously violent filmmakers with whom Ella Taylor subsequently compares Tarantino in her review.

But disturbing violence and discordant, ultra-black humor weren't the only issues audiences had with *Reservoir Dogs*. The casual bigotry and unnerving use of racial epithets, and the sheer volume of profanity and crudity in the dialogue also occasioned considerable shock and awe. In sum, almost *everything* about the film was excessive. "Restraint," "subtlety," and "moderation" seemed the only words that *weren't* in Tarantino's politically incorrect vocabulary. So, any genuine interpretation of *Reservoir Dogs* must account not merely for the film's genre-bending nature, but for its strange infatuation with *excess as such*. And thankfully, while Tarantino himself hasn't offered us much help in this regard, Nietzsche has: what we have in *Reservoir Dogs* is a picture-perfect case of what Nietzsche would call the Dionysian power striving to express itself in a tragic form.

When quizzed by critics about the questionable morality or possible social toll of its many excesses, Tarantino has been consistently dismissive. For instance, in an interview at the Montreal World Film Festival after Peter Brunette reminded him of the five hundred murders committed annually in Washington DC alone, and then wondered aloud about the ramifications of movie violence, Tarantino defended his work by claiming that an artist shouldn't have to worry about the consequences of his art: "If I start thinking about society or what one person is doing to someone else, I have on handcuffs. Novelists don't have to deal with that, painters don't have to deal with that, musicians don't have to deal with that."[10]

Okay. That's an answer all right. But, wherever you stand on the issue, that *kind* of answer is less than philosophically satisfying. It sounds a little too much like he's saying he shouldn't be blamed for something he did simply because others have done it too. Well, maybe they have. But that doesn't mean they *should* have. And it doesn't *explain* Tarantino's decision to do it. In fairness, of course, we should acknowledge that one of the traits common to all great artists (and according to Nietzsche, a trait common to all great *individuals*) is an unwillingness to pander to the demands of the status quo. But in order to determine if the dark and excessive elements in *Reservoir Dogs* and other Tarantino films do something more than merely push the envelope, Nietzsche must help us attribute to them a more profound function.

---

[10] Peter Brunette, "Interview With Quentin Tarantino," in QTI, p. 33.

Oh, and where would *I* put *Reservoir Dogs* at the video store? In either the Foreign or Independent Film section, of course, since that's where the most interesting movies seem to end up regardless of genre or country of origin.

## Devil Dogs: The Nietzschean Case for Artistic Excess

Friedrich Nietzsche was a thinker who had a lot to say about excess as an artistic virtue, a life-*affirming* virtue. So who better than Nietzsche to help us understand Tarantino's unique brand of excess? But not *every* form of excess is a virtue, even for Nietzsche. Endless barrels of blood and countless permutations of the same profane term in a single page of script can wear thin regardless of tolerance levels or proffered justifications. Unless we can discover a meaningful pattern, an effective artistic purpose or a creative significance to Tarantino's characteristic transgressions, then there is little hope that even Nietzsche's thought could help us assign them much lasting worth.

Like Tarantino, Nietzsche was fascinated by artistic depictions of brutality and suffering. In particular, Nietzsche was intrigued by the excessive cruelty and horrible senselessness that characterizes the art of entire periods in Greek history and manifestly lies at the heart of every Greek tragedy. To this decidedly troublesome dimension classicists and art historians before Nietzsche had turned a conveniently blind eye, attributing to virtually all Greek art the noble simplicity and calm grandeur that Winckelmann and Goethe had recognized in Hellenic architecture and sculpture—which is a little like attributing to every American film the characteristics of *Singin' in the Rain* or *It's a Wonderful Life.*

The profound question Nietzsche unflinchingly asked in response to this puzzle (which is the same question he would ask of Tarantino) was twofold. First, what essential truth about Greek (and human) nature are we concealing from ourselves by our refusal to investigate the source and ramifications of art and life's more disturbing aspects (those troubles from which Gene Kelly's angelic leading lady or Jimmy Stewart's bumbling angelic messenger can't rescue us)? Second, how is it that artistic depictions of violence, cruelty, heartbreak, suffering and death do not cause us the same emotional pain occasioned by the real events they reference, but can even arouse in us a form of aesthetic pleasure? Or stated in generic terms, why do artists so compulsively depict the ugly, horrible, and painful as well as the beautiful, and what is it about art that so often allows spectators to find *all* such depictions pleasurable?

According to Nietzsche's *The Birth of Tragedy*, the more sensitive Greek artists recognized in human nature a dialectical struggle between two primordial and ineradicable desires or impulses: an impulse toward the establishment of boundaries and forms, and the impulse toward their erosion or erasure. While it might be tempting to interpret this dialectic as a struggle between good and evil, especially for those of us who espouse Judeo-Christian morals, it would be wrong to do so.

The opposition Nietzsche has in mind is much closer (and certainly indebted) to Kant's distinction between the beautiful and the sublime (a distinction between disinterested pleasure and ecstatic discomfort) and Schopenhauer's relation between will and idea (primordial desire and its phenomenal manifestation); neither element of itself is good or bad, but each occasions a markedly different psychological experience. Unlike even Kant's or Schopenhauer's dualities, however, Nietzsche's pair is *dialectically* antagonistic (each power incites its opposite to greater achievement) and *fundamentally definitive* of who and what we are (the struggle between these powers is internal to our very nature as human beings).

Nietzsche argued that a penetrating *aesthetic* analysis of Greek art and poetry (in opposition to the purely *logical* analyses of Aristotle, Kant, Schopenhauer and Hegel) demonstrates the Greeks to have embodied these dialectical desires in the figures of their two principle art deities—respectively, Apollo and Dionysus.

Apollo was the soothsaying deity of beautiful illusion and measured moderation, the god of the imagistic, figurative, and philosophical arts, whose oracles demanded self-knowledge and denounced ambiguity and excess. The Apollonian impulse thus aimed at taming the wilder emotions, at dismembering the primitive whole of Nature into civilized individuals and unambiguous artistic forms, and at securing that individuality with moral boundaries, calculative reasoning, and contemplative detachment. In *Reservoir Dogs*, Tarantino's prism-like breakdown of the rainbow-hued but homogeneous gang into individual members each designated by a single color (Mr. Brown, Mr. White, Mr. Pink, Mr. Blue, Mr. Orange, Mr. Blonde) is an inspired example of this Apollonian dismemberment, affected in order to secure individual identities and differentiate powers. But like any dismemberment, that separation is itself a violent and painful act, acknowledged in the film by every member's resistance to that separation. Some, like Mr. Pink and Mr. Brown, immediately resist when their names are assigned; others, like Mr. Orange and Mr. White, resist later through a symbolic refusal to maintain their discrete color and thus protect their artificial identity in the gang, revealing to each other their true identity and their prior place in the social whole.

The wine god Dionysus was the Greek deity of intoxicated abandon and communal revelry. He was the embodiment of the musical arts, and represented the impulse toward unity and transgressive freedom from restraint that finds its ecstatic consummation in experiences as diverse as mob violence, sexual intimacy, religious communion, and intoxicated bliss. The repressed pathologies and violent eruptions that doom the *Dogs'* heist to failure in the first place and proceed to erode the integrity of each gang member's "colored" individuality as the film advances are all examples of the Dionysian impulse toward a delight in childish cruelty and a primal need to trespass established boundaries. And the need to gather the gang back into a multi-colored singleness of purpose and musical harmony after the failed heist is a perfect instance of the Dionysian drive to recover its severed parts and redeem them in an intoxicated ecstasy of reunification.

Already we are beginning to glimpse provocative possibilities for interpreting Tarantino's visceral affinity for violence and excess. Even at this early stage we could argue that many of the genre-bending and morally unsettling aspects of his movies are but artistic expressions (by both Tarantino and his fictional characters) of an otherwise sublimated desire for freedom from the alienating rational and institutional restraints that separate us into arbitrary racial, sexual, and religious sub-cultures, into discrete social classes, into legislatively-defined lawmakers and law-breakers, and the like. Such a reading would locate Tarantino's movies securely within the realm of the excessive Dionysian arts, now clearly seen as reactionary responses to the potentially tyrannical Apollonian cravings for order and conformity, virtues that are bought only at the high price of social fragmentation.

To interpret Tarantino in this way would be sufficient to identify him as an observant and astute cultural critic (of which there are far fewer than we need). It would also help explain his work to some extent. Yet, we can push further. Nietzsche argued that the Apollonian arts (which the Dionysian arts dialectically oppose) are themselves reactionary responses to the formlessness and meaninglessness of the merciless, primordial Nature from which we all spring. Nietzsche also observed that while both these impulses are outgrowths of Nature, not every expression of them (however well-intentioned) produces a naturally beneficent or *creative* result. Some end in undeniably *destructive* acts or events. Nietzsche cited the dissolution of families, social disintegration, sexual licentiousness and wanton cruelty typical of the barbarian world as vivid examples of the Dionysian impulse gone horribly wrong. These were the very consequences, wrote Nietzsche, against which the Greeks tried to insulate themselves with Apollonian defenses like laws, morals, religious taboos, and philosophical arguments. But immoderately exercised institutional attempts to legislate order can go wrong as well. Just ask Socrates about the hemlock. The real genius of the Greeks, thought Nietzsche, was revealed by their willingness and ability to bind these two powers together artistically in various creative dynamics which allowed each power a legitimate and controlled form of release. A *dialectically tempered* expression of beautiful illusion and ecstatic excess was the secret behind the Greeks' creative efforts, thought Nietzsche. And while these efforts certainly reached their apex in the perfect balance found in tragedy, Nietzsche didn't argue that every art had to be perfectly balanced or tragic to be praiseworthy; he simply observed that *some* degree of balance should be secured in all art. But is it there in *Reservoir Dogs?* Are Tarantino's Dionysian excesses *creative*, and are they *tempered or balanced* by Apollonian restraints and redemptive manifestations of beauty? That is the crucial question.

## Fur Flies in a Tragic Music-Drama

The excessive nature of the mutilation scene in *Reservoir Dogs* is undeniably disturbing, and in multiple registers: not only does the act itself shock us, so too does the maniacal glee with which Madsen's Mr. Blonde performs the act. Especially shocking is the incongruity we feel between the very real terror of Mr. Blonde's act and its consequences, on the one hand, and the gleefulness of his actions and of the popular music to which they are choreographed, on the other hand. But that dissonance does not render the scene itself gleeful. Quite the contrary, the profoundly dissonant tone established by the music and the acting makes it all much more horrible than it would otherwise be. And without this scene the audience would not be immediately galvanized in critical sympathy for Tim Roth's otherwise plaintive and flawed Mr. Orange when he regains consciousness and prevents Mr. Blonde from perpetrating a still more horrible act (burning the cop alive).

Tarantino says of the scene: "Early on, Harvey Weinstein of Miramax asked, 'What do you think about taking the torture scene out?' Cut it out? I wouldn't. . . . Sure, I think the scene is pretty horrible. I didn't make it for yahoos to hoot and holler. It's supposed to be terrible. But I didn't show it to convey a message."[11] Elsewhere, in answer to a question about the difference between realism and reality, and the recurring images of Mr. Orange slowly sliding down the warehouse ramp into a pool of his own blood, the ever-widening circumference of which measures out the real-time cinematic minutes of his approaching death, Tarantino makes a similar claim: "Tim Roth is lying there saying, 'please hold me.' That scene makes people uncomfortable. They say, 'why don't you move on. You've made your point.' But it ain't about making points! This guy is shot in the stomach and he's begging to be taken to the hospital. You can't deal with that in one or two sentences, and then move on" (Brunette, p. 32). Well, if we take Tarantino at his word and accept his claim that the violence is meant *neither* to provide a puerile, voyeuristic thrill *nor* simply to make a point about violence, then what *is* its function? And how is the violence related to the music?

Music typically functions in an American film either by "Mickey-Mousing" the action (imitating it in perfect synchronization) or by reinforcing—or just *forcing*, in less artistic

---

[11] Michel Ciment and Hubert Niogret, "Interview at Cannes," in QTI, p. 29.

films—an emotional response to other cinematic elements, like dialogue and images. In *Reservoir Dogs* the music is scored in a different way entirely. Tarantino's own take on the music is this:

> I liked the idea of using pop bubblegum music, rock 'n' roll for 14-year-olds. That's what I grew up with as a teen in the '70s. And I thought it's a great ironic counterpoint to the roughness and rudeness and disturbing nature of the film to have this 'What's wrong with this picture?' music playing along with it. In some ways it takes the sting off, in some ways it makes it more disturbing. (Ciment and Niogret, p. 21)

He's right. The music in his films is a major factor in shaping *ironic* rather than reactionary emotional responses to characters and events. Usually the music he chooses is happy, familiar, and satisfying, the melodic equivalent of comfort food. This is precisely why it can serve as such an effective counterpoint to the incongruent violence with which it is often paired. Our eyes are telling us, "you shouldn't like this, look away." Our ears are telling us, "yes, you should like this, keep listening." During the famous helicopter attack in *Apocalypse Now!* Francis Ford Coppola achieved a similar effect by pairing Richard Wagner's rousing and exhilarating "Ride of the Valkyries" with images of indescribable horror and sadness. This makes us feel on a visceral level that something is terribly wrong. It creates dissonance, rather than harmony. A dissonance we feel in our gut, not our head.

But in addition to pairing the music with incongruent images, Tarantino employs music to structure *Reservoir Dogs* from within. This is a highly unusual and artful way to construct a film. An analogue to Tarantino's opening credit slo-mo sequence, where each character is introduced within an allotted screen time equal to two measures of "Little Green Bag," might be the way director Fred Zinneman and film editors Elmo Williams and Harry Gerstad (who won an Academy Award® for their work) cut the climactic scenes in *High Noon* in beat to the Tex Ritter music, increasing the tempo of the edits, measure by measure, to keep pace with the tension-building melody.

Later in *Reservoir Dogs*, Tarantino uses music in yet another way to structure the entire torture scene temporally, as he explains: "what makes [the scene] work is that it unfolds in real time (the time it takes to play a song) and you can't cheat, it has to be played out to the end."[12] But in addition to affecting irony and structuring the syntax and frequency of his cuts, scenes and shots, Tarantino uses music in his films (and this is especially true of *Pulp Fiction*) to provide the tonal core around which the entire film is constructed. It is as if on some deep level the images are *dictated by and added to* the music, rather than the reverse. So, contrary to what Tarantino himself says above, it's not so much that the music forms an ironic counter-point to the images, as it is that the visuals, setting, dialogue and other Apollonian elements form a dissonant counter-point to the Dionysian music. But what philosophical importance can this have? Quite a bit, actually.

Here again, Nietzsche's analysis of tragedy provides us with an interpretive key. Under the assumption that human nature is an evolutionary outgrowth of nature in general, Nietzsche posited a state of primordial union as the origin of the Apollonian-Dionysian antagonism which animates all human life. Music as the originary artistic expression of that primordial oneness is thus the primal *art* (and here again, Nietzsche was heavily influenced by Schopenhauer, who believed music to be a pure expression of the will). Apollonian lyrics and dialogue are but natural responses and imagistic complements to the Dionysian music—the Apollonian dream of a Dionysian sub-conscious, as it were.

Nietzsche says Schiller once confessed that his poetry always began, not with words and images, but with a musical mood. Nietzsche postulates the same origin for tragic poetry. It began with music. The tragic arts began with a Dionysian chorus musi-cally lamenting the death of its god Dionysus, the true hero of every tragedy. The plot, dialogue, drama and spectacle all grew out of and in response to the music of the chorus, like a trou-bled dream grows out of the subconscious remnants of suffer-ings experienced in waking life. When these elements all combined artistically in such a way as to express implicitly their meaning and original significance, tragic music-drama was the remarkable result.

True tragedies were thus perpetually painful, albeit veiled commemorations of a lost primordial unity and "divine" identity.

---

[12] Camille Nevers, "Encounter With Quentin Tarantino," in QTI, p. 7.

They were musical creation myths about the true nature of human being—myths which not only accounted for life, but changed it. The single greatest virtue of Greek art (and perhaps this was Nietzsche's greatest insight) was its capacity to show persuasively what life *could* be, thereby redeeming life by transforming it for the better: "Art is not merely imitation of the reality of nature but rather a metaphysical supplement of the reality of nature, placed beside it for it overcoming."[13]

## The End of the Leash

Recall that Ella Taylor accused Tarantino of being cinematically intrusive during the torture scene, making it an instance of "frighteningly pure art." Philosophically speaking, the scene in question—and the movie—may indeed be pure art, but *not* because the cinema intrudes upon it. In fact, the only intrusive moment in that scene is the manifestly merciful one which occurs at its climax, when Tarantino's camera, like Hitchcock's camera in *Psycho*, pans *away* from the actual violence, thereby excluding it from the frame and leaving the act itself to the viewer's imagination. At least until Mr. Blonde prances back into the frame and starts talking into the severed ear.

*Reservoir Dogs* ends exactly as Nietzsche would say it should: cop and criminal fuse, all the colors and individual identities run back together into a bloody mess, and everybody is rejoined in an orgy of death. The only survivor is Mr. Pink: having crawled out from under the ramp where he hid during the final shootout, Pink grabs the bag of loot and runs from the warehouse—only to be apprehended by police waiting outside. As Stephen Weinberger notes, Mr. Pink is the only member of the gang with a color alias who "remains throughout a professional, thoroughly suppressing any traces of

---

[13] Friedrich Nietzsche, in BW, p. 140. This sentiment is reformulated in numerous places in the text, especially in Sections 24 and 25. But Section 3 contains perhaps its most familiar expression: "The same impulse which calls art into being, as the complement and consummation of existence, seducing one to a continuation of life, was also the cause of the Olympian world which the Hellenic "will" made use of as a transfiguring mirror. Thus do the gods justify the life of man: they themselves live it—the only satisfactory theodicy!" (BW, p. 43).

humanity."[14] In other words, he is the only one who guards his anonymity to the end, who sees through the betrayal, and who feels no compassion or sentimentality or rage. Weinberger only observes this uniqueness; he cannot explain it. Nietzsche can.

What Nietzsche would call the "intoxicated" cruelty unself-consciously expressed by Mr. Blonde is the cruelty that hides in the heart of every character in the film. So too the courage and treachery of Mr. Orange, the mercifulness and loyalty of Mr. White, the hard-boiled amiability of Mr. Blue, and the dilettante intellectualism of Mr. Brown are good and bad characteristics shared by all. Together, the rainbow colors that protect each individual's anonymity constitute the mask of the Dionysian hero: each color is a dismembered part of the primordial whole with which the film begins, parts that can only be restored to full life and oneness by a piecemeal sacrifice of each "human" member, of each separated individual. Mr. Pink's survival betokens the reconstituted Dionysus. All but one must die for all to be rejoined and redeemed.

Some have tried to understand this redemption in terms of religious suffering and post-modern self-realization.[15] But the real redemption realized in *Reservoir Dogs* is not the impossible return to innocence ironically referenced by the opening discussion of Madonna's "Like a Virgin"; it is the redemption proper to Greek tragedy, what Nietzsche calls a Dionysian "augury of restored oneness." And the site of that restoration is art. Film, to be precise. Cinema. And in the end, the cinema intrudes on us only by revealing to us who *we* the viewers are, as if the screen before us were a mirror in which is reflected our own individual virtues and vices, desires and fears, longings and failings.

Greek Apollonian artists managed to create artistic visions, fictional worlds and musical enchantments that were so beautiful and sublime they became the very models after which Greek civilization and culture patterned itself. And Greek Dionysian artists revealed through their music and poetry the primordial truth of those realizations: that at bottom, we are all one, and

---

[14] Stephen Weinberger, "It's Not Easy Being Pink: Tarantino's Ultimate Professional," *Literature/Film Quarterly* 32:1 (2004), p. 50.
[15] Mark T. Conard, "Reservoir Dogs: Redemption in a Postmodern World," in *The Philosophy of Neo-Noir* (Knoxville: University Press of Kentucky, 2007), pp. 101–106.

the fate of every single individual is entangled with that of every other, just as the seemingly individual stories that play out in *Reservoir Dogs* turn out, in the end, to be but facets of the same stone. Or perhaps better said, interlaced themes in the same musical fugue.

Quentin Tarantino has left a lasting mark on film art. No doubt about it. And flaws notwithstanding, *Reservoir Dogs* is a genuine tragedy for the postmodern age. In and of itself that's no small accomplishment. But artistically he's where Clint Eastwood and Sergio Leone were with *Fistful of Dollars* and *For a Few Dollars More*: his originality and infectious daring have earned him a loyal following and well-deserved praise, and the broad strokes of his trend-setting work have displayed real brilliance.

But will Tarantino's delight in wild abandon for its own sake collar his work in the future to dog-runs of silly and destructive excess? Or will the filmmaker whose howl awoke a sleeping art world to a new and exciting presence develop the discipline that produced genuine masterpieces like *Unforgiven* and *Once Upon a Time in the West*, thereby making big dogs out of Tarantino's own heroes, onetime *auteur* pups like Clint Eastwood and Sergio Leone? In short, Tarantino, "Are you gonna bark all day, little doggie—or are you gonna bite?" I hope you bite.

# PART II

## "I Bet You're a Big Lee Marvin Fan"

### Violence, Aggression, Negative Ethics

# 4

# The Moral Lives of Reservoir Dogs

JAMES H. SPENCE

*Reservoir Dogs* is a heist film. A group of criminals is gathered, each is given a color-coded alias, and together they rob a jewelry store. But the robbery goes bad when a clerk sets off the alarm and one of the gangsters—known only as Mr. Blonde—retaliates by killing employees. The police arrive, and the gang must shoot their way to freedom.

If this were the story, it wouldn't be all that interesting. But nearly all of the movie takes place in a warehouse *after* the robbery. It opens with the Reservoir Dogs finishing breakfast in a diner, the credits roll, and suddenly we are in the chaotic post-robbery world. Mr. Orange, who eventually turns out to be an undercover police officer, is wounded during the escape, and at the rendezvous point members suspect that they have been set up. *Reservoir Dogs*, then, is not the story of a robbery, but of something else. It's the story of how the gang deals with a wounded Mr. Orange, Mr. Blonde's murder spree, and the possibility that they have been betrayed. These are all moral themes.

What about the moral character of these Reservoir Dogs? Tarantino's protagonists are always cool, much cooler than we are. They are confident, calm under pressure, articulate, and well-dressed. Usually they are criminals. From their casual use of violence to their refined sense of style, we know that these characters are not like us. Their approach to morality is different as well. Tarantino's characters are not confined by rules or conscience. They seem to make their own rules.

What are we to make of the Dogs, morally speaking? The *Reservoir Dogs: Fifteenth Anniversary Edition* DVD contains a bonus feature offering a psychological profile of several of the characters. Supposedly, the Dogs are immoral psychopaths who fake emotions and sympathy, and use moral words solely to manipulate others. This seems implausible to me, and more so each time I watch the movie. I have become convinced that the movie is *filled* with morality. Not, I should stress, immorality, but *morality*.

## Three Views of Morality

One standard account of morality looks something like this: There are moral rules (perhaps God-given, but we don't need to bother with that here) and these rules form the basis, the most fundamental aspects, of morality. If this view is correct, then the Dogs are obviously immoral. A second way to view morality is to deny that there are any objective values that could justify such moral rules, and conclude that there is really nothing to morality at all. We could call the first view *traditional morality* and the second *nihilism*. Part of the reason Tarantino's movies engage us is this: traditional morality is always in the back of our minds as we watch *Reservoir Dogs*, so it frames the way we view the characters and events and shapes our expectations about how the characters ought to behave. Tarantino cuts across the grain, so to speak, and his characters violate our expectations.

A third possibility is that morality is constructed using the raw materials of human nature and social interaction. On this view, it's a mistake to think that there are objective values built into the foundation of the universe. But it's also a mistake to think that this means that there's no such thing as morality at all. That would mean that human beings have certain natural tendencies which form the basis of morality, and upon which we construct moral rules that provide a way to resolve disputes. In other words, some moral behaviors (helping a loved one in distress for example) come more naturally to us than others (such as paying our debts), but either way they are moral. David Hume distinguishes, in his discussion of justice in *A Treatise of Human Nature*, between character traits that we naturally praise (natural virtues) and those we praise because they are useful to society (artificial virtues).[1] For Hume, calling these latter virtues

---

[1] David Hume, *A Treatise Of Human Nature* (Oxford: Clarendon, 1975).

"artificial" does not diminish their importance; it merely indicates that the standards are constructed by us as a way of preserving peaceful social interaction.

On this view, morality results from certain facts about the human condition: we are both selfish and compassionate, and these opposing tendencies give rise to conflicts which require us to invent rules to help resolve our disputes. Unlike the other views mentioned, the truth of this view depends upon facts about human psychology, because it is human psychology that is the source of morality. Human beings are self-interested, but they possess other characteristics (Jonathan Glover calls them "moral resources") that restrain our self-interested behavior.[2] These moral resources include a natural compassion for others, a deep psychological aversion to killing other human beings,[3] and a concern for what others think of us (Glover calls this concern our "moral identity"). This moral identity is a picture of ourselves as morally good persons, which explains why we believe we deserve the respect of others. Since we value the respect of others, we desire to preserve our moral identity, and this means we are less likely to behave badly. All these features of human psychology manifest themselves as expectations about how we and others should act. In other words, they form the basis of morality.

Natural psychological tendencies aren't enough to keep society running smoothly, of course. We need rules and we need rules about when to break the rules. Our self-interest and our need for food and shelter manifest themselves as a rule about property. Our natural compassion for others manifests itself as a belief that others shouldn't be too greedy. Our aversion to violence manifests itself as a prohibition against killing. In these ways we form a code to live by, and we internalize it, using it as a measure not only for others but ourselves as well.

If this is correct, then we should expect the same natural tendencies, and also the development of something like a moral

---

[2] Jonathan Glover, *Humanity: A Moral History of the Twentieth Century* (New Haven: Yale University Press, 2001).

[3] Lt. Col. Dave Grossman, a psychologist and former army Ranger, provides an extensive argument for the existence of this aversion in *On Killing: The Psychological Cost of Learning to Kill in War and Society* (Back Bay Books, 1995).

code wherever human beings would benefit from having one. Surprisingly, this is exactly what we find. In World War I, for example, unofficial truces between Germans and Allies evolved without any explicit negotiating. Both sides understood how to interact to maintain the peace between their trenches, and would sometimes celebrate holidays together.[4]

We should also find predictable patterns to those rules, and predictable patterns to the psychology of rule breakers—they will do what they can to minimize the damage to their moral identity. When something bad happens, we will try to place the blame elsewhere. When we treat others badly, we try to justify our behavior or place the blame on others. When we seriously harm another human being, we often try to dehumanize that person. On this third view of morality, rules against killing and robbing others emerge out of our human nature and social interactions. Therefore, morality is real, even though there may be no universal, unchanging rules built into the basic structure of our world. Instead, there are psychological facts and social conventions.

I want to use this idea that morality grows out of human nature to think about the moral character of the Reservoir Dogs. The Dogs are violent criminals, but they are human beings, and they behave in exactly the way predicted by this third view of morality. Their motivations are familiar to us, and their excuses and patterns of justification are as well. So while Tarantino knows that he can create tension in his movie by offering cool, attractive, seemingly *amoral* protagonists, in fact he fails to successfully portray an amoral universe. His characters—the Dogs in particular—are not all that different from us. They *can't* be if the movie is going to be the least bit plausible. They feel moral impulses and pressures, they think morally, they debate moral points, and they have a moral code. They are moral in the same way that we are, and therefore the movie offers some indirect support for this third view of morality that I have mentioned.

### "He Don't Tip"

Consider the opening scene. There, as the gang finishes breakfast in a diner, Mr. Pink refuses to tip, which begins an extended

---

[4] Robert Axelrod discusses these unofficial cease-fire agreements in *The Evolution of Cooperation* (New York: Basic Books, 1984).

debate on the ethics of tipping. If these fellows are such cold-hearted bastards, why do they bother? They could easily walk out of that diner with a look sufficiently cold and hard to convince the manager he ought to pay the entire bill himself. Instead, they all have a sense of the right way to behave, and they try to justify these beliefs in ways that are very familiar. Pink doesn't simply refuse to tip; he attempts to justify his belief. And his justification is one we can make sense of, even if we disagree with him. He admits that he would leave some money if he thought the waitress *deserved* a tip, but denies the waitress deserves a tip:

> I don't tip because society says I gotta. I tip when somebody deserves a tip. When somebody really puts forth an effort, they deserve a little something extra. But this tipping automatically, that shit's for the birds. As far as I'm concerned, they're just doin' their job.

Pink is asserting that it is a mistake to treat people the way society expects you to treat them, and that we should instead treat them as they deserve to be treated. I think most people would agree with him about this. The real issue is about whether waitresses *deserve* a tip, and this is precisely what the other Dogs focus upon. Mr. Blonde, the most cold-hearted killer in the bunch, points out that waitresses work hard, and don't make very much money. Pink responds with a number of relevant points: that waitresses aren't starving, that most minimum-wage jobs don't involve tipping, that he doesn't control tax policy, that waitresses have chosen their job, and that they could always quit. He believes that tipping has no real justification, and besides, it isn't his fault if someone else chooses a hard, low paying job. The scene is revealing because it shows the characters reasoning with moral concepts, and doing so in familiar ways. Examine the scene carefully, and we find many, many elements of morality: questions about responsibility, the needs of others, whether tipping is an arbitrary custom, and even the character of the sort of person who doesn't tip.[5]

---

[5] The scene concludes with the ringleader Joe telling Mr. Pink: "Cough up the buck, ya cheap bastard, I paid for your goddamn breakfast," and "See what I'm dealing with here. Infants. I'm fuckin' dealin' with infants." An introduction to ethics could be taught with this scene.

Throughout the scene, the gangsters seem very familiar to us. They are using moral concepts, and using them correctly. Mr. Pink doesn't argue that the waitress doesn't deserve a tip because he is short. Such a claim wouldn't make any sense to us, and he knows that, so it wouldn't succeed in convincing the others and therefore would fail at preserving his moral identity as a reasonable and fair individual. They are all using moral concepts correctly, and, with the possible exception of Pink, they are defending a position that most of us would probably defend. The scene is interesting in part because of the stark contrast between the serious debate about the relatively trivial matter of tipping and the serious business of casual violence that soon follows. There is, no doubt, some disparity between the philosophical debate about tipping and the gangsters' subsequent bloody behavior. It is a mistake, though, to think that the opening scene is an aberration. In fact, the entire movie is infused with morality, and morality is necessary to make sense of the Dogs' behavior. It is, I think, an appropriate introduction to the entire movie.

### "I Don't Wanna Kill Anybody"

Tipping seems a relatively trivial matter compared to the murders that take place in the movie. Despite all the violence, though, we see familiar patterns of motives and excuses—evidence of the sort of psychological and moral restraints discussed by Hume, Glover and others. Specifically, there is evidence that they have some natural sympathies for others (in the opening scene even Mr. Blonde displays some sympathy for the waitress), and that they do not approve of unrestrained violence. When Blonde goes off and kills the store employees needlessly, Pink and White label him a psychopath. White even shows concern for one of Blonde's victims, implying she was too young to die.

Of course, the Dogs are willing to use violence, but there are boundaries. Pink states: "I don't wanna kill anybody. But if I gotta get out that door, and you're standing in my way, one way of the other, you're gettin' outta my way." We might not agree with Pink's choice of careers, but it isn't difficult to understand how he balances self-interest and concern for others. We are more likely to disapprove of Pink's putting himself in such a situation in the first place than we are with the principle that innocent people can sometimes be sacrificed. Even Mr. Orange, the undercover police officer, kills an innocent person when she endangers his life.

Blonde, when confronted about his murder spree, attempts to excuse his actions by placing responsibility on the victims. "I told 'em not to touch the alarm. They touched it. I blew 'em full of holes. If they hadn't done what I told 'em not to do, they'd still be alive." While we think he is wrong about this, the moral logic is appropriate: if he were a police officer warning someone not to reach into their coat, and the victim were a suspected murderer, then the killing would be excused. His attempt to justify his actions seems to prove that he views the situation in terms of right and wrong and that he has a moral identity he is trying to protect.

When we see others suffering we often invent stories to place the responsibility on those suffering individuals, just as Blonde does with his victims. We distance ourselves from the bad in the world to avoid thinking poorly of ourselves. In this way, we protect our moral identity. When violence becomes necessary and commonplace, we dehumanize those we cause to suffer. During war, soldiers routinely invent dehumanizing slurs to describe their opponents. The Dogs use such dehumanizing strategies on the police: when White casually mentions that he killed "a few cops," Pink asks, "No real people?" and White responds, "Just cops."

## "What You're Supposed to Do Is Act Like a Fuckin' Professional"

The Dogs don't really live by their own code, at least not in the sense that each makes rules for himself. Mr. Pink tries that in the opening scene and is rebuffed. The Dogs are supposed to act like professionals. Repeatedly throughout the movie, they appeal to professionalism to influence and evaluate one another's behavior. As professionals, they have a plan. Mr. Blonde deviates from the plan in the store, and is criticized. When Pink begins to think that the plan is going to endanger him, he argues that he should deviate from it, claiming very reasonably that: "the plan became null and void once we found out we got a rat in the house."

A professional avoids unnecessary violence. When discussing Blonde's murders, White states, "What you're supposed to do is act like a fuckin' professional. A psychopath is not a professional. You can't work with a psychopath, 'cause ya don't know what those sick assholes are gonna do next." In this way the code restricts their behavior for the benefit of other gang members.

When violence is necessary, there are still rules. Just as soldiers distinguish combatants from non-combatants, the Dogs distinguish police officers, whom they deem to be legitimate targets, from the protected category of "real people." Police officers exist to put them out of business, so there is no possibility of rules emerging for the benefit of both parties. On the other hand, if the officers were more interested in money than fighting crime, then a truce would be highly likely. Since that isn't the case, there is no reason to come to a truce with the police officers, and so their professional code does not extend to cover them. It does cover "real people" but offers them only weak protection. The real value in the code is protecting the gang (the more violence, the more trouble they are likely to encounter) and helping to resolve disputes among themselves. Recall how Pink jumps between White and Blonde, invoking the professional code, as a way of reducing tensions between them.

Just as non-combatants can sometimes be harmed, so can unco-operative store managers. "If you wanna know something and he won't tell you, cut off one of his fingers. The little one. Then you tell him his thumb's next." Like Blonde, White rationalizes this violence by claiming unco-operative managers deserve what they get: "When you're dealing with a store like this, they're insured up the ass. They're not supposed to give you any resistance whatsoever." So not only is the manager responsible for any physical harm to his body, the thieves aren't really harming anyone at all, since the store has insurance.

It is no wonder that we often find fictional gangsters explaining "It's just business," or referring to themselves as soldiers. If these fictional characters are to be believable, they need to have some sort of moral identity. Viewing themselves as soldiers and businessmen is one way of doing this. It minimizes the moral distance between their work and other occupations, and gives them a moral frame of reference. But I think it is more than that. We often find real criminals invoking ethical codes, referring to themselves as soldiers, and trying to excuse their behavior for the same reasons.

## "This Rotten Bastard"

Moral themes provide more than dialogue filler throughout the movie. They are, in fact, essential to the plot of the movie. The entire movie turns on Mr. White's taking responsibility for Mr. Orange and the gang's desire to learn the identity of the rat. There would be nothing left of the plot if these elements were taken out. The climax, in which White's loyalty to Orange meets the gang's desire to get the rat, makes these moral themes explicit. Here we have a debate about the relative moral characters of Orange and Blonde:

> **MR. WHITE:** Joe, trust me on this, you've made a mistake. He's a good kid. I understand you're hot, you're super-fuckin pissed. We're all real emotional. But you're barking up the wrong tree. I know this man, and he wouldn't do that.
>
> **JOE:** You don't know jack shit. I do. This rotten bastard tipped off the cops and got Mr. Brown and Mr. Blue killed.

White refuses to believe that Orange is the rat: he is loyal to the end, willing to stand by Orange against his long-time friend, and leader of the gang, Joe, despite the evidence accumulating against Orange. This loyalty creates the tension that leads to the climax and resolution of the movie. How does the gang know that Orange is the rat? Orange makes implausible claims about Blonde's actions because he is unfamiliar with Blonde's character. Everyone in the gang knows that Blonde is a cold-hearted criminal, but they also know that he was willing to spend time in jail rather than be a rat himself. When Orange claims he shot Blonde because Blonde was going to betray the gang, they don't believe him. Nice Guy Eddie confronts Orange:

> The man you killed was just released from prison. He got caught at a company warehouse full of hot items. He could've walked away. All he had to do was say my dad's name. But instead he shut his mouth and did his time. He did four years for us, and he did

'em like a man. And we were very grateful. So, Mr. Orange, you're tellin me this very good friend of mine, who did four years for my father, who in four years never made a deal, no matter what they dangled in front of him, you're telling me that now, that now this man is free, and we're making good on our commitment to him, he's just gonna decide, right out of the fuckin' blue, to rip us off?

So it's not only White's loyalty to Orange that brings the movie to a climax, it is also Nice Guy Eddie's certain knowledge (and ours as well) of Blonde's character. He would never betray the gang.

## An Amoral Universe?

If the Dogs are completely immoral psychopaths then they are *always* working an angle, using moral language as a way to manipulate others to achieve their own goals and to fool others about their true nature. But this isn't the least bit plausible. The Dogs pass judgment on one another's character, they explain actions that need explaining, and justify actions when we expect someone to justify an action. Importantly, much of the moral discussion occurs *within* the gang, and in circumstances where nothing is at stake.

In a sense, the description of the Dogs as amoral manipulative sociopaths gives them too much credit. It makes them into ideal, purely autonomous, purely rational creatures who just happen to disregard conventional morality. Human psychology is more complex than that and all human beings work hard to make their ideals, beliefs, actions, and moral identity cohere. Even Mr. Blonde endures imprisonment rather than becoming a rat. It is only on a thin, false view of human psychology that a person could subtract their perceived moral evaluations of a situation and calculate solely according to the tangible effects to self interest. Most of us do not, and perhaps could not, think this way, even if we tried. I would not know how to begin if someone were to ask me to consider the possibility of selling my mother for a million dollars, reflecting on only the practical aspects of the question.

I think the points discussed in this paper count against both the idea that the universe is amoral and to a lesser extent that there are universal moral rules. I'm not sure there is any way to completely rule out this second possibility, but I think the discussion here provides some reason to be skeptical. First, the Dogs seem to understand a lot about morality—responsibility, fairness, and desert, and so on. They appeal to these concepts and use them correctly. So it's unclear where their mistake is, except that we disapprove of their behavior and they violate widely shared norms. Second, the traditional view has nothing to say about the phenomena I have discussed in this paper. It can incorporate the psychological facts about human beings once they are discovered—as the truths of human psychology are learned, the theory will find a way to accommodate them. But it flattens the moral and psychological world of the Reservoir Dogs. It has nothing interesting to say about the points I have mentioned above and is hardly a fertile ground for predictions about human behavior. It also has a practical problem. The Dogs are not all that different from us, and a false confidence that we are moral may allow us to become more like them.

Readers of this essay may be inclined to conclude that my argument is directed towards excusing the behavior of the Dogs. That is to miss the point entirely. Reflection on the behavior and attitudes of the Dogs helps us better understand the nature of morality. It may simplify our lives to boil everything down to rules and rule-breakers, good ordinary people and the morally deficient minority. Unfortunately, this misleads us into thinking that morality itself is a simple thing, consisting of only rules that any ordinary person can understand and act upon. The point, rather, is that our preoccupation with *individual* wrongdoing, rather than the psychological and social conditions that foster such behavior, may contribute to making the world a worse place.

We're now in a better position to understand why, if this view is correct, the gang should not be considered amoral. If Hume is correct, they have much of what it takes to be moral. They have sympathies for others, they have conventions regarding appropriate behavior, and they use moral language and reasoning. Perhaps most difficult for this view is explaining the authority of morality. If morality is nothing more than feelings and agreements, why bother? I think Hume's response is appropriate here. We cannot help but take our moral judgments seriously. You, the reader, believe it is important to be treated fairly and to be thought of as someone who treats others fairly. Your

conscience tugs at you. You use moral language, and other people understand what you are saying. You want others to think
highly of you. You want to be thought a professional, not a rot-
ten bastard.[6]

---

[6] An early draft of this chapter was presented to the Department of Philosophy
at East Tennessee State University. Many thanks for the helpful, thought-
provoking comments. I would also like to thank Jason Grinnell for careful
comments.

# 5
# Revenge and Mercy in Tarantino: The Lesson of Ezekiel 25:17

DAVID KYLE JOHNSON

> You read the bible, Brett? Well, there's this passage I got memorized, sort of fits the occasion. Ezekiel 25:17: "The path of the righteous man is beset on all sides by the iniquities of the selfish and the tyranny of evil men. Blessed is he who, in the name of charity and good will, shepherds the weak through the valley of darkness, for he is truly his brother's keeper and the finder of lost children. And I will strike down upon thee with great vengeance and furious anger those who attempt to poison and destroy my brothers. And you will know my name is the Lord, when I lay my vengeance upon thee."
>
> —Jules Winnfield, *Pulp Fiction*

As it appears in *Pulp Fiction*, "Ezekiel 25:17" is not an actual biblical quote; no English translation of any portion of Ezekiel (or any other book for that matter) is worded quite like the "cold blooded shit" Jules says to "a motherfucker" before he "pops a cap in his ass." But the lesson that Jules eventually derives from the "verse" is quite biblical: one ought to show mercy. In fact, Tarantino's films abound with acts of mercy—acts of mercy that we are meant to admire.

It seems, according to Tarantino's films, that *mercy* should be common practice. And yet *justified revenge*—the seeming opposite of mercy—is a common theme, as well as a common motivating factor, for characters in Tarantino's films—and it seems that applause is intended for them. For example, the Bride's "Roaring Rampage of Revenge" in the *Kill Bill* saga is not portrayed as morally heinous, but as justified; in the end, "The lioness has been reunited with her cub, and all is right in the jungle." It seems that, according to Tarantino's films, if we were ever wronged as they were, *we would be morally justified in taking revenge on our enemies like they did.*

Now whether or not Tarantino uses his movies to communicate the specifics of his own moral views is unclear. (Art, sometimes, is just art and not intended to communicate anything.) But what is clear is that watching Tarantino's movies (and taking them at face value) leaves one with the impression that, although mercy should be common practice, revenge is justified. For simplicity's sake we will call this "Tarantino's view." (Although—and I must be clear on this point—this is only a name; I am not ascribing any particular view to Tarantino himself.)

Tarantino's view is quite common—his movies wouldn't be enjoyable for so many if it wasn't—but one is forced to wonder whether sense can be made of it. Are not these two claims—that *mercy ought to be shown* and that *revenge is morally justified—* inconsistent? How can one be morally justified in enacting revenge if one should be merciful? In this chapter, I'll show that, contrary to appearances, *Tarantino's view* is consistent.

## Revenge versus Retribution

Revenge is a dish best served cold.

—Old Klingon Proverb

We must define both mercy and revenge if we are to maintain clarity in our discussion. Although we will say more about specific definitions of mercy later, a broad definition of mercy will do for now. We will say that *mercy is considerate treatment of others, especially those under one's power.* Revenge, however, is not as easily defined and, to do so, we must distinguish it from something with which it is often confused: retribution.

What is retribution? Take some person who wrongs another; call that person the *offender.* An action that is carried out on the offender accomplishes retribution when the action is negative (one can't accomplish retribution with a foot massage), the action is intended as punishment for the offense, is proportionate to the offense, and the offender is aware that it is intended as punishment. So, in short, we might say that retribution is accomplished when "a penalty is inflicted for a reason (a wrong or injury) with the desire that the [offender] know why this is occurring and know that he was intended to know."[1]

Revenge has these qualities as well, and in fact is a type of retribution; but revenge has additional qualities that set it apart. Retributive punishment can be administered by anyone; revenge, on the other hand, is personal and, thus, only those who are wronged by the offender can get revenge on the offender. Revenge is fueled by emotion and desire to *see* the offender suffer—not simply a desire to ensure that the appropriate price is paid. Revenge sets no limit on what harm can be inflicted and, in fact, the amount of punishment that is doled out is dependent solely on what the person who seeks revenge deems appropriate.

Examples from Tarantino can help us clarify the notions of retribution and revenge. Consider the alternate ending to *Natural Born Killers*,[2] where—after leading the serial killers Mickey and Mallory out of prison—Owen Taft (their "guardian angel") kills both of them with a shot gun at point blank range. Many would suggest that Mickey and Mallory deserved to die for their crimes, but even if that is so, Owen killing them accomplishes neither revenge (he was never personally wronged by them) nor retribution (he was not intending to punish them for their crimes, nor did they view his action as such).

For an example of retribution, we can look to the movie *True Romance* where Clarence kills Drexl, his new wife Alabama's pimp. He specifically acknowledges that he is haunted by the fact that someone as morally repugnant as Drexl is "breathin' the same air as [him] . . . getting' away with it every day" and admits that Drexl doesn't "deserve to live" and thus wants to kill him . . . and does so. Clarence wants to punish Drexl for his immoral behavior—and even wants to ensure that he knows that is why he is being punished (that is why Clarence

---

[1] Robert Nozick, "Retribution and Revenge," in *What Is Justice?*, edited byRobert Solomon and Mark Murphy (New York: Oxford University Press, 2000), p. 214.

[2] Tarantino wanted *Natural Born Killers*, for which he wrote the screenplay, to be his directing debut, but it was given to Oliver Stone instead. Stone didn't do it at all as Tarantino envisioned, and consequently Tarantino never watched it. (See Jami Bernard, *Quentin Tarantino the Man and his Movies*. (New York: Harper, 1995), Chapter 6.

makes Drexl open his eyes and look at him before he kills him). Since Clarence has never been personally wronged by Drexl, we can't call this an act of revenge. But we can call it an act of retribution.

But, for a perfect example of an act of revenge, we can look to O-Ren Ishii, in *Kill Bill*. As she pushes a samurai sword into the chest of her father's murderer, Boss Matsumoto, she says to him "Look at me, Matsumoto . . . take a good look at my face. Look at my eyes. Look at my mouth. Do I look familiar? Do I look like somebody you murdered?" Clearly, in this case, a victim of the offender—fueled by emotion—is punishing the offender, for his offense—with the punishment that she deems necessary—and is ensuring that he knows he is being punished for that offense. This, we might say, is a *textbook case* of revenge.

So revenge, unlike retribution, is personal, emotional, includes a desire to see the offender suffer, and sets no limit on punishment. Retribution is simply the accomplishment of appropriate punishment of a wrongdoer by anyone. It is revenge, not retribution, that is the main focus of this article and of many of Tarantino's films. And it is the "Tarantinian" suggestion that revenge is justified that shall be evaluated.

## "Justified" Revenge in Tarantino

Examples of revenge abound in Tarantino's films. In *Pulp Fiction*, Marsellus exercises revenge on Zed—for anally raping him—by blowing off his genitals with a shot gun and then promising to get "medieval on his ass" with a pair of pliers and a blow torch before he finally kills him. At the end of *Reservoir Dogs* we have the perfect "revenge" circle. Joe Cabot wants revenge on Mr. Orange because he set them up and shot Mr. Blonde to whom Joe owed a debt of gratitude. Mr. White—on the assumption that Orange is not a cop (but a good kid and his friend)—threatens immediate revenge on Joe if Joe shoots Orange. Nice Guy Eddie threatens revenge on White if White shoots Joe (his dad), and—after Joe does shoot Orange, White shoots Joe, and Eddie shoots White—White shoots Eddie for shooting him. And when Orange—as an act of loyalty—reveals to White that he is a cop, White—quite distraught—shoots Orange in the head as a final act of revenge before the credits roll. These films are silent about the justification of these particular acts of revenge, but some other films don't follow suit.

It is hard to watch *Death Proof* without concluding that the girl's act of revenge on Stunt Man Mike is meant to be applauded—I know I did the first time I saw it! (Embarrassingly, I saw it for the first time in a theater.) However, for a clear portrayal of revenge as morally justified, one need look no further than *Kill Bill*. The "roaring rampage" of the Bride (Beatrix Kiddo) in *Kill Bill* is motivated solely by desire for revenge. Bill and the Deadly Viper Assassination Squad (or "D.iV.A.S."—the acronym Tarantino coined for the group consisting of O-Ren Ishii, Verntia Green, Elle Driver, and Budd in the original script) attempted to kill her and her unborn child—at her wedding rehearsal no less—for simply wanting to quit her life as a hit man, "jetting around the world, killing human beings, and being paid vast sums of money" (*Kill Bill Volume 2*). After she awakes from her coma—inflicted upon her by Bill shooting her in the head—she finds her unborn child gone, presumes the child to be dead, and then sets out to individually kill each D.iV.A.S. member, Bill himself, and anyone who gets in her way. She is fueled by emotion to punish those who wronged her and the appropriate punishment is set by her standards: that is, she seeks revenge!

My friend Jason Southworth pointed out to me that the entire *Kill Bill* saga can be interpreted as a symbolic story of Bruce Lee getting revenge for the Americanization of Asian culture. Beatrix's outfit in *Volume 1* is Lee's from *Game of Death*; the Crazy 88s resemble Lee's portrayal of Kato, The Green Hornet's sidekick [a role that he found demeaned him and the martial arts]; the music played before that scene is the Green Hornet's theme; and David Carradine, who plays Bill, got the lead role in *Kung Fu* over Lee. Of course, it could also be that Tarantino just likes throwing in Bruce Lee references—but I love viewing the movies this way.

That Beatrix's quest is portrayed as morally justified is very clear. As Beatrix herself points out:

> When fortune smiles on something as violent and ugly as revenge, at the time it seems proof like no other, that not only does God exist, you're doing his will. (*Kill Bill Volume 1*)

And as Budd points out:

> I don't dodge guilt. And I don't Jew out of paying my comeup-
> pance. That woman deserves her revenge. And we deserve to die.
> (*Kill Bill Volume 2*)

And the *Kill Bill* saga ends with a blessing on the Bride's actions: "The lioness has been reunited with her cub, and all is right in the jungle." It seems clear: in *Kill Bill* vengeance is portrayed as morally justified.

## Mercy in Tarantino

> The truth is, you're the weak. And I am the tyranny of evil men. But I'm tryin', Ringo . . . I'm tryin' real hard to be the shepherd.
>
> —Jules Winnfield, *Pulp Fiction*

Examples of mercy abound in Tarantino's films, almost as much as examples of vengeance do. In *Kill Bill Volume 1*, Bill shows Beatrix mercy when he—as she lays in her hospital bed—recalls the "goodbye forever" poison syringe assassination order. And in *Kill Bill Volume 2*, when she shows up to kill him, Bill shows Beatrix mercy by allowing her time with her daughter before also giving her a fair opportunity to kill him. In *Pulp Fiction*, Butch hunts down Marsellus and would even blow off Marsellus' head, were he not stopped by Maynard the "pawn shop shop-keep." And yet, when the tables turn, and—while Marsellus is being anally raped by Zed—Butch is able to escape, Butch does not leave Marsellus to this awful fate, but instead rescues him, in a obvious act of mercy. In return, Marsellus shows mercy to Butch by forgiving the wrong Butch inflicted on him by refusing to throw the prize fight.

But the most notable example of mercy is Jules Winnfield's. Jules and Vincent narrowly escape death—by the "miracle" of Vincent and he being missed by multiple bullets fired at them from point blank range. Jules "feels the touch of God" and thus concludes that Ezekiel 25:17 instructs him to give up being "the tyranny of evil men" (by being a cold blooded hit man) and instead to become "The Shepherd." As he enters the "transitional period" between his two lives, the restaurant where he and Vincent are eating is robbed. But instead of killing the thieves (which he actually envisions doing in the original version of the *Pulp Fiction* script), he begins his new "Caine-from-Kung-Fu-style" life with an extreme act of mercy: he buys their lives, letting them escape with a large amount of stolen money—$1,500 of it his own.

I don't think much of an argument is needed to show that these films glorify these acts of mercy. After all, Bill admits that he owes Beatrix better than to "sneak into her room in the night, like a filthy rat, and kill her in her sleep." Such a thing would "lower" him (*Volume 1*). And Ezekiel 25:17 is the moral lesson of *Pulp Fiction*; God gives both Jules and Vincent a chance to be shepherds (Vince's rejection of that chance leads to his death). It is clear: according to Tarantino's films, mercy should be common practice.

## What's Tarantino's View?

It's mercy, compassion, and forgiveness I lack, not rationality.

—Beatrix Kiddo, *Kill Bill Volume 1*

It certainly seems that these two claims—that *mercy should be common practice* and that *revenge is justified*—are inconsistent. How can one be justified in enacting revenge if one should be merciful?

Acts of revenge in Tarantino's films are just what one would expect them to be: acts driven by the victim's emotional desire for satisfaction after personally suffering a wrong at the hands of the offender. But, in Tarantino's films, mercy is never exercised in lieu of such vengeance.

Consider the acts of mercy we have discussed so far. In *Kill Bill Volume 2*, Bill recognizes the wrong that he did to Beatrix—he was a "real bad daddy"—and likewise recognizes that he has no claim of vengeance upon her. In fact, he seems to recognize her claim of vengeance on him and—even though he reserves the right to defend himself—he feels obligated to give her a fair shot at killing him. In *Pulp Fiction*, Butch shows Marsellus mercy, but he has no right of revenge on Marsellus. (In fact it is the other way around; Butch wrongs Marsellus by refusing to throw the prize fight after he has promised to do so and accepted Marsellus' money for doing so.) Thus, the mercy that Butch shows Marsellus is not in lieu of a right of vengeance.

Marsellus has a right of vengeance on Butch, but doesn't waive that right until Butch saves his life. Marsellus views Butch's action as an action that lifts his right of revenge and thus Marsellus isn't merciful in lieu of revenge either.

Lastly, consider Jules's act of mercy in the final scene of *Pulp Fiction*.

> **JULES:** Normally both your asses would be dead as fuckin' fried chicken. But you happened to pull this shit while I'm in a transitional period and I don't wanna kill ya, I wanna help ya. But I can't give you this case cause it don't belong to me. Besides, I've been through too much shit over this case this morning to just hand it over to your dumb ass. Now, I want you to go in that bag and find my wallet.
>
> **PUMPKIN:** Which one is it?
>
> **JULES:** It's the one that says "bad motherfucker." (Pumpkin finds the wallet with the words "bad motherfucker" embroidered on it.) That's it. That's my bad motherfucker. Open it up; take out the money. Count it. How much is there?
>
> **PUMPKIN:** About fifteen hundred dollars.
>
> **JULES:** Okay, put it in your pocket, it's yours. Now with the rest of those wallets and the register, that makes this a pretty successful little score.
>
> **VINCENT:** Jules, you give that fucking nimrod fifteen hundred dollars, and I'll shoot him on general principle.
>
> **JULES:** No, Yolanda, Yolanda, he ain't gonna do a goddamn motherfucking thing. Vince, shut the fuck up!
>
> **YOLANDA:** Shut up.
>
> **JULES:** Come on Yolanda, stay with me baby. Now I ain't givin' it to him, Vincent. I'm buyin' somethin' for my money. Wanna know what I'm buyin' Ringo?
>
> **PUMPKIN:** What?
>
> **JULES:** Your life. I'm givin' you that money so I don't hafta kill your ass.

Jules isn't ignoring a right of vengeance; neither Ringo nor Yolanda have personally wronged him. He is stopping them from doing something that would require him to kill them: taking his case, killing anyone in the diner, continuing their life of thievery, or leaving with his *bad motherfucker*. And notice that this is consistent with the commands of Ezekiel 25:17, which doesn't demand forgiveness but simply calls Jules to "shepherd the weak through the valley of darkness."

Thus, it seems that Tarantino's view is this: Mercy is a praiseworthy—and even desirable—thing. Perhaps it is even obligatory in certain circumstances if we take Ezekiel 25:17 seriously. But it does not trump the right of revenge; when an offender wrongs a victim, the victim's obligation to show mercy is lifted and revenge is morally justified. (Actually, Tarantino doesn't think *all* acts of revenge are morally justified. I'll say more about this.)

Perhaps we can most clearly articulate Tarantino's view by delineating mercy. *Considerate mercy*—sparing others pain when possible (even if inconvenient)—is desirable and perhaps even obligatory. *Forgiving mercy*, however, where one forgives those who have wronged him or her, is not morally obligatory. Granted, someone who exercises forgiving mercy is nicer (more virtuous) than one who doesn't; but one who does not forgive is not doing anything morally wrong. So it seems that Tarantino's view is that compassionate mercy ought to be shown, but not in lieu of vengeance; forgiving mercy can be dispensed with.

Like Beatrix, it seems that Tarantino's view lacks mercy, compassion, and forgiveness, but not rationality; the view is perfectly consistent. Consistency, however, although required for truth, does not guarantee truth. So, one must still ask, is Tarantino's view correct about mercy and revenge? It certainly seems that the general point about mercy—that it is a good thing—seems right. But isn't vengeance something that most philosophers frown upon?

## Tarantino and Asian Philosophy[3]

That bitch ain't gittin' no Bushido points for killin' a white trash piece of shit like me with a samurai sword.

—Budd, *Kill Bill* [original script]

---

[3] For this section, a great many of my thanks go to my good and long time friend, Caleb Holt. Caleb is a third degree black belt in Kaishu Ki Kempo Karate and a Renshi (Assistant Instructor) in the discipline: he inspired (and wrote) much of this section.

Some might try to find justification for Tarantino's view in Asian philosophy. After all, Bushido—the warrior code of ethics derived from Asian philosophies like Buddhism, Zen, Confucianism, and Shintoism that emphasizes "loyalty, self sacrifice, justice, sense of shame, refined manners, purity, modesty, frugality, martial spirit, honor, and affection"[4]—does suggest that acts of vengeance are justified in many circumstances. However, although some acts of vengeance that occur in Tarantino's films, like O-ren's killing of Boss Matsumoto, might be justified under the Bushido moral code, most of them would not be.

The great and lasting essence of Bushido centers not upon combat, the techniques of war, the killing of men or the concerns of self, but rather upon the total negation of all passion and desire. For the warrior truly to be a warrior, she must enter into a calm, empty place; she must give herself up and die. Only in this way can she achieve her end and vanquish her enemy. Bushido, in its essence, exists in a master-servant dynamic.

Samurai in feudal Japan were first and foremost retainers, warriors attached to a daimyo or regional lord. It was their duty to live and die for their lords. Samurai who failed in their capacities were either cast aside to become ronin ("wave men") or ordered to commit seppuku (ritual suicide). Failure in feudal Japan was considered a dishonor. Loss of any kind, particularly in battle was equally dishonorable. A samurai's failure reflected negatively upon not only himself but equally upon his lord distributing shame on a grander scale.[5]

The clearest evidence that Bushido cannot be used to justify "Tarantinian" acts of vengeance can be found in *Kill Bill*. Beatrix—given her training—is supposed to operate under the Bushido moral code. However, there is no room in Bushido for Beatrix's claim of revenge on Bill or any of the D.iV.A.S. She breaks from Bushido the moment she breaks from Bill. Bill is her lord; she is his samurai. He gives her training, protection, payment, and affection, all components required from a daimyo to his retainers. She in return is to give him loyalty, fidelity, and her life. And not only is Beatrix's quest for revenge unjustified, but because of her abandonment, Bill, as far as Bushido is concerned, is justified in trying to end her life. Truth be told, when

---

[4] Nippon Steel, *Nippon: The Land and Its People*. Japan: Nippon Steel Human Resources Development Company, 1988, p. 329.

Beatrix wakes up from her coma, if she were to follow the Bushido code, instead of vowing revenge on all who wronged her, she would commit ritual suicide for failing to protect her friends and fiancé in the El Paso wedding chapel. All in all, Bushido would view Beatrix's actions as immoral. Her motives are self-centered and she is filled with passion, rage, and a great homicidal thirst; these are all abominations in Bushido. This is also why Bill's actions are not justified according to Bushido: he is only justified in killing Beatrix, not everyone in the wedding chapel!

Interestingly enough, the only "Bushido exemplar" is Hattori Hanzo who has vowed, since his student Bill rejected the Bushido code, never again to create an object which kills people, but abandons that vow when he learns that Beatrix intends to assassinate Bill. His student has gone evil and Hanzo has a moral responsibility to fix the problem. When the answer comes in the form of the yellow-haired warrior, Hattori Hanzo is justified, according to Bushido, in breaking his vow to ensure that this wrong is righted. But this is the only example of "Tarantinian" revenge that is justified by Bushido. So it's fairly clear that Bushido could not be used to defend Tarantino's view.

Of course, one could try to go outside Bushido in the Eastern traditions—to Buddhism and Hinduism—to find justification for Tarantino's view. But I don't think one would have much luck. Both religions subscribe to Karma and the notion that everyone will ultimately get what they deserve. Revenge is thus unnecessary, and enacting revenge may make you deserving of something you don't want. So Asian philosophy can't be used to defend Tarantino's view.

## Western Philosophy and Tarantino

**JULES:** Oh man, I will never forgive your ass for this shit; this is some fucked up repugnant shit.

**VINCENT:** Jules, did you ever hear the philosophy that once a man admits that he is wrong, that he's immediately forgiven for all wrong-doings; have you ever heard that?

**JULES:** Get the fuck out my face with that shit! The mother-fucker said that shit never had to pick up itty-bitty pieces of skull on account of your dumb ass.

—Vincent Vega and Jules Winnfield, *Pulp Fiction*

The most notable Western moral code that speaks against revenge is the Christian one. Jesus told us to love our enemies, pray for those who mistreat us, and turn the other cheek.[6] The Apostle Paul even specifically tells us not to seek revenge.[7] Thus it seems fairly clear that one can't be a Christian and seek vengeance. But Christianity doesn't corner the morality market—and I even doubt that all Christians would agree with my interpretation of the above passages—so certainly much more needs to be said.

In modern philosophy, it's commonly assumed that revenge is not morally justified. So, one might expect to find, in the classical philosophers, a commonly accepted knock-down argument against the moral permissibility of revenge. This, however, is not the case. Many classic philosophers consider whether "retribution" or "rehabilitation" should be the goal of government punishment, but most of them say nothing about the moral permissibility of *personal* revenge. They do agree that a government allowing citizens to seek personal revenge is ill-advised because it would lead to social unrest (perhaps even chaos), but this doesn't tell us about revenge's morality; the fact that something should be illegal doesn't entail that it is immoral. A few have said a little about the moral permissibility of personal revenge—and at first glance it seems that they oppose it—but when one takes a closer look, it becomes clear that they actually leave the question of revenge's moral justification open.

Hobbes (1588–1679), for instance, says that the natural law frowns upon vengeance.

> The fifth precept of the Law of nature is: That we must forgive him who repents, and asketh pardon for what is past. . . . The sixth precept of the naturall Law is, that in revenge . . . and punishments we must have our eye not at the evill past, but the future good. That is: It is not lawfull to inflict punishment for any other end, but

[5] For more on Bushido see John Newman, *Bushido: The Way of the Warrior* (New York: Gallery, 1989); Noel Perrin, *Giving Up the Gun: Japan's Reversion to the Sword, 1543–1879* (Boulder: Shambhala, 1979); Inazo Nitobe, *Bushido:The Soul of Japan* (Tokyo: Tuttle, 1969); Conrad Schirokauer, *A Brief History of Chinese and Japanese Civilizations* (Fort Worth: Harcourt Brace Jovanovich, 1989); H. Paul Varley, *Samurai* (New York: Dell, 1970).
[6] Luke 6:27–29.
[7] Romans 12:17–19.

that the offender may be corrected, or that others warned by his punishment may become better.[8]

Thus one is tempted to conclude that Hobbes doesn't think vengeance is morally justified. But such a conclusion would be hasty. Later Hobbes admits that if someone doesn't repent for his wrongs, nature doesn't demand forgiving mercy.

> But Peace granted to him that repents not, that is, to him that retains an hostile mind . . . that . . . seeks not Peace, but opportunity, is not properly Peace but feare, and therefore is not commanded by nature.[9]

And presumably, like Jules, he wouldn't let admitting wrongdoing qualify as repentance. And more importantly, since Hobbes didn't view the natural law as morally binding (it only describes what is prudent for one to do) whether or not vengeance is in accordance with the natural law is irrelevant to vengeance's morality.[10] Thus it seems that Hobbes leaves the question open.

John Locke (1632–1704) suggests that one should not seek vengeance on an abusive tyrant.

> Must the people then always lay themselves open to the cruelty and rage of tyranny? Must they see their cities pillaged . . . their wives and children exposed to the tyrant's lust and fury . . . and all the miseries of want and oppression, and yet sit still? . . . I answer: Self-defence is a part of the law of nature; nor can it be denied the

---

[8] *De Cive: Liberty*, Chapter III: Of the Other Laws of Nature, p. 18.

[9] *De Cive*, p. 18.

[10] Those who know Hobbes know that he suggests that the only moral obligation we have is to obey the state. Thus one is tempted to conclude that vengeance would be morally off limits, if the state condemned it. But *this* might not even be right! Hobbes, at least in one place, admits that one is not morally bound to follow the rule of the state if doing so requires one to sacrifice one's life or honor. And since many view vengeance as a defense of one's honor, it would seem that, according to Hobbes, vengeance could be justified even if the state forbade it. But it should be noted that Hobbes saying this is quite confusing, given other things that Hobbes says about the absolute authority of the state. See Sharon A Lloyd, "Hobbes's Moral and Political Philosophy," *Stanford Encyclopedia of Philosophy (Fall 2006 Edition)*, URL = <http://plato.stanford.edu/archives/fall2006/entries/hobbes-moral/>.

community, even against the king himself: but to revenge themselves upon him, must by no means be allowed them; it being not
agreeable to that law.[11]

So at first glance it seems that Locke would suggest that
revenge is never justified; if it is not justified when a tyrant is
subjecting you to "all the miseries of want and oppression,"
then it would seem never to be. But once we read further, we
realize that such actions are not off limits because they are acts
of revenge, but because they inappropriately cross social barri-
ers. Such actions

> exceed the bounds of due reverence and respect. [Those wronged]
> may repulse the present attempt, but must not revenge past vio-
> lences: for it is natural for us to defend life and limb, but that an
> inferior should punish a superior, is against nature.[12]

Locke is not condemning revenge but the punishment of supe-
riors. (Like Bushido, Locke would condemn the Bride's revenge
on Bill.) But he leaves open the question of punishing—taking
revenge upon—your equals.

Friedrich Nietzsche (1844–1900) argued that resentment
(clearly an emotion that fuels revenge) tends to poison one from
within. Thus one might think that Nietzsche would argue that
revenge is never morally justified. However, such a conclusion
is hasty. As Murphy points out,[13] Nietzsche is suggesting that
resentment is not in your self-interest because, given the laws of
society, it is usually repressed and thus acts as a poison. Given
that fact, it seems unjustified to conclude that Nietzsche condemned *expressed resentment* in the form of revenge; if you can
get away with it—like O-Ren and Beatrix—expressed resentment will not poison. So, it seems, Nietzsche too leaves open
the question of revenge's moral justification.

The only classical philosopher I know of who explicitly
speaks against revenge is Socrates (469–399 B.C.E.), who sug-

---

[11] John Locke, *Second Treatise of Civil Government*, Chapter 19, paragraph 233.
[12] Locke, Chapter 19, paragraph 233.
[13] Jeffrie Murphy, "Getting Even: The Role of the Victim," in *Philosophy of Law*,
sixth edition, edited by Joel Feinberg and Jules Coleman (Belmont: Wadsworth,
2000), p. 791.

gests that desires for vengeance and harming one's enemies are immoral. But he never actually presents a satisfactory argument to this effect; he merely relies on his "intuition" that "true moral goodness is incapable of doing intentional injury to others."[14] So it seems, if we are to *show* that revenge is not morally justified, we need to go beyond the classical philosophers and seek out contemporary arguments.

Some might argue against the moral justification of revenge by pointing out that "two wrongs don't make a right." Those who offer up this "saying" as an argument against the moral justification of revenge, however, would be begging the question: that is, they would simply be assuming the truth of what they are trying to prove. To assume that vengeance is "answering wrong with wrong" is to assume, without argument, that vengeance is wrong. If vengeance is morally permissible, then a wrong followed by vengeance is not a case of "two wrongs" but a case of "a wrong and a right." Thus, a separate argument against revenge needs to be put forth.

To do so, some might argue that we are not morally qualified to enact revenge; only God knows the intent of the wrongdoer and only he is without sin and thus morally worthy of "casting the first stone."[15] But that perfect knowledge and moral character is required to qualify one to enact revenge is, at the least, unclear.[16] It seems that we can be "sure enough" about an offender's intentions and as long as we haven't done something just as bad as the offender, we are not being hypocritical by punishing them. (Even though O-Ren is not completely without sin, the fact that she has never killed anyone's parents in cold blood entails that she is not a hypocrite for punishing Boss Matsumoto.) So this argument seems wanting.

Some argue against revenge by suggesting that it does no good. After all, even though O-Ren isn't a hypocrite, killing Boss Matsumoto doesn't bring her parents back. But, although it is true that seeking revenge doesn't "undo" the offense, it is far from clear that revenge accomplishes "no good" at all. The offender does get what she or he is due (thus justice is accom-

---

[14] Gregory Vlastos, *Socrates: Ironist and Moral Philosopher* (Ithaca: Cornell University Press, 1991), p. 196.
[15] Romans 12:19 and Deuteronomy 32:35.
[16] See Murphy, pp. 792–93.

plished) and the victim gets satisfaction and perhaps even peace of mind. If a desire for revenge possesses a person it might harm more than it benefits—and if that is the case, revenge is unadvisable—but it's hardly obvious that revenge does no good *at all*.

If universal pacifism—the position that *all* actions of violence are wrong—is true, then clearly vengeance would be morally unjustified. But many don't find universal pacifism plausible. It entails that even actions of self-defense, both personal and social, are morally unjustified; and this means that Alabama in *True Romance* should not have defended herself against the hit man Virgil, and that we should not have opposed Hitler with force. Most find this implausible and in the same way that we can offer of up an argument for self-defense, it seems that we can offer up an argument for revenge: It seems perfectly clear that *we have a moral obligation* not *to harm people who have not wronged us.* However, what could this possibly mean but that, when one does wrong us, the obligation not to harm them has been lifted? Why even bother to point out that we have an obligation not to harm others who don't wrong us, if we still have such an obligation even after they harm us? Wouldn't we then just have an obligation not to harm in any circumstance? And isn't that just pacifism? Thus it seems that, if one wrongs us, we are morally permitted to seek revenge; the obligation not to harm has been lifted.[17]

Given that we have found no convincing argument against it, and have seen a convincing argument for it, it seems that revenge can be justified.

## Are We Going Too Far?

I can tell you with no ego, this is my finest sword. If on your journey, you should encounter God, God will be cut.

—Hattori Hanzo, *Kill Bill Volume 1*

---

[17] Mackie, although he is talking about retribution, not revenge, acknowledges that this argument seems to have some force. However, he adds that it seems that most still won't think that punishment is permissible, unless it is combined with an obligation to punish; but I find that unpersuasive and he says nothing more on the issue. See J.L. Mackie, "Retributivism: A Test Case for Ethical Theory," in Feinberg and Coleman.

So, it seems, western philosophy makes room for Tarantinian revenge. But perhaps Tarantino goes too far. fter all, with revenge, there is no limit to the punishment's severity and its severity is determined by the avenger alone; this entails that the punishment could end up being much worse than the offender's original crime. In *Pulp Fiction*, Lance tells Vincent that punishment for keying someone's car should be death. "No trial, no jury, straight to execution." In *Jackie Brown*, Louis kills Melanie in the parking lot of the Del Amo Mall because she won't stop bugging him. (The final straw is her making fun of him for forgetting where he parked.) And such actions seem wrong.

I tend to agree, and would suggest that revenge that "oversteps its bounds" in this way is not morally justified. So I offer my defense of revenge with this caveat: not all acts of revenge are morally justified, but revenge can be morally justified if the inflicted punishment reflects the original crime—in other words, if the punishment is "due." But Tarantino's films offer this caveat as well. I don't think that the above examples are portrayed as praiseworthy. Notice also that, in *Pulp Fiction*, when it is suspected that Marsellus Wallace dropped Antwan Rockamore (a.k.a. Tony Rocky Horror) down four stories into a greenhouse for giving his wife a foot massage—even though Vincent suggests that Tony was "playing with matches" and should have expected to get burned (PF)—both Jules and Vincent acknowledge that he went too far.

> **Jules:** Now look, just 'cause I wouldn't give no man a foot massage, don't make it right for Marsellus to throw Antwan off a building into a glass motherfuckin' house, fuckin' up the way the nigger talks. That shit ain't right. Motherfucker do that shit to me, he better paralyze my ass, 'cause I kill the motherfucker, you know what I'm saying?
>
> **Vincent:** I ain't sayin it's right. But you sayin' a foot massage don't mean nothing, and I'm saying it does.

Even though "undue punishment" is frowned upon, one might complain that Tarantino's view seems to suggest that under certain circumstances the killing of innocents is morally justified. After all, Tarantino suggests through the voice of Hattori Hanzo:

When engaged in combat, the vanquishing of thine enemy can be the warrior's only concern. This is the first and cardinal rule of combat. Suppress all human emotion and compassion. Kill whoever stands in thy way, even if that be Lord God, or Buddha himself. (*Kill Bill Volume 1*)

This quote is often attributed to Rinzai, "a ninth-century Chinese monk who developed a school of Buddhism that focused on 'sudden enlightenment'"[18] and would seem to suggest the killing of innocents is justified if innocents stand in the way of due punishment. But I don't think that Tarantino's view really takes things that far (nor does the quote entail that one should). Beatrix does take this advice to heart when she fights the Crazy 88s, but this is only because the Crazy 88s are not innocent; they are sworn protectors of O-Ren. If they had simply refused to protect O-Ren she would have not touched them. (In fact, in the movie she offers this way out to Go Go, and in the original script she makes the same offer to Mr. Barrell—O'Ren's #2 who doesn't appear in the film—and he takes it!) But the most convincing evidence that Tarantino's films don't promote the killing of innocents in the name of vengeance is seen in the scene that precedes the above quote where Beatrix kills Vernita.

> **VERNITA:** You have every right to wanna get even—
> **BEATRIX:** But that's where you're wrong, Vernita. I don't want to get even. To get even, even Steven, I would have to kill you, go into Nikki's room, kill her, then wait for your old man, Dr. Bell, to come home and kill him. That would make us even. No, my unborn daughter will just hafta be satisfied with your death at her mother's hands.

Since "due" punishment would entail the killing of innocents, Beatrix refuses it. Beatrix knows that this is, morally, going too far and settles for only killing Vernita. So it seems that there is room for Tarantino's view; it is not only logically coherent, but I think it is defensible. As long as the punishment administered fits the crime and doesn't kill innocents, revenge is morally permitted.

---

[18] www.beliefnet.com/story/163/story_16301_1.html.

Some may be appalled that I am defending such a view but to them I say three things:

1. I'm not saying that, if wronged, seeking revenge is morally obligatory; only that it is morally permissible. (We can't shake a morally disapproving finger at O-Ren for avenging her parent's death.)

2. I'm not saying that one should seek revenge if wronged. If you can't be sure that your act of vengeance is morally justified—that your desired punishment fits the crime of a guilty personal offender—you ought not seek revenge, and such things are hard to be sure of. (Besides, "loving your enemy" seems to have the moral high ground and seeking revenge is illegal. Although revenge is permissible, the non-avenger is more virtuous.)

3. This view, I think, is shared by the majority. As Murphy points out, this is why people enjoy revenge movies like Tarantino's and applaud when the victim finally kills the villain in the end.[19]

Of course, the majority sharing the view doesn't make it right; but I think it does entail that one can't be appalled at its defense.

---

[19] Murphy, pp. 788–89

# 6

# "I'm a Bad Person": Beatrix Kiddo's Rampage and Virtue

RACHEL ROBISON

Beatrix Kiddo (codename: Black Mamba), the main character of Quentin Tarantino's *Kill Bill* series, goes on a "roaring rampage of revenge" to kill everyone who was involved in her attempted murder.

Are the actions of the Deadly Viper Assassination Squad morally okay? Is Beatrix's revenge morally okay? Let's see how several different ethical theories would answer these questions. Most of these theories will conclude that the Squad's actions are morally impermissible. Yet I believe that the Deadly Viper Assassination Squad operates according to a bastardization of virtue ethics. Looked at in this way, their actions may actually turn out to be permissible.

## Consequences

One way of analyzing whether an action is permissible or impermissible is to look at the consequences that result from that action. One of the most popular theories of this kind is *utilitarianism*. This type of theory is advocated by philosophers like John Stuart Mill[1] and Jeremy Bentham.[2] From this point of view, the only thing with intrinsic value (the only thing that is valuable for its own sake) is happiness. So in order to make the right moral decision, an agent should perform whatever action

---

[1] John Stuart Mill, *Utilitarianism*, second edition (Indianapolis: Hackett, 2001).
[2] Jeremy Bentham, *An Introduction to the Principles of Morals and Legislation*, (Mineola: Dover, 2007).

promotes the greatest amount of overall happiness or (in those cases where there is no net happiness) prevents the greatest amount of overall unhappiness.

To see how this theory works, let's look at the first killing we see in the movie, the death of Vernita Green (codename: Copperhead). At first, all we know about the situation is that there is a standoff between two beautiful women who are somehow very well trained in martial arts. At this point, we need to look at the happiness or unhappiness that both parties would experience were Beatrix to kill Vernita. We know that Beatrix would derive a great amount of happiness from killing Vernita. Assuming that Vernita has an equally strong desire to stay alive, utilitarianism might not be able to tell us whether the killing is morally permissible or not. All this changes when we see a school bus pull up in front of the house and Vernita's young daughter Nikki arrives home. At this point, we need to factor in not only the happiness that Beatrix would experience and the unhappiness that Vernita would experience, but also the happiness or unhappiness that Nikki would experience. Presumably Nikki would experience a great amount of unhappiness if her mother were killed. When all of these elements are factored into a utilitarian calculus, it is clear that the action is morally impermissible.[3]

This is a case where we are looking at immediate happiness or unhappiness. What is really important is the happiness or unhappiness that is promoted for all agents involved in the long term. For example when Beatrix receives training from Pai Mei, his behavior seems to leave something to be desired. She is constantly afraid of losing her arm or having her eyes ripped out of their sockets. However, in the long term, Pai Mei's actions may be justified because of the happiness that Beatrix experiences when she is in possession of the power that the master imparts. So an action that seems unjustified at the time that it occurs is ultimately justified when we look at the long-term happiness or unhappiness of the agents involved.

However, there are some problems with this kind of utilitarianism. Take, for example, psychotic Go-Go of the Crazy 88.

---

[3] At this point, for the purpose of ease of explanation, I am leaving out the fact that both women are deadly assassins. I will touch on this detail later.

Go-Go derives a great amount of pleasure from killing and she will do so with little provocation. She kills a man at a bar just because he said "yes" when she asked him if he would like to have sex with her. Imagine that the man she killed had no family or loved ones that would care if he was dead. Also suppose that the man has lived a fairly miserable life and isn't too sad about dying. It may actually turn out that crazy murderous Go-Go is justified in killing the man because she will derive a greater amount of pleasure than the amount of pain she causes. This seems counter-intuitive.

A modification of utilitarianism that attempts to avoid such a problem is *rule utilitarianism*. This can be distinguished from the *act utilitarianism* we have been discussing so far. Act utilitarianism looks at the specific consequences that result from any particular action. Rule utilitarianism is concerned with the happiness that is promoted as a general rule from the action that is performed. From a rule utilitarian perspective, Go-Go's actions would not be morally permissible. Because murdering another person as a general rule promotes more unhappiness then it does happiness, all such instances of murder are morally impermissible.

This distinction will help us in our discussion of revenge. Let's look at Beatrix's revenge. She kills four of the world's most deadly assassins and blinds a fifth. We need to weigh her happiness against the unhappiness of the assassins. We also need to factor in the happiness that would be experienced by the families of the victims of the people the assassins killed upon receiving the news of the assassin's death. Finally, we need to factor in all of the lives saved by killing these four people and their associates. From an act utilitarian perspective, this action may be morally praiseworthy. From a rule utilitarian perspective, however, the action is impermissible because deadly revenge as a general rule leads to more negative consequences than it does positive ones.

There is no textual evidence in the screenplay that suggests the squad takes themselves to be operating according to a utilitarian theory of morality. However, there is one other form of consequentialism that we should consider, ethical egoism. According to this theory, an action is morally permissible if it promotes the agent's long-term self interest. In a situation like Beatrix's, seeking revenge may actually be in her long-term self interest. The relief she seems to feel at the end of the movie when she is laughing on the bathroom floor in her cheap motel is evidence of this. However, there is no textual evidence in the movie that Beatrix thinks she is acting in accordance with ethical egoism. In fact, there is textual evidence to suggest that this is not the theory the squad operates on. Take, for example, Bill's words to Beatrix immediately following his attempt on her life. "Do you find me sadistic? You know, Beatrix, I'd like to believe that you're aware enough even now to know that there's nothing sadistic in my actions. At this moment, this is me at my most masochistic." This quote suggests that even though Bill knows his actions are not in his own long-term self interest, he is motivated to perform them anyway. This is not consistent with an Ethical Egoist account.

## Duties and Intentions

A second way of determining whether an action is right or wrong is to look at the duties and intentions of the agent performing the action. This approach is typically referred to as "deontology." The philosopher that is the most famous for advocating this kind of theory is Immanuel Kant.[4] According to Kant, reason gives us access to the moral law. The moral law manifests itself in commands or imperatives that we are obligated to follow. For Kant, the supreme principle of morality is the Categorical Imperative. This is the principle from which all of our moral obligations can be derived.

There are two formulations of this imperative that we will be concerned with here—the Formula of Universal Law and the Formula of Humanity. The Formula of Universal Law states that you should

> act always according to that maxim which you can, at the same time, without contradiction, will to be universal law.

A maxim is usually of the following form: I will perform action A to achieve purpose B. In order to follow the Formula of Universal Law, we must imagine what would happen if our

---

[4] Immanuel Kant, *Grounding for the Metaphysics of Morals*, third edition (Indianapolis: Hackett, 1993).

maxim were universalized. In other words, we must imagine what would happen if everyone did what we are planning to do. Once we have universalized our maxim, we must check for what Kant oddly refers to as "contradictions." There are two different types of contradictions that may arise, contradictions in conception and contradictions in will. If the maxim is universalized and no contradiction occurs, then the action is morally permissible. If the maxim is universalized and a contradiction does occur, the action is impermissible. If failing to perform the action creates a contradiction, then that action is morally required.

A contradiction in conception occurs when, if you universalize your maxim, it no longer works. To illustrate how this works, let's look at the arrangement that Elle Driver (codename: California Mountain Snake) makes with Budd (codename: Sidewinder). She wants his Hattori Hanzo sword and agrees to give him a million dollars in exchange for it. She arrives at his trailer as promised with a briefcase full of large bills. Ultimately, however, she has no intention of parting with the money as she promised. Underneath the cash is a deadly Black Mamba snake. The snake bites Budd multiple times about the head and face and, as Elle points out, "In Africa, the saying goes 'In the bush, an elephant can kill you, a leopard can kill you, and a black mamba can kill you. But only with the mamba is death sure.' Hence its handle, 'Death Incarnate.' Pretty cool, huh?" Budd dies and Elle is in a position to keep the sword and the money. In this case, our maxim would be to promise to do something that we were never planning to do in order to obtain some advantage or benefit. If we universalized this maxim, it would no longer work because no one would trust one another and no such agreements would ever be made.

A contradiction in will arises when a person would not rationally will to live in a world in which the maxim is universalized. For example, during a staff meeting, O-Ren Ishii (codename: Cottonmouth) chops off the head of a person with a dissenting opinion. In this case, our maxim is to kill a person for expressing an opinion contrary to our own in order to achieve some sense of satisfaction or to get rid of the dissenting opinion. If we universalized this maxim, we would have a world in which no one could speak freely. A rational person would not will to live in a world in which this maxim is universalized. All rational persons would, at various times, wish to have their positions known. Therefore, O-Ren's actions are impermissible.

The second formulation of the Categorical Imperative, The Formula of Humanity, states that

> one should act always in such a way as to treat humanity, whether in the form of oneself of another, as an end in itself and never merely as a means.

This means that we should respect one another's ability to make autonomous choices. We shouldn't use people. For example, consider Buck, the hospital orderly who has sex with comatose patients and accepts money from other men in exchange for guarding the room while they do the same thing. Buck's actions are morally impermissible because he is not recognizing Beatrix as an end in herself. He is treating her as a mere means to obtain sex and money.

Now let's consider revenge from this perspective. The kind of revenge that Beatrix is engaging in will always be impermissible on this view. Killing is wrong according to both formulations of the categorical imperative. If we universalize the maxim that we should kill in order to be vindicated, a contradiction in will occurs. A rational person would not will to live in a world where they have to fear for their life if they offend someone. The Formula of Humanity yields the same result. When Beatrix kills, she is treating her victims as a means to her vindictive end. She is not only disrespecting their ability to make autonomous decisions, she is actually permanently depriving them of that ability.

Is this the system they seem to be acting on? There may be some textual evidence to support the claim that it is. When Bill comes to Budd with the news that Beatrix is out to kill them all, Budd says, "That woman deserves her revenge . . . and we deserve to die. But then again, so does she." This quote suggests the idea of a person getting what they deserve, which is a deontological concept. However, Budd seems to be using it in an eye-for-an-eye, Code-of-Hammurabi kind of way. There is no sophisticated deontological theory in play here. We will see that there is more substantial textual evidence to suggest that Beatrix and the squad operate according to a different moral code.

## Virtue Ethics

At this point one might be tempted to conclude that the Deadly Viper Assassination Squad acts without any regard for ethics. As we have seen, the actions they engage in are impermissible from both consequentialist and deontological perspectives. However, members of the squad do not act with complete reckless abandon. There is a certain code they follow such that some members of the squad are more ethical than others. In this section I will discuss a third theory that more closely approximates the ethical code the Deadly Vipers appear to be acting in accordance with. In fact, I will argue that there is some textual evidence for the claim that they take themselves to be acting on such principles.

Let's begin by gathering the evidence from the screenplay. At the end of *Kill Bill Volume 2*, Bill says

> Superman did not become Superman; Superman was born Superman. When Superman wakes up in the morning, he's Superman. His alter ego is Clark Kent. His outfit with the big red "S," that's the blanket he was wrapped in as a baby when the Kents found him. Those are his clothes. What Kent wears, the glasses, the business suit, that's the costume. That's the costume Superman wears to blend in with us. Clark Kent is how Superman views us. And what are the characteristics of Clark Kent? He's weak, he's unsure of himself . . . he's a coward. Clark Kent is Superman's critique on the whole human race. Sort of like Beatrix Kiddo and Mrs. Tommy Plympton.

This quote suggests that the squad does not act without consideration for ethics. Essential to any theory the squad would accept is an element that takes into consideration neither duties nor consequences, but the kind of character a person has. Bill is pointing out that there is something admirable about Beatrix and others like her that is not present in the average person. She is courageous and strong. These character traits are virtues.

This emphasis on character is present on a number of occasions in both movies. At the beginning of *Kill Bill Volume 1*, Beatrix lies in a coma as a result of an unsuccessful attempt on her life. Elle arrives at the hospital to finish the job. She makes a phone call to Bill to apprise him of the situation. He tells her not to kill Beatrix, insisting that she deserves better. Bill consid-

ers killing Beatrix in her sleep to be cowardly. Cowardice is a
trait of character to be avoided by members of the squad.

This sentiment is also present in Elle's reaction to the news
that Budd has killed Beatrix. She is appalled and says (on
Budd's "deathbed"):

> Now in these last agonizing minutes of life you have left, let me
> answer the question you asked earlier more thoroughly. Right at
> this moment, the biggest "R" I feel is regret. Regret that maybe the
> greatest warrior I have ever known, met her end at the hands of a
> bushwhackin', scrub, alky piece of shit like you. That woman
> deserved better.

This is a strange response for someone who has made multiple
attempts on Beatrix's life herself. Although all members of the
assassination squad are ruthless killers, there is something particularly contemptible about Budd. For example, when Beatrix arrives
at Budd's trailer, he shoots her in the stomach. Beatrix duels with
all the other members of the squad she encounters without the use
of firearms. Budd is too cowardly to engage her directly.

Elle isn't much better. During Elle's face-off with Beatrix, she
tells her that she killed Beatrix's former master. A look of terror
crosses Beatrix's face. Surely whoever was strong enough to kill
Pai Mei must be the best warrior of them all. When Beatrix
learns that Elle killed her master by poisoning his fish heads,
however, the fear dissipates and she knows she can certainly
take anyone who would stoop to that level of cowardice.

## The Virtues of Superhumans

The theory that these assassins seem to take themselves as acting in accordance with is some bastardization of a Virtue Ethical
theory. Virtue Ethical theories are present in both Plato and
Aristotle. Such theories focus on building good character.
According to this theory it is persons that are evaluated, not their
actions. For Aristotle, human beings are able to flourish by living their life in accordance with reason. Not all people are able
to live their lives in accordance with reason. It's virtue that
makes living a reasoned life possible.

For Aristotle, virtuous people will utilize reason to find what
he calls the "golden mean." The mean in this sense is not an

average, but rather the appropriate course of action that a virtuous person would engage in when utilizing reason in a particular situation. The appropriate course of action, in turn, will make reference to a pair of extremes, which the mean falls between. For example, let's look at courage. I pick this virtue because it seems to be the one the Squad cares the most about. A courageous person will utilize reason to find the mean in a given context. Courage is a mean between the two extremes of cowardice and rashness. The Deadly Viper Assassination Squad is a group of well-trained warriors. They are proficient in many forms of combat. It is unnecessary for them to resort to killing people in the swiftest or easiest way possible regardless of the circumstances. So when any of them attempts to kill another member of the Squad in this way—by ignoring their proficiency—it is dishonorable. This is a code of honor that they have in virtue of their extensive training. When they ignore it, they are acting in an uncourageous way. Here, consistent with the Aristotelian version of the virtue theory, context binds courage to honor. Under these circumstances, they have not reasoned as a courageous person would. They have not found the mean; rather, they are acting in a way that is too close to rash.

Granted, this may not be the way that most people would act under the circumstances. However, the earlier quote from Bill seems to suggest that the Squad views themselves as being super-human in some way. A twisted virtue ethical system may support his claim. The Squad may be more virtuous, at least in terms of courage, than anyone else. Friedrich Nietzsche argues that most moral systems are antithetical to the flourishing of truly excellent human beings.[5] He argues that a revaluation of values occurred which caused people to value things that do not contribute to the production of a higher class of people. There is evidence that the assassins see themselves as a higher class of people, people who are more virtuous in many ways than the average person. They don't feel they need to value the things that common people value. In order to truly flourish as assassins, the Squad can't look to consequentialism or deontology because these theories prevent the creation of people who

---

[5] See Sections 44, 56, 61–62, 203, 211–12, 242, 272, and 296 of Nietzsche's *Beyond Good and Evil* (London: Penguin, 2003).

are truly great. A virtue ethical perspective allows the squad to flourish.

From Beatrix's perspective, she must defend her honor. Bill disrespected her when he killed her friends and attempted to kill her. Beatrix is not only justified in seeking revenge; she would be cowardly if she did not. As a courageous person, under the circumstances, reason dictates that she should defend her honor.

At the end of the movie, after using the five-point-palm-exploding-heart technique on Bill, Beatrix expresses her concern about being a bad person. Bill responds by saying, "You're not a bad person. You're a terrific person. You're my favorite person." From their warped view of virtue ethics, maybe he is right.

# 7

# A Sword of Righteousness: *Kill Bill* and the Ethics of Vengeance

TIMOTHY DEAN ROTH

"That woman deserves her revenge . . . and we deserve to die." So says Budd, one of the five assassins singled out for destruction by the mysterious "Bride," played by Uma Thurman. "But then again," Bud continues after a long pause, "so does she."

Vengeance is the theme of Quentin Tarantino's *Kill Bill*, his most ambitious (and bloody) film. Betrayed by Bill and his mercenaries, the Bride draws up a "death list" of her five would-be assassins, who she believes killed her unborn daughter and nearly herself. Armed with the greatest samurai sword ever made, the Bride goes on a killing spree that brings a whole new meaning to the word "Mother."

Tarantino exploits the revenge story in *Kill Bill* for maximum trash-and-gore effect. But behind what looks to be a straightforward revenge epic, Tarantino interjects moments of genuine emotional pain and glimmers of conscience that transcend the film's grindhouse aesthetic. These moments introduce an ambiguity about the Bride's murderous mission, uncovering the ethical questions posed by the act of vengeance.

## The Inequities of the Selfish and the Tyranny of Evil Men

Like all three of his previous films, Tarantino's *Kill Bill* is filled with characters whose morally self-defined worlds inevitably come into conflict, revealing a more primitive and basic moral reality. Tarantino uses violence and human depravity as a kind

85

of crucible that burns away all superfluous concerns until all that's left is an irreducible, and sometimes humorously unexpected, moral epiphany. This "moment of clarity" is a realization of the most universal and ancient "golden rule": "Love your neighbor as yourself," as the Old Testament has it.

Of all human impulses, the desire for revenge is one of the easiest to understand because it appeals to our innate sense of equity. There's a reciprocity to evil action that's a product of an unspoken understanding that we, as sentient beings who all feel happiness and pain, are equals. Thus the eighteenth-century B.C. maxim from Hammurabi's law code—the simple but self-evident rule "an eye for an eye and a tooth for a tooth."

Revenge is itself an implication and extension of the golden rule. It's something we all intuitively understand, which is why we find revenge stories so engaging. I drive a cab for Washington State's Social and Health Services. On one recent trip to the hospital, two women were talking about *Kill Bill*. "It's a woman getting revenge," one of them said. "Bill went and messed her up good, so she went and messed *him* up good. That's how it works!" See what I mean? (Incidentally, one of my regular clients survived a coma after she put two bullets in her head. Truth really is stranger than fiction.) The Bride's revenge, according to this woman, needs no justification. It's her natural right to "get even."

## And I Will Strike Down Upon Thee with Great Vengeance and Furious Anger

There's a rare Japanese poster for *Kill Bill Volume 2* that features Uma Thurman dressed in a white wedding gown and holding her samurai sword at the ready. In a superimposed banner lies the surprising tag line: KILL IS LOVE.

The phrase is reminiscent of the seemingly incongruous words that appear over the gateway to Dante Alighieri's Hell:

> Justice inspired my exalted Creator.
> I am a creature of the Holiest Power
> of Wisdom in the Highest and of Primal Love.[1]

---

[1] *Inferno*, Canto 3, lines 4–6. Robin Kirkpatrick, *The Divine Comedy I: Inferno* (London: Penguin, 2006).

These words are from Dante's *Divine Comedy*, the definitive literary synthesis of medieval ethical, aesthetic, religious, and political philosophy. It's also a work that stands on the verge of Renaissance humanism. Tracing a thread through Thomas Aquinas, Saint Augustine, and Aristotle, Dante gets medieval on our asses by presenting a holistic inquiry into what it means to be fully human. Dante borrows heavily from Aquinas who believed that God's very essence was his own Being. Aquinas's idea, in turn, comes both from Aristotle's conception of the "Uncaused Cause" and Exodus 3:13–15 in which God reveals his name as Yahweh—"I AM." God's nature, Aquinas and Dante believed, is Truth and Love, the two primary and essential characteristics of Being. Because humans are created in the image of God, one is only fully human, according to Dante and Aquinas, if one rightly exercises reason and love. To fail to do so is to deny one's own humanity.

The degree to which one sins against love and reason determines the nature of the punishments described in Dante's *Inferno*. There are several interesting parallels between *Kill Bill* and *Inferno*. They feature a heroine named Beatrix and Beatrice, respectively; both Dante and Tarantino adapt their aesthetic to fit the nature and place of the sinner; and both view vengeance as a logical extension of love.

Dante uses the method of *contrapasso* as the aesthetic principle that determines each sinner's punishment. That is, the punishment is a concrete, physical embodiment of the spiritual condition (not simply punishment-fits-the-crime as many assume). The greatest sinners in Dante's hell, for example, are forever encased in ice, a vivid and horrific allegorical statement that sin ultimately results in the reduction of all human freedom and possibility.[2]

Tarantino uses a similar method in his punishments, often, like Dante, with acerbic humor. The knife-fighter Vernita is killed with the Bride's knife. O-Ren is killed by "Japanese steel" (those who live by the sword die by the sword). The loathsome, trailer-trash desert hermit, Budd, is killed by a snake. Elle Driver's hubristic inability to see the generosity of Pai Mei's "cruel tutelage" results in her blindness. And Bill, of course, dies of a broken heart.

---

[2] Kirkpatrick, lxxv.

Tarantino also adapts his aesthetic approach to each situation just as Dante's poetic language differs according to each stage of his journey. And both exhaust every conceivable technique of their respective arts in the process. (The effortless versatility with which Tarantino does this is one of the great joys of watching *Kill Bill*.) The Crazy 88 chapter, for example, is respectfully parodic in its tribute to Japanese cinema. An astonishing animé sequence is utilized to tell the story of O-Ren's childhood. The Budd scenes are presented in a style reminiscent of the spaghetti westerns of Sergio Leone. And the Pai Mei chapter is shot in grainy 16mm film, with extreme camera zooms, typical of low-budget Bruce Lee films.

More importantly, both Dante and Tarantino view vengeance as a form of truth-telling. Vengeance presupposes one's dignity by calling one to account for their crimes against others, and against their own humanity. The act of vengeance is an unambiguous declaration that evil is a reality. By contrast, the act of vengeance is also a statement that love, goodness, and righteousness are moral realities by virtue of the fact that they have been violated. The implication is that without the reality of justice there's no reality to mercy.

Dante makes this clear in his depiction of the Lukewarm and their non-place in Hell. Because these indifferent people never chose good or evil in their lifetime, they occupy a nowhere-land where they forever chase a blank banner. For Dante, the Lukewarm would not understand the generosity and self-sacrifice of forgiveness and mercy, since they are unable to properly reflect on their own offenses. To punish them would likewise be a waste. "The world allows no glory to their name. Mercy and Justice alike despise them," Dante concludes.[3]

Tarantino doesn't make films about lukewarm people. He deals in the luridly entertaining lives of outlaws and assassins, thugs and thieves. The crooks in *Kill Bill* are fully aware that they "deserve to die," as Budd says. Budd even seems proud of the fact that he "never cheats his way out of his comeuppance." It's a statement of his inherent dignity (what little remains, anyway) as a rational and autonomous moral agent.

The Bride's revenge is, whether right or wrong, an act of love: for herself as one who is violated; for her missing daugh-

---

[3] *Inferno.* Canto 3, lines 49–50. Kirkpatrick, p. 23.

ter; for her innate sense of righteousness; and for her emotionally necessitated reconciliation with her former lover, Bill.

## Blessed Is He Who Shepherds the Weak Through the Valley of Darkness

It's clear that the Bride "deserves her revenge," that there's a certain heroic righteousness in her quest to kill her tormentors, and that their deaths are just. Her vengeance is even potentially life-saving given that all her victims are hired assassins and gangsters. Why, then, might we conclude that her mission of "bloody satisfaction" is, in fact, immoral?

Tarantino suggests that it's precisely because the act of vengeance perpetuates a never-ending cycle of violence. It's also to commit the Dantean sin of reducing one's self to the imprisonment of excessive passion. This obsession results in a continuation rather than reconciliation of the murderous act. Tarantino illustrates this cycle through multiple stories-within-stories of orphaned children who seek revenge for their murdered parents.

We first encounter the orphan story when the Bride kills Vernita in front of her young daughter, Nikki. "It was not my intention to do this in front of you," she explains coldly. "But you can take my word for it; your mother had it coming." Then with antithetical tenderness she tells her, "When you grow up, if you still feel raw about it, I'll be waiting." That Nikki *will* feel raw about it is implied by Tarantino's placing of O-Ren's orphan story shortly after.

As a child, O-Ren witnesses the ruthless murder of her parents at the hands of the evil Yakuza boss, Matsumoto. As a young teenager, she gets her revenge by killing Matsumoto at an "advantageous" moment. She goes on to become a skilled mercenary who forms her own Yakuza clan, the Crazy 88s.

There are subtle indications that the Bride, as well as Bill and his younger brother Budd, are also orphans. Bill is said to have been in need of father figures "like most men who never knew their fathers." And when asked why her family won't be attending her wedding, the Bride replies, "I don't have anyone." Later we glimpse the Bride as a child. She's wearing the same pigtails that both Nikki and the young O-Ren are seen wearing. The dizzying effect of these stories-within-stories reveals the dreadful and terrifying prospect of the proliferation of violence upon violence in a never ending whirlwind of hatred.

Although it's Hattori Hanzo who provides the Bride with her "instrument of death," he is, in fact, the moral conscience of the film. He offers several observations on the nature of revenge in vivid aphorisms. (There's a reason why the sage who creates the flawlessly piercing sword is Hattori Hanzo rather than Pai Mei.)

The first moral crisis comes when the Bride kills Vernita in front of Nikki. She knows her actions will have repercussions, perhaps even guaranteeing her own death at the hands of an older Nikki. As we see her troubled expression, we hear Hanzo describe the single-minded blindness of revenge: "For those regarded as warriors, when engaged in combat, the vanquishing of thine enemy can be the warrior's only concern. Suppress all human emotion and compassion. Kill whoever stands in thy way, even if that be Lord God, or Buddha himself."

On her way to kill O-Ren we hear Hanzo warn: "Revenge is never a straight line. It's a forest. And like a forest it's easy to lose your way, to get lost, to forget where you came in." These words echo Aristotle's qualification of revenge: "it is not easy to define how, with whom, at what, and how long one should be angry, and at what point right action ceases and wrong begins."[4]

Finally, while handing her the sword he's made (something he'd vowed never to do again) he says, "I can tell you with no ego, this is my finest sword." He continues, with a touch of regret in his voice, "If on your journey you should encounter God, God will be cut." It's a subtle indication that her mission of revenge may well cause pain to more than just her victims.

## And You Will Know My Name Is the Lord When I Lay My Vengeance upon Thee

"When fortune smiles on something as violent and ugly as revenge," the Bride tells us, "it seems proof like no other that not only does God exist, you're doing his will." Clearly the Bride identifies herself as an agent of God, and in the wisdom tradition of the Hebrew Prophets, she's right. Well, partly.

---

[4] *Nichomachean Ethics,* Book IV, Chapter 5, in *Introduction to Aristotle,* edited by Richard McKeon (New York: Modern Library, 1992), p. 414.

Personal identification with God, whether conscious or unconscious, is a common literary motif in the stories of the Old Testament. The story of Samson, for example, is that of a man continually betrayed by the women he falls in love with. This story is set in the larger context of the book of Judges which relates how Israel (God's Bride) continually breaks God's trust. By sympathizing with Samson's heartache the reader sympathizes with God.

Identification is a recurring theme with Jules Winnfield in *Pulp Fiction*, in which Jules sees himself as an agent of God's wrath. During his religious epiphany he consciously seeks to re-interpret his situation from the divine point of view. This divine empathy culminates in Jules's pardon of Pumpkin and Honey Bunny. This act of mercy changes the way he interprets his Ezekiel 25:17 speech. He takes on the merciful rather than the vengeful perspective of God. When Jules repeats Ezekiel 25: 17 to "Ringo," there's a surprising tenderness to his voice, though his conclusion is no less dramatic. He even changes the impersonal "my name is" and "thee" it to the more direct and intimate, "you will know *I am* the Lord when I lay my vengeance upon *you*."

Like Jules, the Bride identifies her actions as a personal expression of God's anger. "Her revenge is very Old Testament," Uma Thurman herself has noted.[5] The Hebrew Prophets often indicate that God makes certain nations and people instruments of his wrath against Israel, and vice versa, implying that the avenger "is doing God's will." But God's wrath, according to the Prophets, is far from simple. There's a dual nature to God's wrath as sharply delineated as the two sides of a Hanzo sword. Vengeance in the scriptures (as Jules and Dante understood) is always a paradoxical act of love. And mercy is always a paradoxical act of wrath.

The prophets Isaiah, Ezekiel, and Jeremiah all predicted judgment would come upon Israel for idolatry and social injustice. But as one Old Testament scholar clarifies, "'Judgment' is not a negative concept in the Bible; it is an intervention by which justice is brought about by punishing evildoers and

---

[5] Uma Thurman, "Samurai Sistas." Interview in *FiRST* (October 2003).

upholding the righteous."[6] Even so, the Prophets usually portray God as reluctant to punish.

This reluctance can be seen in the story of Elijah. When Elijah impatiently demands that God reveal his true self, God tells him, "Go outside and stand on the mountain before the Lord; the Lord will be passing by." As he waits, Elijah sees the characteristic symbols of God's wrath: wind, earthquake and fire. But, as the account goes, God was not in any of these signs. To Elijah's surprise, "After the fire there was a still, small voice."[7] At this moment God passes by and Elijah witnesses God's essential nature.

The story of Jonah is another instance where a prophet is angry at God for being merciful. After preaching God's impending judgment to the people of Nineveh they repent and are forgiven. Jonah's furious response is comical: "This is why I fled when you first called me. I knew that you are a gracious and merciful God, slow to anger, rich in clemency, loathe to punish."[8]

Herein lies the ethical divide between divine vengeance and human vengeance. Human vengeance is never borne of a pure and holy love for the purpose of repentance and forgiveness. We also don't patiently wait as God does; we typically want our bloody satisfaction right now. It's a forest, as Hattori Hanzo says, that obscures the true way, like the forest at the opening of Dante's *Inferno*. Dante portrays the vengeful in Hell as forever wallowing in sludge. Eternally tearing each other to pieces, their anger is never (and could never be) satisfied. In Dante's *Purgatorio*, the vengeful are made to wind their way slowly through a thick cloud of smoke that chokes their lungs and stings their eyes. They are barely able to make out their path. Even if their wrath against their neighbor was just, it was inevitably polluted by an emotionally constricting desire for injury that is ultimately sadistic. "The wrath of a man does not accomplish the righteousness of God," the Apostle James said.[9] And the full text of the golden rule, which is seldom heard,

---

[6] Richard J. Clifford, "The Major Prophets, Baruch, and Lamentations," in *The Catholic Study Bible* (Oxford: Oxford University Press, 2006), p. 284.
[7] 1 Kings 19:1–18 (NAB).
[8] Jonah 4:2.
[9] James 1:20.

urges the reader: "Take no revenge and cherish no grudge against your fellow countrymen. You shall love your neighbor as yourself. I am the Lord."[10]

The Bride has a right to her vengeance, but sometimes the ethical choice impels us to act more freely than our rights demand. To continue the cycle of violence, as the Bride does when she makes the innocent Vikki motherless, is to participate in the very evil that is being redressed. In the words of the prophet Bono: "We must not become a monster in order to defeat a monster."[11] Sometimes the ethical choice is inherently unfair. But self-surrender and the extraordinary act of forgiveness are, in fact, the end of violence.

## The Finder of Lost Children

After the bloody adrenaline rush of *Kill Bill Volume 1*, moviegoers eagerly anticipated more retina-searing action in the sequel. It was natural to assume that Tarantino would conclude the epic with a jaw-dropping battle between the Bride and Bill that no one could foresee. Tarantino delivers, but he does so by confounding the audience's expectations.

In contrast to *Kill Bill Volume 1*, *Kill Bill Volume 2* portrays the Bride in a position of weakness rather than strength, of defense rather than advance. Though she certainly tries, she fails to land a single blow with her sword. As far as her "kill-crazy rampage" goes, the only person she kills in *Kill Bill Volume 2* is Bill, and even then, her deadly blow is an act of self-defense (Bill, without warning, swipes at her with his sword). In fact, *every* killing by the Bride, in both movies, is an act of self-defense. The only exception is her one-on-one duel with O-Ren, which they mutually engage. Even when she kills Vernita it's a reflexive act (Vernita surprises her with a gun hidden in a box of cereal). According to Aquinas, she's at least partially off the hook since "the act of self-defense," he states, "can have a double effect: the preservation of one's own life; and the killing of the aggressor. . . . The one is intended, the other is not."[12]

---

[10] Leviticus 19:18.
[11] U2, *Vertigo Tour*, 2005.
[12] *Summa Theologica* II–II, 64, 7 as quoted in *Catechism of the Catholic Church* (New York: Doubleday, 1997), pp. 603–04.

Contrast that with the other murders in the film: Matsumoto's unprovoked and gratuitous murder of O-Ren's parents, Gogo Ubari's absurdly random killing of a Tokyo businessman, O-Ren's furious beheading of Boss Tanaka. As for numbers three and four on the Bride's list, Budd is killed by Black Mamba (the Bride's code-name), just not the Black Mamba we expect. And, oddly enough, the Bride doesn't grace Elle with a noble samurai death. Instead she plucks out her other eye and leaves her humiliated and flailing about in rage.

The biggest surprise of *Kill Bill Volume 2*, however, is the Bride's discovery of BB. In a movie where The Bride is constantly caught off guard, she is totally unprepared for the shock of suddenly realizing her daughter is still alive. That she pretends to die of a bullet from BB's imaginary gun underscores the fact that this vengeful, seemingly indestructible woman we feel we've come to know, has "died." We find out that BB is both the reason why the Bride "quit the life" and the reason she went on a "kill-crazy rampage."

These details come into the light thanks to Bill's "truth serum." As Bill interrogates the woman whom we now know as Beatrix, she's forced into an act of confession, contrition, and penance—a cathartic process that prepares her, and us, for the final confrontation. As Bill drills her, he insists that underneath all her ruses, Beatrix is in essence a "natural born killer" (a reference to Tarantino's eponymous screenplay). Beatrix concedes this fact, but she goes on to relate how her discovery that she was pregnant changed her so fundamentally that her new identity as Mother supersedes all other identities. It's a conversion epiphany similar to the one Jules experiences. Just as Jules goes from The Tyranny of Evil Men to The Shepherd, Beatrix goes from Killer to Mommy.

Finally we come to the sublimely anti-climactic duel between Beatrix and Bill. By this point the film has all the inevitability of a Greek tragedy. There can be no turning back for the Bride, and Bill has destroyed any chance of regaining her trust. "You and I have unfinished business," Beatrix tells him. "Baby, you ain't kiddin'," Bill responds as he slashes at her unexpectedly. Stunned, Beatrix falls back on her chair desperately trying to wield her own sword. She never gets the chance. After Bill knocks her sword away, Beatrix is left holding nothing but the sheath. In an absurdly witty re-enactment of their sexual romance, Bill thrusts at her while she very skillfully sheaths his sword. She then proceeds to break his heart—literally.

In a masterful way, Tarantino infuses this deadly scene with grace and humor. When the Bride hits Bill with the deadly "Five Point Palm Exploding Heart Technique," he has a few seconds left to make his peace with her. His death becomes, in this moment, their reconciliation, and there is a look between them of mutual forgiveness and tenderness. Her revenge, it turns out, is bittersweet. Earlier in the film, Budd, assuming that Beatrix is dead, asks Elle, "So, which one are ya filled with: relief or regret?" It's clear by the look in Beatrix's face, as she watches Bill die, that it's quite a lot of both.

In the final scene of *Kill Bill Volume 2*, we see Beatrix lying on a bathroom floor as she finally releases all of her conflicting emotions, crying out repeatedly the last words of the film: "Thank you." It's an expression of gratitude for the hope of a new life beyond violence. It's the moment when the film transcends the boundaries and limitations of its genre. And like Jules's conversion in *Pulp Fiction*, it comes as such a surprise—a tender heart within the context of a brutal and standoffishly cool genre—that its very existence seems miraculous.

"This film is about justice and redemption," Uma Thurman has stated.[13] In an interview concerning the redemptive value of *Pulp Fiction* Tarantino revealed the heart of his approach to screenwriting: "I never said, 'I'm gonna write a redemption story.' But . . . that's what ended up coming out, because that's what I really believe in."[14] By the end of the film, it begins to look as though The Bride really has, in the words of Hattori Hanzo, "encountered God."

In a world without grace, everyone in *Kill Bill* gets exactly what they deserve. The surprise of the film is that grace somehow pries its way in, without seeming obligatory or contrived. When Beatrix prayerfully whispers, "thank you," it's the film's still, small voice.

---

[13] Uma Thurman, "The Making of *Kill Bill Vol. 1*." Miramax, 2003.
[14] Quentin Tarantino, "Celluloid Heroes." 1995 interview by Chris Willman in *Quentin Tarantino: Interviews*, edited by Gerald Peary (Jackson: University Press of Mississippi, 1998), p. 147.

# 8

# Stuck in the Middle with You: Mr. Blonde and Retributive Justice

JOSEPH ULATOWSKI

> If they hadn't done what I told 'em not to do, they'd still be alive.
> —Mr. Blonde, *Reservoir Dogs* (1991)

> Whoever has committed Murder, must *die*.
> —Immanuel Kant, *Metaphysics of Morals* (1797)

None of the memorable scenes of Quentin Tarantino's *Reservoir Dogs* have affected viewers so much as the one in which Mr. Blonde (Michael Madsen) tortures a cop while dancing to "Stuck in the Middle with You" by Stealer's Wheel. Some viewers have argued largely on the basis of this scene that the violence in *Reservoir Dogs* is entirely gratuitous and that the film is thus morally indefensible as a work of art (call this the "orthodox view"). Oliver Conolly writes:

> The infamous scene in *Reservoir Dogs* in which someone's ear is cut off is not of any interest in terms of any insight into the psychology of the characters in the film. It is hard to see how it could interest anyone except someone with a particular interest in that particular form of torture.[1]

We can easily see that this must be mistaken. The fact that a person would gleefully cut off someone's ear gives us a great deal of insight into that person's psychology, just as the differing

---

[1] Oliver Conolly, "Pleasure and Pain in Literature," *Philosophy and Literature* 29 (2005), p. 314.

reactions of the other members of the gang to this action give us insights into theirs.

We may also learn something about the moral universe of the movie by thinking about the reasons given by the other characters for why Blonde's treatment of Marvin the cop either is or isn't a cause for concern. If we look at the perspective of the characters for whom it is not a problem, we may find that their acceptance of his brutal behavior has larger repercussions for our understanding of real-world philosophical problems. In particular, we may discover that some of the "gratuitous" attitudes toward violence displayed by these criminals are not all that different from some of the attitudes that underlie certain widely-accepted theories of justice and punishment.

In contrast to some film critics and philosophers of film, I maintain that Blonde is a far more complex character than someone who just enjoys shooting—and presumably killing—people. The naive belief that Blonde is nothing more than a psycho torturing for the fun of it stems from the critics' assumptions about the correct theory of punishment. Given a different theory of punishment, we can make better sense of Blonde's actions.

Let's look at two theories of punishment: the utilitarian theory, probably held by the critics who misunderstand Blonde's actions, and the retributive theory, which makes those actions appear more understandable.

But first, what is a theory of punishment?

## Theories of Punishment

A theory of punishment attempts to provide a justification for an authority to inflict some penalty on a person for a wrongdoing. Any theory of punishment requires:

1. proper authority,
2. form,
3. proportionality.

First, the person or entity administering punishment must have the proper authority to do so. Governments have the legal authority to punish citizens for committing crimes, and parents have the moral authority to reprimand their children.

Second, the *form* of punishment administered should be appropriate to the crime: for example, minor moving violations might draw a fine, whereas murder might incur the death penalty.

Finally, the punishment should be proportional to the wrongdoing—that is, the amount of punishment inflicted, in whatever form, should not exceed, or fall short of, the degree of the original infraction.

Punishment can be defined in a *negative* or a *positive* way: that is, it may involve either the intentional deprivation of some good, right, or privilege belonging to a person, or the requirement of some restitution or compensation to make up for a person's wrongdoing. If Smith is arrested for driving drunk, a judge may revoke his driver's license or send him to jail, whereas if Jones is caught stealing merchandise from a store, she may be required to do community service or pay a fine. Of the two theories I will describe, the utilitarian theory emphasizes a positive approach, whereas the retributive theory emphasizes a negative one.

## The Utilitarian Theory of Punishment

The utilitarian theory of punishment justifies punishment if maximizing people's general happiness is a likely consequence of carrying out the punishment. One version of the utilitarian theory, which has probably influenced critics who condemn the violence in *Reservoir Dogs* as gratuitous, may be stated as follows:

> Punishing a person is morally justified if and only if some future good, such as incapacitation to commit another harmful act, rehabilitation, or deterrence, is served.

The utilitarian theory of punishment is a forward-looking theory rather than a retrospective one because it justifies punishment based upon the consequences that follow from the wrongdoer's actions, rather than focusing on the wrongdoer's actions.

The utilitarian position as stated above may seem plausible, but there are objections to it. For example, if a person holds high political office or is otherwise influential in the community, then punishing that person may have undesirable effects. It may compromise the well-being of the commonwealth or even start a riot. Since this would not maximize social utility, the pure form of the theory outlined above would seem to dictate that we ought not to punish the influential person, or at least not as severely as others. Most fair-minded persons in our own society would probably agree that social status ought not to be a consideration in an acceptable theory of punishment.

The utilitarian theory may also seem to justify harsh penalties for minor offenses and light penalties for major offenses if these penalties have the best effects generally. For instance, imprisoning or even executing a person for violating speeding laws might deter others from speeding, but harsh penalties for minor offenses and light penalties for major offenses are unfair because the penalty doesn't fit the crime. Again, most persons would agree that the amount of punishment ought not to be given according to the effects it will actually produce; instead, the amount of punishment ought to be determined by the seriousness of the crime.

These objections and others like them are easily addressed with a few modifications, and in fact most contemporary versions of the utilitarian argument are sophisticated enough to fend off such objections. The more fundamental objection out of which these specific ones emerge, however, is the one that leads us to our second theory.

The objection runs like this: according to the utilitarian theory, some good must be gained to justify punishment. But if the punishment depends for its justification on some future good—on the likely effects it will produce—then it seems to lose sight of the crime that has been committed. We shouldn't punish a person only if it will be advantageous for the community; instead, we should punish a person because he or she has done something wrong, and therefore *deserves* it.

## The Retributive Theory of Punishment

This brings us to the retributive theory of punishment.[2] Whereas the utilitarian theory uses the foreseen consequences of punishment (the good or bad effects) to argue that some sanction is

---

[2] For a broad overview of different forms of retributivism, see Ted Honderich, *Punishment: The Supposed Justification Revisited*, revised edition (Ann Arbor: Pluto Press, 2006).

morally justified, the retributivist says that we are justified in punishing a person simply on account of the fact that the person has done wrong. According to the demands of justice, wrongdoers deserve to suffer. John Rawls writes:

> Punishment is justified only on the ground that wrongdoing merits punishment. It is morally fitting that a person who does wrong should suffer in proportion to his wrongdoing. That a criminal should be punished follows from his guilt, and the severity of the appropriate punishment depends on the depravity of the act. The state of affairs where a wrongdoer suffers punishment is morally better than one where he does not, and is so irrespective of consequences.[3]

If the retributive theory is correct, society has a moral duty to punish wrongdoing, not just a practical interest in doing so. The retributive theory is retrospective or backward-looking, in that it doesn't depend on the outcome of some action to justify punishment. Two problems vex the retributive theory. We have to decide who deserves to be punished, and the theory has to be defended against the charge that it is nothing more than a form of retaliation.

According to retributivism, only wrongdoers, those people guilty of doing something wrong, may be punished for their actions. Rawls says, "What retributivists have rightly insisted upon is that no man can be punished unless he is guilty" (p. 7). Therefore, on the retributivist's view, moral culpability is both a necessary and sufficient condition of liability to punitive sanctions.

Some retributivists maintain that we do wrong if we don't punish the man who has done wrong by doing the same to him. Retributivism can then be seen as a form of retaliation (*lex talionis*, the law of retaliation or 'an eye for an eye'). According to *lex talionis*, criminal acts should be punished by like acts. The classic early modern (1797) statement of retribution as *lex talionis* is by Immanuel Kant:

> Even if a civil society resolved to dissolve itself with the consent of all its members—as might be supposed in the case of a people

---

[3] John Rawls, "Two Concepts of Rules," *Philosophical Review* 64 (1955), pp. 4f.

inhabiting an island resolving to separate and scatter themselves throughout the whole world—the last murderer lying in prison ought to be executed before the resolution was carried out. This ought to be done in order that everyone may realize the desert of his deeds, and that blood-guiltiness may not remain upon the people; for otherwise they will all be regarded as participators in the murder as a public violation of justice.[4]

Kant insists on equivalence of punishment not only in quantity but also in quality of punishment. Such equivalency seems to justify retaliation or revenge.

All retributivists hold that punishment should be graded in proportion to desert, but they're not all committed to any particular penalty as being deserved. So, *lex talionis* is not something common to all theories of retributivism.

## Mr. Blonde, the Utilitarian Theory, and Retribution

Mr. Blonde's violent behavior is best understood as exacting a form of retributive justice upon his enemies. He punishes his enemies because—according to his judgment—they deserve it. Blonde's actions, from the perspective of the social code he observes, are within the confines of a consistently retributivist approach to punishment. Unlike the utilitarian, for whom some gain in human happiness justifies the violence of punishment, Mr. Blonde does not need to justify what he does in terms of subsequent consequences. Blonde punishes Marvin because Marvin has attempted to thwart his plans and is thus "blameworthy."

In addition, the cops killed Blonde's collaborators. An implicit moral rule or principle is that no one should harm another. This is also known as the *harm principle* and it was most clearly articulated by John Stuart Mill. Mill writes, "the sole end for which mankind are warranted, individually or collectively, in interfering with the liberty of action of any of their number, is self-protection."[5] The cops violated the harm princi-

---

[4] Immanuel Kant, *The Metaphysics of Morals* (Cambridge University Press, 1996), p. 106 [6:333].
[5] John Stuart Mill, *On Liberty and Other Essays*, edited by John Gray (Oxford University Press, 1998), p. 7.

ple when they killed Blue and Brown. For Blonde, it could be that the persons who violate the harm principle deserve punishment. So Blonde believes he is justified in punishing the cop.

On these two accounts, Blonde's actions appear to be retaliatory rather than strictly retributive. The first interpretation argues that Blonde is justified in punishing the cop because his plans were thwarted. Anybody's plans may be interrupted, but that doesn't warrant torturing a person. Blonde's getting back at the cop is not righting a wrong. Similarly, on the second view, Blonde's torturing the cop is the result of the harm done to his fellow burglars. The difference between revenge and retribution is that the former is done for an injury or harm, while retribution is done for a wrong. What we have to show is that Blonde's actions aren't done because of a special tie to the events as these two interpretations suppose.

It might be objected that the cop doesn't deserve what Blonde does to him, that slicing the cop's ear off and trying to set him on fire is too harsh. This objection is about the proportionality of Blonde's actions.

One complicating factor cannot be dismissed here: Blonde is clearly sadistic. Even some of his colleagues seem convinced of this. At one point, Mr. White (Harvey Keitel) remarks, "this guy's a fucking psycho." Not only does Blonde kill without remorse people who get in his way, he seems impervious to human suffering and he even takes delight in inflicting pain and terror. He jokes and dances as he taunts Marvin. He tells Marvin that he doesn't care if he "knows anything" (the original pretext for holding Marvin captive and beating him up is to attempt to find out from him who tipped the police off to the robbery), but that the thought of torturing a cop "amuses" him. After cutting off Marvin's ear, Blonde speaks into it mockingly before tossing it aside. Marvin's pleas that he has "a little kid growing up" are answered with callous disregard ("You through?") as Blonde douses him in gasoline and lights a match ("Have some fire, Scarecrow"). If it were not for Mr. Orange's intervention (in the form of a bullet that blows Blonde away), Blonde would not hesitate to burn Marvin alive.

Is Blonde's sadism relevant? There is a distinction between acting on a principle and acting in accordance with a principle. One might, for example, act in accordance with a moral law without being motivated buy the moral law. Consider the case of someone who refrains from committing a violent crime solely because they fear the consequences of getting caught. Such a person would not be acting on a moral principle, but would be acting in accordance with a moral principle (such as "do not harm"). Similarly, if one has a great deal of evidence for some proposition, but believes that proposition on the basis of something a fortune teller told her, she would have justification for her belief, even though she wouldn't be justified in holding her belief (as her belief was formed in a dubious way). The same general point can be made about Blonde's actions. Clearly Blonde is acting on his sadistic urges, but his actions can (at least to some extent) be justified by retributivism, even if he is not personally acting on a retributivist principle.

## Mr. Rawls and the Decision Procedure

Mr. Blonde's actions do accord with a pure retributive theory of punishment. But pure retributivism is susceptible to serious problems. Do Mr. Blonde's actions accord with a more defensible version of retributivism? Let's look at a version of retributivism presented by James Sterba, incorporating ideas from H.L.A. Hart and John Rawls.

In the 1960s, the famous legal philosopher H.L.A. Hart developed a modified form of retributivism.[6] Hart says that punishment is only justified when inflicted on someone who has committed an offense with *mens rea*. *Mens rea* is a legal term meaning 'guilty mind'. In other words, no one is to be punished unless they freely chose to do something unlawful, with knowledge of the circumstances and the consequences. Hart also insists that punishment must serve in the reduction of crime generally. So in Hart's account, in addition to retribution, a social utilitarian aim must also be furthered for punishment to be justified.

Further developing Hart's theory, Sterba applies to it Rawls's concept of "justice as fairness." Rawls put forward the idea that what is just is what is fair, and what is fair is something that can

---

[6] Hart is combining some features of utilitarian theory with those of pure retributive theory, to develop a stronger theory of punishment which overcomes the weaknesses of both theories. H.L.A. Hart, *Punishment and Responsibility: Essays in the Philosophy of Law* (Oxford University Press, 1968), pp. 1–27.

be captured by imagining that we get to choose some social arrangement without knowing in advance what position we will occupy within that arrangement. For instance, we would choose the best arrangement for allocating income to people, without knowing whether we would personally have the highest or the lowest income. We would give special weight to the worst off position (since we might be in that position). What we would choose would then be fair.[7]

Sterba adapts Rawls's notion of fairness to come up with a form of retributivism as fairness.[8] Fair principles for the legal system would be those that anyone would find acceptable without knowing what position within the legal system they would be placed in. Sterba's approach saves pure retributivism from its biggest problem: that actions are more likely to be done out of revenge. I think that Sterba's argument can be used to show that Blonde's actions are a reflection of retributivism as fairness.

According to Sterba, representatives in the original position will not choose principles that maximize utility because

> a necessary requirement for selecting [principles] would be that the representatives did not experience any risk aversion when they imagined themselves as possibly turning up in any of the represented positions in a system which maximized utility. (*Demands of Justice*, p. 69)

If any representative believed that the principle didn't improve the conditions of the least desirable positions, then on Rawls's account they would not choose those principles.

Sterba's legal enforcement system includes some safeguards against problems that may arise. First, his system will not punish excusable behavior because Hart's account only punishes people if they commit an offense with the cognitive and volitional conditions of *mens rea*. Second, his system would not punish innocent people, since it doesn't justify punishment via utility maximization. Finally, Sterba argues that since the criminal would have been able to avoid his fate if he had chosen to

---

[7] Rawls, *A Theory of Justice*, revised edition (Cambridge, Massachusetts: Harvard University Press, 1999).
[8] James P. Sterba, *The Demands of Justice* (South Bend: University of Notre Dame Press, 1980), pp. 63–83.

abide by the reasonably just laws of society, we decide the basic principles of legal enforcement with the interests of the victims in mind (p. 77).

The last safeguard is controversial, and it is one with which Blonde may not agree. The victims of the crime and the criminals who perpetrate them both have some claim to be in the least desirable position in a legal enforcement system. Sterba acknowledges this, but he believes that the criminals aren't the least advantaged.

However, if the criminal were the product of a violent environment and if our environment shapes our character, then there is no way that she could have chosen to do otherwise. To choose to do something other than she did may be perceived as sacrificing her well-being. Since well-being is everyone's concern, the criminal could not have chosen a different path.

Support of this interpretation comes directly from Blonde. After Eddie arrives at the warehouse, Pink and White confront Blonde about his psychotic behavior. White doesn't want to leave Blonde with the captured cop "because this guy's a fucking psycho." Blonde went crazy in the store blowing away everyone in sight. Blonde says: "I told 'em not to touch the alarm. They touched it. I blew 'em full of holes. If they hadn't done what I told 'em not to do, they'd still be alive." When a person is in a hostage situation, an implicit principle is to do as the hostage taker tells you to do. If a hostage doesn't listen to the hostage taker, then she should expect the hostage taker to punish her. We might think of the hostages and the hostage takers as parties in a contract where the parameters of the contract are created and instituted by the persons setting it up. Since the people violated the rules, they were the wrongdoers. Because Blonde is a retributivist, they deserve to be punished.

Blonde couldn't have chosen to do anything else than blow the people full of holes. He says, "Fuck'em, they set off the alarm, they deserve what they got." Blonde understands that he and the others are in a precarious position. They're robbing the jewelry store. If they're caught, they'll go to jail. Going to jail is not in the interest of Blonde or the others. For Blonde not to shoot the people would be to sacrifice his own well-being and the well-being of his collaborators. The people in the jewelry store made it more likely that Blonde and the others would go to jail by sounding the alarm. Blonde takes it upon himself to make the people understand that they've done something wrong. So, to his mind, he's justified in blowing a few away, and he couldn't have done otherwise because that would be endorsing their actions and sacrificing his own well-being.[9]

---

[9] I am grateful for comments on a draft of this chapter by Richard Greene and K. Silem Mohammad, and I would like to thank Kathleen Evers, Heather Figaro, Rich Mancuso, Dave Moreshead, Ed Page, and Allen Terrell for discussing the topic of this paper years ago after I had watched the movie for the first time. Though they weren't privy to reading drafts of this chapter, the discussions we had played a large role in the formulation of my ideas.

# PART III

## "Why Don't You Tell Me What Really Happened?"

### Time, Causality, Experience

# 9

# "I Didn't Know You Liked the Delfonics": Knowledge and Pragmatism in *Jackie Brown*

K. SILEM MOHAMMAD

> . . . as we know, there are known knowns: there are things we
> know we know. We also know there are known unknowns: that is
> to say, we know there are some things we do not know. But there
> are also unknown unknowns: the ones we don't know we don't
> know.
> —Donald Rumsfeld

The characters in Quentin Tarantino's films frequently draw
attention to what they and others don't know, know they don't
know, and don't know they don't know. In *Reservoir Dogs*
(1992), Mr. Blonde (Michael Madsen) answers the question of
what happened to Mr. Blue (Eddie Bunker) by rehearsing a set
of possibilities that tells us no more than that he hasn't got a
clue: "Either he's alive or he's dead or the cops got him or they
don't." In another scene, Mr. Pink (Steve Buscemi) rattles off
this piece of impeccable reasoning: "I can say *I* definitely did-
n't do it, 'cause I know what I did or didn't do. But I cannot
definitely say that about anybody, 'cause I don't definitely
know." In *Pulp Fiction* (1994), Mia Wallace (Uma Thurman)
asks Vincent Vega (John Travolta) whether the gossip he has
just repeated to her is a "fact," and he replies, "No it's not, it's
just what I heard."

**MIA:** Who told you this?
**VINCENT:** "They."
**MIA:** They certainly talk a lot, don't they?
**VINCENT:** They certainly do.

"They" talk a lot, but They as well know only what They have heard: the circle of unknowledge disguised as information perpetuates itself. All the same, this imperfect, received version of knowledge is what They have to go on, what will have to do.

Tarantino's fictional universe, one might say, is one that is characterized by a heavy incidence of *aporia*. Aporia, a Greek word meaning roughly "doubt," is the classical philosophical method by which Socrates continually leads the interlocutors in Plato's dialogues to examine what they believe, or think they believe, until they are forced to admit that they cannot sustain those beliefs. They end up bereft of their false convictions, in a state of aporia. Jacques Derrida (1930–2004) applies the concept broadly to a general epistemological condition of unknowing, gapping-out, unreadability, impasse. Statements of knowledge and attempts at reasoning in Tarantino's films frequently start from and/or end up at a position of aporia.

## "Is That Rutger Hauer?" Aporia and Aspect-Change

An amusing and significant moment in *Jackie Brown* (1997) occurs when ATF agent Ray Nicolette (Michael Keaton) and LA police officer Mark Dargus (Michael Bowen) are getting Jackie (Pam Grier) ready for a money pick-up at the Del Amo Mall in Torrance, California. Ray is speaking into his recorder, itemizing materials to be used in the operation, and he comes to the shopping bag in which Jackie will carry the money. He describes it as purple, and Mark interrupts him to observe that it is white. Ray is thrown off. The color of the bag is not that important; nevertheless, Ray's momentary intellectual paralysis is telling. He looks at the bag, begins to clarify that the bag is in fact white with a purple pattern, then catches himself when he realizes the absurdity of the interlude. He comes up against the aporia of the situation, the space of doubt that threatens his need for organizational precision and categorical certainty. Wisely realizing that to linger in that space will be counter to the efficiency of their operation, he elects to move on.

Ludwig Wittgenstein (1889–1951) would describe Ray's aporia in this scene in terms of *aspect perception*. In Part II section ix of his *Philosophical Investigations,* Wittgenstein invokes the now famous figure of the duck-rabbit:[1]

Wittgenstein uses the duck-rabbit as an example of the phenomenon of aspect-change. A person looking at the picture might first see it as a duck, and then a rabbit, or vice versa, but nothing in the picture has actually changed. In fact, it is difficult to say that anything has changed, although it seems so to the observer. As Wittgenstein puts it:

> The expression of a change of aspect is the expression of a *new* perception and at the same time of the perception's being unchanged.

The philosophical import of Wittgenstein's thought-experiment (or *Gedankenexperiment*) concerns the way in which words like "know" tend to lose their coherence outside the context of the particular rules of the "language games" in which they are used. The duck-rabbit example illustrates the way in which we can become convinced that actions we perform are not just actions, but things or states of being. So for example when we stop seeing the duck-rabbit as a duck and start seeing it as a rabbit, we are tempted to say either that something in the picture or something in our perception (or both) has changed, that a physical phenomenon of some kind has occurred. What actually happens, Wittgenstein says, is just that we *describe* our experience differently from one moment

---

[1] Ludwig Wittgenstein, *Philosophical Investigations* (Oxford: Blackwell, 1953, 1958, 2001). Wittgenstein borrowed the duck-rabbit from a book by American psychologist Joseph Jastrow.

to the next in the specific "language-game" (*Sprachspiel*) we use to account for the way we register aspect-change—a game I myself play in referring to "aspect-change" as a noun, as though it were a substantive thing. It is this difference in description that makes it seem as though we have had two qualitatively different perceptions.

A couple of examples from *Jackie Brown* may help to flesh out the concept. At one point, illegal gun dealer Ordell Robbie (Samuel L. Jackson) glances at the movie his girlfriend Melanie Ralston (Bridget Fonda) is watching on TV, and thinks he recognizes the actor:

> **ORDELL:** Is that Rutger Hauer?
> **MELANIE:** No, that's Helmut Berger.

Similarly, earlier in the film, Melanie looks at a dark-haired actress in the "Chicks Who Love Guns" video and giggles: "Demi Moore." Philosophical questions one might ask about these scenes are: does Ordell see the actor differently before and after he knows it is not Rutger Hauer but Helmut Berger? Does Melanie see the actress differently from the way she would see her if she did not make the mental connection to Demi Moore? According to Wittgenstein's position as outlined above, the answer would be yes—but only within the particular language-game in which the phrase "to see differently" is used in this way. It would be a misunderstanding, Wittgenstein would say, to look for a "mental state" or other tangible epistemological condition corresponding to the expression. The meaning of the phrase is its meaning in *use*.

Tarantino is fascinated with the idea of differing perspectives on a single action or series of actions. In *Reservoir Dogs*, *Pulp Fiction*, and *Kill Bill*, he structures entire narratives as staggered temporal sequences in order to force our awareness of how our consciousness of the present is conditioned by past details that may have seemed insignificant or irrelevant at the time they occurred. By changing the order of events within the sequence of the filmstrip, the significance and relevance of such details is made more conspicuous, if not necessarily more clear.

*Jackie Brown* stands out in comparison to these other films because its narrative is chronologically pretty straightforward: events are portrayed mostly in the order in which they are supposed to occur. The one major exception is the long sequence depicting the money switch-off at the Del Amo Mall, in which the exchange is viewed first from Jackie's perspective, then from the perspective of criminals Louis Gara (Robert DeNiro) and Melanie, and finally from that of bail bondsman Max Cherry (Robert Forster). Even here, however, the order of events is not actually changed, only repeated from different angles. Unlike the other films, where the point of the skewed narrative is to affect *our* perception of the action, and thus to influence the interpretation we place upon the entire series of events that make up the story, the repetition of the switch-off in *Jackie Brown* serves primarily to emphasize the differing experiences of the *characters* in their relation to a single event. And the viewer may well ask: why? The events depicted could just as easily have been edited into a conventionally cross-cut sequence in which we see the bag hand-off from Jackie's perspective, Louis and Melanie waiting in the dress shop from Max's perspective, the parking lot escape from Louis and Melanie's perspective, and so on, without any retreading of the same details. The revelation that Jackie has given Melanie a dummy bag with only a top layer of actual money, for instance, occurs after the sequence has already played out.

Since the replaying of the switch-off doesn't serve any expository narrative function, one might object, it could be seen as a case of sloppy filmmaking, or of pure aesthetic surface for the sake of pretentious flashiness. However, one motivated function of the sequence has to do precisely with its "failure" to resolve into an information-bearing structure. All the gestures of exposition are there, all the conventions by which we have been trained as moviegoers to recognize the clever unfolding of pertinent details are in place. But the filmic device adds up to nothing. The multiple vantage points of perception ultimately do neither us nor the characters much good. Jackie pulls it off, of course, but the scene in which she rushes out into the openness of the mall to let Ray and Mark know that the bag has been "stolen" is so convincingly staged from her position of subjective experience (the camera pans around her in continual motion, signaling what seems like her genuine panic) that once we realize she is play-acting, we feel as though our perception has changed. What has changed, of course, is only the *aspect* in which our perception is experienced.

The film plays on our aspectual perceptions in various ways from start to finish. During the opening titles, we see a profile of Jackie in a medium shot, in her flight attendant's suit, apparently walking very smoothly and steadily from right to left in front of some colorful wall tiles. It's only after a moment that we realize why the motion is so fluid: she is actually on a moving sidewalk at LAX. For a brief moment, that is, we see her *as* walking, before we correct ourselves and see *that* she is standing still on a mobile platform. Again at the end of the film, we hear a refrain of the same music that plays during the title sequence: "Across 110th Street." As Jackie drives off in her car, we slowly start to see that her lips are moving, that she appears to be singing along to her car radio. What we had assumed was extra-diegetic music (that is, music that is not part of the world of the film as the characters experience it) is actually diegetic.[2] What we see and hear remains consistent, but our aspect perception changes. This change, moreover, can only be registered via an aporia: a temporary space or gap of understanding within which we try to re-conceptualize and re-describe our experience so that we can make sense of it.

## "My Ass May Be Dumb, but I Ain't No Dumbass": Ordell's Aspectual Smarts

Although nearly everyone in *Jackie Brown* is subject to the disorienting effects of aspect change and related mental aporias, some characters are more aware than others of the ways in which these effects can be harnessed for their own benefit. One of those characters is Ordell Robbie (Samuel L. Jackson). From the time we are first introduced to Ordell, we can tell that he's all about control achieved through the manipulation of appearances, a trait signaled by his wielding of the remote while showing Louis the "Chicks Who Love Guns" promotional video. Ordell chuckles gleefully as he adjusts the volume to enhance the sound of automatic weapon fire at just the right moments, as though he were directing reality according to his whims.

---

[2] Complicating this realization, however, is the fact that we hear the music start before Jackie gets in her car. Is the music truly diegetic, or does Tarantino make Jackie seem "magically" to hear the extra-diegetic soundtrack?

(Later in the film, Melanie reveals to Louis that the Hermosa Beach apartment where this happens is not actually Ordell's, as it at first appears not only to Louis, but to us as well. "I live here," she says; "he just drops in and out." Tarantino waits till halfway through the film to let us know this: it's yet another example of the way our perceptions are subjected to a change of aspect, causing us to reevaluate assessments we may have made earlier.)

Ordell prides himself on his own ability to take advantage of others by manipulating their perceptions. He brags to Louis Gara about the way he has fooled his little "country" girl Sheronda: "I took her to my place in Compton and told her it was Hollywood." When the hapless Beaumont Livingston (Chris Tucker) runs afoul of the law in the process of assisting Ordell in his gun-running business, Ordell tries to reassure him with soothing arguments about why he is not really in danger of receiving a severe sentence. The brunt of his argument rests on the claim that the police are "just fucking with" Beaumont. This is Ordell's trademark strategy: to convince the people he means to manipulate that any fear they may have of getting caught and jailed is the result of authority figures fucking with their minds. The irony here, of course, is that no one fucks with people's minds more habitually than Ordell, and that his reassurances that people's minds are being fucked with by others are his main means of fucking with their minds himself. Ordell's greatest fear is of being sold out by his accomplices, so it is in his self-interest to convince them at every turn that it is in *their* best self-interest not to co-operate with the authorities: that the benefits of their continued partnership with him outweigh the benefits of ratting him out. As Ordell says,

> if you know Beaumont, you know there ain't no way in hell he can do no ten years. And if you know that, you know Beaumont's gonna do any goddam thing Beaumont can to keep from doin' those ten years including telling the Federal government everything they want to know about my ass.

Ordell frames everything in terms of logical chains: if you know one thing, you know another, corresponding thing, and another. Theoretically, if you know enough things, and how the knowledge of each hooks up with the knowledge of all the others, you have all the power. You are able to stay ahead of the game and work everything to your advantage. Whether it actually works out this way is another thing, as we'll see.

The moment we first realize the extent of Ordell's capacity for ruthless mind-fucking is when he goes to see Beaumont shortly after bailing him out of jail (through Max Cherry Bail Bonds). Beaumont thanks Ordell energetically for his help, and Ordell plays the benevolent protector, telling Beaumont about the high-powered lawyer he has lined up to defend him, and so on. Then Ordell tells Beaumont he needs his immediate help on a job. He tells Beaumont that he needs to sell some guns to some Koreans, and he would like to have a back-up man with him in case anything goes wrong. Beaumont is immediately apprehensive, and asks what the "problem" is. Ordell responds with the helpful distinction: "It ain't no problem, man, it's more like a situation." He downplays the danger of the job, just as he downplays the risk Beaumont faces when he goes up for sentencing on the charge he has just been arrested on. He applies the same explanation to both situtations: just as the police are just "fucking with" Beaumont, he and Beaumont will just be "fucking with the Koreans." Beaumont is still resistant, even when Ordell accuses him of ingratitude. Finally, Ordell pulls out his winning argument: the promise of "chicken and waffles" when the job is done! Beaumont accompanies him down to his car, where he is told to get in the trunk and hide. He gets in, still reluctant, and Ordell slams the trunk down on him, gets in the car, drives around the block (to the accompaniment of "Strawberry Letter 23" by the Brothers Johnson), stops, gets out, goes back, opens the trunk, and shoots Beaumont.

It's worth noting here that Ordell's strategy is not entirely successful in this instance. Beaumont isn't ultimately swayed by Ordell's reassurances, but by a crude appeal to his appetite. For all Ordell's subtle machinations, his arguments based on what given parties know or don't know aren't all that persuasive. He wastes a long time trying to engage Beaumont rationally, when he could just have played the chicken and waffles card at the beginning. He ought to know better. As he himself explains to Louis earlier in the film, he manages to sell guns to his clients based not on the truly relevant information about the specific models, but based on the clients' superficial associations of the guns with characters from movies. "The Killer [John Woo in the movie of the same name] had a .45, they want a .45," he explains, even though the truth is that the .45 Magnum "has a serious fucking jamming problem." Louis is impressed by Ordell's savvy, though much of what he says goes over his head: "He knows a lot," he observes to Melanie, who replies disdainfully, "He's just repeating stuff he's overheard."

If Melanie is right—and she seems pretty perceptive, even though she's apparently perpetually stoned—Ordell himself has no special claim to significantly greater analytical skills than many of the persons he scams. (At one point she remarks: "He moves his lips when he reads. What does that tell you?") Nevertheless, he prides himself on such skills, and he seems disappointed when other people are not matches for him. He *wants* to lure Beaumont into the trunk through persuasive reasons alone. Ordell's self-image centers around being perceived as smart, but he's blind to his own limitations. When he says late in the film, "My ass may be dumb, but I ain't no dumbass," he is trying to play an aspectual mind game akin to the duck-rabbit example, but it doesn't seem to occur him that someone whose ass is dumb is a dumbass no matter how you rearrange the terms.

## "You Rationalize": Jackie Brown's Pragmatism

The other main character in *Jackie Brown* who trades on a special ability to manipulate people's perceptions is Jackie herself. At first, Jackie looks like she's in danger of suffering the same fate as Beaumont, as Ordell goes through the same steps to bail her out and then do her in so she won't squeal. Once again, we see Ordell's preoccupation with mental games, as he says to Max at the Bail Bonds shop regarding the police's potential case against Jackie after she is caught with drugs (and a lot of money) in her flight bag upon getting off work as a flight attendant at LAX: "They fuckin' with her: they call that shit "possession with intent." (To Ordell, certain words have a special, almost magical significance: he is fascinated with the rhetorical and poetic power they represent. After telling Max that someone "blew Beaumont's brains out," he stops and reflects on his own phraseology, "Hey, that shit rhymes: *Blew Beaumont's / Brains out!*" (That shit is actually alliterative, but whatever.) Once again, Ordell wants to think of himself as in control due in considerable part to his command of the chief instrument of reason: language.)

Ordell shows up at Jackie's house directly after Max drives her there from jail, and begins his cat-and-mouse game. He tries to intimidate her by walking through each room, forcing her backwards as he goes, and flicking the light switches off one by one. We realize that the game is not one-sided, however, when Jackie, who has stolen a gun from Max's glove compartment, turns it on Ordell and reverses his strategy: the switches start getting flicked back up as she assumes the upper hand. Ordell tries to keep his cool, protesting, "I was just playing with you," and resorting to his old routine by expressing his concern that she might be overly concerned with the power the law has over her: "Police start fucking with your mind."

Max too is concerned—for less selfish reasons—that the police might be able to counter-manipulate Jackie, and Jackie tries to persuade him that his concern is misplaced:

JACKIE: Max, you said it yourself. Ray wants Ordell. He doesn't give a shit about the money. The money won't convict him. Guns will.
MAX: You're rationalizing.
JACKIE: Well, that's what you do to go through with the shit you start, you rationalize.

Much of *Jackie Brown* comes down to a competition between Jackie, Ordell, and the law to see who "rationalizes" most successfully, which seems here to have less to do with its everyday sense of "making up weak justifications" than with its stricter technical sense of "employing reason in an effective way to make calculations." When Jackie tells Max that she has Ray and Mark believing that Ordell is afraid they are on to him, he cautions her: "You know, a good cop will never let you know that he knows you're full of shit." Although his warning turns out to be unnecessary, the principle behind it is one that Jackie fully appreciates and anticipates. "All [they] needed was a reasonable explanation," she responds. Notice the role that "reason" plays in this passage. Ray and Mark value reason not because of its value as a mode of determining actual truth value, but as an indication that they have not neglected their duties in the course of pursuing their main objective. The reason in the reasonable explanation need not be sound; it need only be identifiable as something one might legitimately call reason. What matters is that the rules of their particular police language game are adhered to, not whether the pieces moved in that game retain their use in other contexts.

Jackie's awareness of this, and her ability to make accurate predictions about Ray and Mark's behavior based on this awareness, are central to the attitude that I believe accurately characterizes her handling of the situation: one of sharply analytical pragmatism. Pragmatism is a philosophical approach first developed in the late nineteenth and early twentieth centuries by thinkers like Charles S. Peirce, John Dewey, and William James. One of the central tenets of pragmatism is that concepts like truth, knowledge, reality, and so forth are to be gauged by their utility with respect to a specific context, rather than by some absolute measure of validity. It is more complicated than this, of course, and the idea of pragmatism is often banally misrepresented as a simplistic credo along the lines of "whatever it takes to get the job done." I maintain, however, that one can draw meaningful connections between specific concepts expressed in *Jackie Brown* and the ideas explored by philosophers like the pragmatists and Wittgenstein in his duck-rabbit example (Wittgenstein was not, properly speaking, a pragmatist, but there is some overlap between pragmatist theory and his own, especially in his account of language-games).

Notice the similarities between Jackie's treatment of rationality and reason and Ordell's, shortly after Ordell discovers that Louis has botched his role in the switch-off:

**ORDELL:** I don't wanna hear no fucking excuses, Louis.

**LOUIS:** I ain't giving you excuses . . . I'm giving you fucking reasons.

**ORDELL:** Oh, you gonna tell me the reason you lost every goddamned cent I got in the world? You gonna tell me reasons? Let me tell you the reason, motherfucker: the reason is your ass ain't worth a shit no more. [*Ordell shoots Louis dead.*]

Like Jackie, Ordell sees reason as a term that functions differently in different language games. Louis wants to use it in the familiar "language-game of giving information," as Wittgenstein puts it. He wants to explain to Ordell why he shouldn't be held accountable for his incompetence, in as rational a manner as his intellect can muster. Ordell, on the other hand, has no patience for this language-game. His language-game is the language-game of demonstrating his aggression and superiority. In that game, "reason" *means* more or less the same thing that it means in Louis's game, but its *use* is quite different. How pragmatic Ordell's application of the term is, it must be said, is another matter.

Jackie's (and Max's) pragmatism shows its strength most clearly in its adaptability to the aporias and unknowns that render right action so murkily uncertain. Ordell is taken aback by developments that don't correspond to his preset expectations. "I didn't know you liked the Delfonics," he says suspiciously as he gets in Max's car and turns on the stereo. Unpredictability throws him off. For Jackie and Max, by contrast, uncertainties are a constant fact of life, and are what "rationalizing" helps to negotiate. Max gives his partner Winston some instructions in preparation for the final showdown at the Bail Bond shop, and Winston expresses his faith in Max's judgment:

> **WINSTON:** I don't have to know what I'm doing, just long as you know.
> **MAX:** I think I do. Good enough?

To know the difference between what one knows one knows and what one only thinks one knows is to possess a great advantage over someone who takes "know" to be a reliable, constant index of certainty. What Jackie and Max appreciate, whether consciously or instinctively, is that knowledge, like any other term, has its limits, and those limits are determined by the type of language-game being played. To hold out for a limitless knowledge, outside of language altogether, is vain and counterproductive. In a world where aporia is a reliable constant, conscious uncertainty is more pragmatic than rigid certainty.

# 10

# Vinnie's Very Bad Day: Twisting the Tale of Time in *Pulp Fiction*

RANDALL E. AUXIER

## *Faire des Singeries*, or Monkey See, Monkey Do

There's nothing *essentially* new in Quentin Tarantino's *Pulp Fiction*, and that's part of the point, as he often says in interviews—to use every Hollywood cliché, but to present these in combinations that the audience has not seen before. It's Hollywood with a (Jack Rabbit Slim's) twist contest.

Aristotle once insisted that the whole "poetic art" was just one big imitation of life (and that includes film, although Aristotle wasn't much of a movie-goer). For about two thousand years after Aristotle said that, everybody agreed—until one day in the late eighteenth century when some Germans and a few renegade Brits got bored with watching French soldiers kill everybody, and started insisting that the poetic art is *really* the expression of the artist's feelings, not mainly an imitation of life. They said it out of pure spite. That really pissed off the French army, because they liked Aristotle.

The French, who were the champions of "classical aesthetics," had an especially snooty way of reading Aristotle. They said you have to follow the rules in order to make worthy art, and especially you have to have three things to make a story work, the "three unities" is what we now call them: unity of (1) time, (2) place, and (3) action. You have to tell your audience, at least vaguely, *where* the characters are, and keep it constant. And they also thought you should present the events in their proper temporal sequence, so that no one gets confused. You can see where this is going, I'll bet. In the movie industry, even in

Tarantino movies, there is a dude whose job it is to assure the "continuity" of the set and props to make sure things don't move around from one cut to the next and one scene to the next. He's sort of the master of time and space in the movie universe—or perhaps he's just Aristotle's Gallic slave boy.

But really time and place are just unities of *action*, which is what all the fuss is actually about. Aristotle says: "The truth is that . . . imitation is of one thing, so in poetry the story, as an imitation of action, must represent one action, a complete whole, with its several incidents so closely connected that the transposal or withdrawal of any one of them will disjoin [that is the time requirement] or dislocate [that is the place requirement] the whole"[1]

The French were quite inflexible about this "requirement" back in those days. At first they had long-winded arguments with the Germans and the Brits (the French even accused Shakespeare of being a bad playwright because he liked to mess around with the three unities), but eventually it just had to become a shooting war. This was called the Battle of Classicism and Romanticism. The Germans pulled out the big guns to hold the center, like Goethe and Beethoven, and finished with a heroic charge by Wagner (commanding some Vikings and a detachment called the Light Brigade); the Brits reinforced with Byron and Shelley and Keats (all regrettably killed in action), and deployed Coleridge and Wordsworth to protect the flanks. The French eventually moved on to Africa to kill people who didn't have quite so many guns. The three unities were in full retreat. People started writing whatever they damn well pleased while the Sun King turned over in his lavish rococo grave. It's amazing the things people will fight for.[2]

---

[1] Aristotle, *Poetics*, translated by Ingram Bywater [god, I love that name], in *The Basic Works of Aristotle* (New York: Random House, 1941[a very bad year]), lines 1451a30–34.

[2] Some of you will say that I am gratuitously picking on the French in this essay. I may be, but I am not the one who built a cryptic critique of French cinema into *Pulp Fiction*. Watch it again, and watch for all things French, and see whether you think this was my idea or Tarantino's. Pay close attention to Fabienne's conversation with Butch about why she has not properly valued his father's watch. That's Tarantino telling you that French cinema has lost its sense of film time, and if Fabienne will ever just get on that damned chopper, she might learn a thing or two about how important time is in a movie.

## *Le Big Mac*, or *"Garçon* means 'Boy'"

Americans don't give a shit about such things. That's why we serve (bad) beer at the McDonald's in Paris and call the sandwich "Le Big Mac." We're mocking them and they just eat it up (complaining all the while). And then they pay us good money to watch our supposedly inferior movies (and that's what they are, "movies," not "films"). We're laughing all the way to the bank. That's our revenge on the French for their uppity ingratitude and hypocrisy. That and Michael Moore. They must know, I mean they *must*, that we set up that whole *Fahrenheit 9/11* thing just to see if they were really so far up their own asses as to honestly give that joker the *Palm d'Or* for that ridiculous string of pulp celluloid. They went for it, and for Le Big Mac. Idiots.[3]

Tarantino doesn't read Aristotle, and he doesn't imitate life; he imitates other art. And no one, I mean *no one*, is having more fun than our boy Tarantino. It ought to be a crime. In France it *is*. He bats around the three unities like a kitten. And he's no romantic either. If Tarantino were actually expressing his *feelings* in his movies, we would have to wonder about whether he should be locked up. Of course, Mel Gibson should be locked up regardless of whether he's imitating or expressing.[4] Maybe we should put him in a birka and send him to *gay Paris*.

But with Tarantino, this imitation/expression thing actually makes a real difference. He is imitating other art—well, just other movies. Part of the reason he can get away with making us cringe so often is that we know he is toying with the art form, and with us, and it is thoroughly playful. Yes, we wonder about him a little bit, but not too much, once we get his game. One of the techniques discussed over and over in Tarantino interviews, reviews, and criticism, is his boyish experimentation with showing us what

---

Otherwise she will make us all late for the train. To put it more plainly, the French have forgotten the *audience*, and are wasting their time. You may not believe me now, but watch it again and ask yourself "why, in this story, is Fabienne French?"

[3] Say, you know what they call a "monkey wrench" in France? They call it "clé anglaise." "Clé" means "key," and I think you know what "anglaise" means. Sour grapes from Waterloo, I'd guess.

[4] Here is a case where the Aussies pulled one over on *us*. Ask an Aussie if he or she likes Mel Gibson's films. See if you don't get an evasion, with just a hint of a wry grin that says "he used to be our problem, but he's your problem *now*."

was *not* on the screen in some classic scene he imitates, and *not* showing us what they originally showed us. He knows we will fill in the other part ourselves. It gives us something to do. Tarantino is always playing this game—look at the classic movie (even a B or a C movie), ask yourself what you're *not* seeing that you *want* to see, reframe the scene from a new perspective, and then let everybody fill in the rest. It's great fun.

By contrast, Mel Gibson thinks something like: chain the viewer to a seat like poor Alex in *A Clockwork Orange* and administer the Ludovico Technique. Leave nothing to the imagination, and be certain your movie-goer is no longer able to think when it's over, or to get the images out of his poor brain ever afterwards. It is not fun. It is abuse. So while Tarantino is about art imitating art for the delight of us all, Gibson is about art imitating Nazi prison guards for the sake of . . . only God knows what. Some part of us apparently likes to be tortured (after all, we elected Bush and Cheney twice, sort of), but not our *best* part. Just say no.

But that old argument the philosophers used to have over whether art is imitation or expression can help us a little bit. No matter how hard he may try, an artist can't really imitate anything without placing an original stamp on the final product. It happens, one way or another, as decisions are made about what to leave in and what to leave out. And we love Tarantino because he lets *us* play along, participate in the movie, place our own stamp on the film in all the places that he activates our imaginations with whatever he left out of the frame. On the other side, Gibson expresses himself, alone, and forbids us, with a cat-o'-nine-tails if necessary, to see *anything* but what he shows us. If Tarantino is the *enfant terrible* of contemporary directors, Gibson is surely the *rex tyrannis*. I could be wrong about this, but I would wager a Hanzo katana that not one person who truly admires and understands Tarantino also likes Gibson's films. There is a reason. Some people like to have fun, others just want to be tortured.

### *Laissez les bon temps rouler*, or *Tempus Fugit* (When You're Having Fun)

Much ink has been spilt over the temporal sequencing of *Pulp Fiction*, but the critics and writers are not often familiar with the philosophy of time. The point that intrigues me most is that Tarantino points out (in an interview he did with Charlie Rose in 1994) that for all of its disjointed sequencing, there is nothing confusing about the movie—it is easy to follow, so long as you pay attention. Tarantino made this remark with perfect confidence, and indeed he is correct. Anyone who watches the movie can untangle its temporal sequence with a little effort. Tarantino invites us to do so. However, this feat of untangling is easier to accomplish *intuitively* than *intellectually*.

There are really two ways of understanding time. There is "clock time" and there is "experienced time." They aren't the same at all. Sometimes an hour on the clock seems like it takes forever to pass, like when you're at the dentist or watching a Mel Gibson film. Other times, an hour just seems to fly by, like when you're watching *Kill Bill* the way it was intended to be seen—all four hours at once. A philosopher named Henri Bergson (1859–1941) wrote a bunch of books about the differences between "clock time" and "experienced time."[5] People who like movies love this guy Bergson, because all the way back in 1907 he started writing about how movies do what they do—using light and the movement of machinery (the camera and then the projector) to create the illusion that real time is unfolding before our eyes.

Bergson thought that "clock time" wasn't really "time" at all; we just invent ways of turning time into *space* (that way we can artificially "even out" the dentist chair experience and the

---

[5] I know that his name sounds French, but he was born in England, his parents were Polish and English-Irish, and the attitudes of the French are not Bergson's fault. They regard themselves as too hip to read Bergson now, even though he wrote in French and won the Nobel Prize for literature. Oh, and his coolest books are *Time and Free Will* (London: Allen and Unwin, 1910 [1889]); *Laughter: An Essay on the Meaning of the Comic* (New York: Macmillan, 1913); and *Creative Evolution* (New York: Holt, 1911 [1907]). The part where he talks about the film projector and its relation to time is in Chapter 4 of *Creative Evolution*. Another French philosopher (who wasn't very French in my opinion) named Gilles Deleuze wrote a book on Bergson called *Bergsonism* (New York: Zone, 1988), and then applied the theory to cinema in a very cool book called *Cinema One: The Movement Image* (Minneapolis: University of Minnesota Press, 1986). You really should check out the Deleuze. I know Tarantino isn't an avid reader of philosophy, so I'm not saying he read this, but if you want to understand how he does what he does and why it has the effect on you that it has, it's pretty hard to beat Deleuze's theory.

experience of the Tarantino movie). Think about it for a second. Look at the calendar on your wall. It's a bunch of little squares arranged on a rectangle. That's space, *mon ami*, not time. The calendar just sort of sits there, being the same, and only your *act* of reading the calendar, anticipating the next days and remembering the last ones, brings it to life. It's the same with a clock, hanging there in space, being an arrangement of circles and lines. Yes, it moves, but you have to admit that it isn't very interesting to watch it move. It's just spatial arrangements imitating the experience of time.

A movie is sort of like a clock combined with a calendar: lots of little squares strung together with a motor to make them move. But it's really all just space and machinery. So Bergson says, "real time" is in our *experience* of things, not in the way we turn those experiences into spatial arrangements that imitate the experience. If that is right (and it is) then the "real" movie is *not* the string of celluloid running through the projector; the real movie is what's happening to *you* when you sit through it. Tarantino gets this. How many times has he said that the key to being a good director and writer is to be a good movie-goer? Pay attention to what you are experiencing when you watch a movie. Aristotle said as much in his clear emphasis on the audience in his *Rhetoric* and *Poetics.*

It is true that a movie is made by turning every single second into something like a calendar: we storyboard the script down to the level of the "shot," analyze each one down to the last detail, and then create the illusion of continuity by setting actions into motion within the narrow limits of the shot. In this case, actors are like machines adding motion to the temporal limits of the "shot." As soon as they've gotten the shot, what was "experienced time" for the actors is now just a series of still pictures, but we can re-assemble the pictures any way we like. Yet, a mere assemblage of pictures does not make a "movie." The movie becomes a *real* movie when someone sees it, experiences it in his own "real time". . . with popcorn, or KY jelly, or whatever you like to bring along to enhance your experience. A projector just running a film, no matter how well made, but with no one watching, may still be a "film," but it isn't a movie.[6]

------

[6] I have sometimes wondered whether commercial movie theaters run the film

So we're watching *Pulp Fiction*, and that devilish director has instructed the editor to put the whole thing out of sequence.[7] We all know that most movies are shot out of sequence (which makes movie-acting an interesting challenge), but Tarantino also wants us now to *experience* it out of sequence. He is far from the first to try this, but he may be better at it than others. Part of the reason he wants us to do that is that it helps us understand *his* world, just how free he is to play around with the art form. Christopher Nolan, by contrast, presents *Memento* out of sequence to convey to us the confusion of his main character, Leonard Shelby. But where Nolan is (carefully) confusing us for an effect, he is not exactly inviting us into his world. With Tarantino, we become aware that he can put things just anywhere he wants them. He wants us to *experience* what that is like for him to have that freedom, so that we can appreciate the decisions he made and share his playful delight at the effects. Yes, he is playing with us, but he is not *toying* with us; he is toying with the three unities for our edification.

Even Tarantino cannot tell a story without the three unities—no one can—but he can toy with them in ways that *enhance* the story, if he's good (and he is good). Aristotle's point (if those old French fuddy-duddies had *read* him a little more closely) was not that the three unities *must* be preserved at *all* costs; his point was don't *confuse* your audience, needlessly, if you want to tell a good story—non-French audiences will put up with very little of being confused, and most importantly, the audience wants *catharsis*. That means, the audience wants to give *you*, the playwright, the filmmaker, a piece of their time, of their *experience*, and they will give you their "willing suspension of disbelief"

---

through the projector at the appointed clock time even if no one buys a ticket. I'll bet some do. I'm sorry, but that's just weird.

[7] Of course, Tarantino's and Avery's script was already presented "out of sequence" so that even the actors never saw it "in sequence," which is perhaps why even the actors couldn't really answer the question as to what the movie was about in interviews. Each of them had digested his or her character's *perspective* on the events, but even the actors would have been hard pressed to identify the "main" character. So it isn't really that the film was just edited out of sequence, it's that Tarantino and Avery had already conceived of it *in* sequence, varied it in their imaginations for the anticipated effect (on the audience *and* the actors) and then edited the script to reflect the temporal choices they settled upon.

(they will pretend what you are showing them is "real"), so they can have a certain *kind* of experience, and when it is over, well, they want to *feel* better. So if you want the audience to experience catharsis, you should keep in mind that the three unities are important. It's not like Tarantino doesn't know that.

Yet, toying around with the three unities can create an enhanced experience, and can bring the audience closer to the filmmaker's art. Putting the vignettes out of sequence can (and *does* in the case of *Pulp Fiction*) force us to focus more of our attention on the characters. But we don't focus on their development, or even on their likely destinies in the story—I mean, halfway through the movie we already know that Vinnie bites the big one. Rather, we focus on who these people are, how they think, what their values are. Since we don't know which characters are more important, we pay attention to *all* of them. Thus, Tarantino invites us to enjoy his characters, just for who they are, and uses time-twisting to give us that experience. But whereas Hitchcock, for example, likes to create a *distance* between the filmmaker's art and the audience, to conceal his art so that, frankly, he can toy with their psychology, and whereas Gibson wants to do experiments in mind-control, Tarantino is like a boy in his tree house. And you are invited to join the club. Yes, it's *his* tree house, but all you need is the password, and he'll give you all the clues you need to get in. He doesn't want to control you, or toy with you, he just wants to play. You already know the game. It's just good (not so clean) fun, and time flies when you're having it.

## *Un Ménage à Trois*, or It's Three, Three, Three Plots in One

With *Pulp Fiction*, it is easy to experience the movie and "get it," intuitively. As Tarantino told Charlie Rose, it isn't confusing at all. Focus on the characters and don't worry too much about the order of events. Trust Tarantino. He has a plan. But actually sitting down and graphing the "objective" sequence of events is more challenging than just sort of "understanding" what happened. I couldn't resist taking the script and putting it in temporal sequence, just to see how it looks. This is how it happens:

The whole sequence unfolds on three different days. The movie begins around 7:00 AM on one day and the first event is

Vincent Vega (John Travolta[8]) and Jules Winnfield (Samuel L. Jackson) driving to a "hit." The last event is Butch Coolidge (Bruce Willis) and Fabienne (Maria de Medeiros) driving off on poor dead Zed's chopper.[9] Butch has just shot Vinnie, after catching him with his pants down. All the other events in the movie happen in between.[10] The first day is mainly Jules's story. The second day is mainly Vinnie's story. The third day is mainly Butch's story.

It is written in the classic style, a plot, "Vinnie's very bad day" (okay, three days, all bad), and two subplots, Jules and Butch. The rest of the characters support either the main story of Vinnie, or one of the subplots, or two of the subplots, or one subplot and the main story, or both subplots and the main story. The three main characters play supporting roles in each other's stories to varying degrees. Then each story includes discussion of the other stories in the dialogue. It isn't all that complicated.

---

[8] No one calls Vincent Vega "Vinnie" in the movie. This is by design, I suspect. Tarantino knows we will think of him as Vinnie Barbarino from *Welcome Back Kotter* in any case. I am calling him "Vinnie" because that's who John Travolta is and will always be.

[9] I would like to point out that when you say the alphabet in French, the last letter of the alphabet is pronounced "Zed."

[10] It may seem like only one continuous day, but Tarantino makes clear in a number of places that the story of Jules Winnfield's exit from the hit-man profession happens on one day, that Vinnie's date with Mia is not that same night, but the next night. An indeterminate amount of time passes between Vinnie's date with Mia and the night that Butch wins the fight he was supposed to throw; Butch's exit with Fabienne is the morning after his fight. The coffee shop stand-off is on day one, and that day includes the visit to Jimmie's house and Monster Joe's Truck and Tow, and also the scene at the bar where Vinnie first encounters Butch. How that evening passes we are not told. The next thing that we see is day two, beginning with Vinnie's visit to Lance the drug dealer, before his date with Mia. The third day is indicated because Mia has recovered from her overdose and Marsellus is back from Florida by the time of Butch's fight, so it may be a few days later, but since Marsellus is still wearing the mysterious bandage on the back of his head, it is not long enough for a minor wound to heal. The interesting events in the back of the Pawn Shop store unfold the following morning. If you don't just love the character of The Gimp, you just aren't quite playful enough to be in this tree house. I mean was The Gimp gratuitous or what? I admit I haven't figured out why he's in the script, but I'm working on it.

The McGuffin[11] of Butch's story is a watch handed down from Butch's father—a *time*piece of course, and Butch simply cannot go into the future without it; he would sooner die. The clues about time throughout the movie are everywhere: there is a gratuitous clock ticking in the background in scene after scene. Tarantino wants us to know what time it is, but he buries the time references like clues to a treasure in the constant banter and in the background. He wants us to piece the actual temporal sequence together. He dares us to do it. Why? Because it's fun; it's a *clé anglaise* Tarantino wants us to discover for ourselves. Obviously he (and Avery) conceived of the story roughly in order, at first, and then monkeyed around with it until it made a different kind of sense, showed us different things about these characters than we could have seen in the regular sequence, and concealed things we surely would have noticed. Tarantino builds the "dare" into his subtitle: "Three Stories . . . About One Story . . ." So what's the "one story" and what are the "three stories"? He even puts in the ellipses to clue you in to the fact that *you're* supposed to fill in the blanks. I couldn't resist. It's too much fun.

One of the concealed things that everyone would immediately notice, if the movie unfolded in temporal sequence, is that the entire movie is about "Vinnie's Very Bad Day" (okay, three days in one story). Out of sequence it isn't even obvious that Vinnie is the main character, but in sequence the whole movie is a story about how he screws up just one time too many. Placing the movie out of sequence leads us to pay *more* attention to the supporting characters than we otherwise would, as I mentioned. We don't know if the movie is about Vinnie, or Jules, or Butch. This is our unholy trinity: we are led to have *some* sympathy for each of them, in spite of their, shall we say,

---

[11] This is the term Hitchcock used to describe the object of desire that motivates the plot's action—something that has to be retrieved for some reason. *The Maltese Falcon* is the classic example. It makes no particular difference what the McGuffin is, so long as there is *something* the characters want, simply *must* have. It can be a lot of fun to look for the McGuffin in a film—there can be more than one, and they are often quite revealing. See Thomas E. Wartenberg, "Ethics or Film Theory: The Real McGuffin in *North By Northwest*," in *Hitchcock and Philosophy: Dial M for Metaphysics*, edited by David Baggett and William A. Drumin (Chicago: Open Court, 2007), pp. 141–155.

"flaws." So those are the three stories, but *Pulp Fiction* is a story about Vinnie. When we look at it this way, the thing that becomes undeniably clear is the moral of the story. Butch and Jules walk away and Vinnie dies. The question is why? What is Tarantino's point? I may be wrong, but I think I've got it figured out. There is something about the way that Butch and Jules think, about the way they see life and face its challenges that Vinnie just doesn't get.

## The Mexican Stand-off, or Three Well-Dressed, Slightly Toasted Mexican Men

It's impossible not to notice how Tarantino loves to cross-reference and inter-mix his movies, so there are clues in other movies about how to understand *Pulp Fiction*. Everyone knows that Vincent Vega is Vic Vega's brother, and Vic is the scariest of all the scary characters in *Reservoir Dogs*. And it is as plain as the nose on your face that the entire script in *Reservoir Dogs* was designed to set up a show-down imitating the Mexican Stand-off in *The Good, the Bad and the Ugly*, when Blondie, Angel Eyes, and Tuco stand almost endlessly in the Sad Hill Cemetery, while the audience sweats. By the time it is over with, we are all ready to shoot Sergio Leone for torturing us (we loved it, it's so *not* like Mel Gibson), and then we later find out that we were screwed—Tuco's gun wasn't even loaded, and Blondie knew it all along. We love that too.

Tarantino *knows* that we know the game and that we love it. So in *Reservoir Dogs* he gives us a Mexican stand-off in which we cannot see how *any* of the characters can back down, and then he makes us wait. We wonder whether someone's gun isn't loaded and someone else knows it. But no, everyone has bullets. And no, no one backs down. Tarantino shows us what we actually *wanted* to see in *The Good, the Bad, and the Ugly*, but Sergio Leone hadn't left that option for himself—the movie would have been over and no one would have gotten the treasure (which was the McGuffin in this case). In *Reservoir Dogs*, Tarantino saves the stand-off for the end of the movie. By the time we come to it, he can do anything he wants, and we all know it. We have absolutely no idea what he will do. That's fun. But Tarantino cannot stand to settle on just one ending for such a great scenario.

Taken in sequence, the Mexican stand-off in *Pulp Fiction* would have happened in the middle of the movie—after the visit to Monster Joe's Truck and Tow, but just before Jules delivers the mysterious glowing briefcase (which is the McGuffin of Jules's story) to Marsellus Wallace at the bar.[12] Having the Mexican stand-off in the middle would be no good at all, as anyone can plainly see. Of course, by showing it out of sequence, Tarantino frames the movie with the Mexican Stand-off, and then has *everyone* walk away, having gotten some of what they wanted, but sacrificing something to get it.[13] That works.

But Tarantino's stand-offs are very different. In both movies, instead of playing off of greed, self-interest, and the survival instinct, he makes each scenario revolve around loyalty. This raises the Mexican stand-off to a much higher ethical plane. The reason no one can back down in *Reservoir Dogs* is because each is loyal to a person or a principle that he simply cannot violate. Joe Cabot and Nice Guy Eddie know that Vic Vega has been loyal to them, because of the years he spent in prison to protect them, and that is why they know Mr. Orange, who killed Vic, is the undercover detective. They would rather die rather than let Orange live. This establishes the "loyalty of the Vegas," or the family honor, in the Tarantino universe. This is an important point to notice. But where loyalty is easy for Vic (he is simply *made of* loyalty), his little brother Vinnie has to struggle with the idea. Vinnie doesn't lack courage, but he is weak-willed; Aristotle calls this weakness of the will "incontinence." Incontinent people fare poorly in Tarantino's ethical world. As Winston Wolf so memorably puts it, "Just because you *are* a character doesn't mean you *have* character."

## Character Flaws

Aristotle makes a point about characters that is pretty hard to deny: "the agents represented must be either above our own

---

[12] The bar is called "Sally LeRoy's." LeRoy is a French name.
[13] The original script has Jules imagining the bloody outcome and then snapping back into the present. Tarantino did shoot the daydream segment, but wisely left it out of the final film—it disturbs the stand-off too much. But of course, he put it in the out-takes on the DVD, as he knew he would when he made the final edits, so he knew we would still get to see what we wanted to

level of goodness, or beneath it, or just such as we are."[14] Now, if you want to tell a good story, one that brings catharsis, you don't have that many choices. You can start with good men and teach us that they are more like us than we thought (the tragic fall), or you can start with bad men and show that *they* are more like us than we thought. *We* are pretty boring, which is why we go to the movies.

You would think that the French, for all their love of Aristotle, would understand this simple point. But they are still quite peevish about the defeat of Classicism; Aristotle is now their ex-husband, and now they must pretend they never were married to him. Now the *modes du temps* is to be more *avant-garde* than Thou. Yeah, right, whatever. Anyway, French directors love to show people who are better than us becoming worse than us, people like us getting worse than bad people, and people who are worse than us getting worse than they already were. Sometimes they show people like us doing nothing at all. Anything else is a "Hollywood ending" and beneath their aesthetic dignity.[15]

---

see, which is really whether anyone would do us the kindness of shooting Amanda Plummer (who is most annoying).

[14] Aristotle, *Poetics*, line 1448a4.

[15] I think you still doubt me about this concealed critique of French cinema. Okay, explain this: why does every important character, except Butch, have a French name: Jules, Vincent, Marsellus, Mia, Lance, and most of the minor characters, Maynard, Raquel, Roger, Brett (which means someone who is a Breton, the French invaders of 1066 included Bretons) . . . the list goes on. You will say, "Ah, but it is just a coincidence, what about Butch?" Well, Butch tells us, and I quote: "I'm an American. Our names don't mean shit." By implication, Tarantino is trying his best tell us to pay attention to what the non-American names mean. Why, pray tell, do Butch and Esmerelda have a conversation about the meanings of names? You have to pay *attention* if you want into the tree house. Now, Quentin, this part of the footnote is just for you, when you read this: You're thinking that "Yes, he got the French thing, but he missed the Spanish thing." Not so. I certainly caught the Spanish names—Yolanda, Ringo, Esmerelda, and I certainly noticed when Butch says good night to Esmerelda, he says "*bon soir*" and she replies "*buenas noches.*" And I know Sergio Leone shot *The Good, the Bad, and the Ugly* in Spain, so I do know the "true" identities of Esmerelda's three slightly toasted Mexican men. And, yes, I even watched the Spanish subtitles under the French dialogue on the DVD, just as you hoped some of us would. Hilarious. But someone else will have to write the essay on your Spanish subplot. I just don't have the time.

Tarantino, without exception, starts out with people who are worse than we are and shows us how they aren't so *very* bad. That's how we get catharsis. Think about Jimmie's wife in *Pulp Fiction*, the vignette he calls "The Bonnie Situation."[16] Here you have two vicious killers and a dude they call "The Wolf" dashing around, like their heads are fire and their asses are catchin', to clean up evidence of poor Marvin's mishap,[17] and the principal thing that motivates this rush is . . . what Jimmie's *wife* will say when she gets home and the house is full of killers covered with blood? Now that, *that* would be pretty bad, if Jimmie got in *trouble* with his wife. It's pretty hard to deny that Tarantino is consciously moving these killers in our general direction. But that isn't the Moral of the Story. It's just a condition for catharsis. Nothing fancy is going on here, just a boy in a tree house playing cops and robbers with Aristotle.

But the rules are a little different in this game. In most movies the audience knows within the first five minutes who will be the main character. That is no fun. In *Pulp Fiction*, you might watch the movie nine times and still not immediately grasp which is the main character. As I said, Vinnie is the main character in the movie, which isn't obvious until the script is put into sequence. When it is, it becomes very clear that Vinnie is a bumbling anti-hero who becomes the victim of his own carelessness. None of his character flaws—selfishness, laziness, hubris, careless inattention, even weakness of the will—is his "central flaw." And we are supposed to overlook the fact that Vinnie is a ruthless killer, because frankly, everyone he kills is at least as bad as he is. As the Wolf says, "Nobody who'll be missed," at least by us.[18] There will be no serious investigation, and you, my dear middle-American, have nothing to fear from Vincent Vega. Tarantino is not going to get preachy about character flaws in any case. The

---

[16] Bonnie is a French name. And since when is "Jimmie" spelled with an "ie" at the end? Oh, wait. I think I do know of a language in which they spell "Jimmie" that way. . . .

[17] You don't want to play "Marvin" in a Tarantino film. Marvin was the police officer who got his ear cut off by Vic Vega in *Reservoir Dogs*, and then met with a pretty bad end. By the way, "Marvin" is a French name.

[18] They're all bad people, except maybe Marvin, and that was *definitely* an accident.

Moral of the Story does not come from some lesson about what makes a hit man a bad person.

Apart from Vinnie, it is pretty hard to miss that Butch, filled with testosterone and pride as he is, has a soft spot for his dear departed dad, and dangerous though he is, he puts up with whining from Fabienne that none of us would begin to tolerate.[19] And Jules, well, he is *trying* to be the shepherd. He is by far the most dangerous of the dangerous boys, but even he believes in miracles, scolds blasphemers, and reads the Bible.[20]

## *Le temps de me laver les mains*, or Bathroom Loyalties

It is easy to miss, but Vinnie's "incontinence"—and I mean this in the ordinary sense of the word—is the master key to the movie, and the monkey wrench. That's the password to Taratino's tree house. Everything bad that happens to Vinnie is signaled by what's happening in the bathroom. The "fourth man" with the hand cannon is hiding in the bathroom when Vinnie and Jules make the "hit" in the apartment, but Jules takes the hint and Vinnie doesn't get it. Vinnie is in the bathroom when Honey Bunny and Pumpkin pull their guns at the coffee shop to create the Mexican stand-off. Vinnie is in the bathroom when Mia Wallace mistakes his heroin for cocaine (saving them both from an impending and very disloyal tryst). And Vinnie is in the bathroom when Butch returns for his beloved watch, which is the end of Vinnie.

We do see Jules in the bathroom once, and we do see Butch there once: each is washing off the stain of a former life he intends to leave behind. And Tarantino makes it very, very clear that Vinnie does not wash his hands, showing him emerging

---

[19] I don't guess I really have to point out that not only is Fabienne French, she whines *because* she is so very French. And she wants blueberry pancakes because she isn't terribly well-connected to the way things really are; she'll have to settle for buttermilk pancakes, since this is an American movie.

[20] I know very well that you already looked it up. I mean Ezekiel 25:17. No, it does not quite say what Jules says before he "caps someone's ass," but it's not that far off. Call it *license poétique*. Here is the passage in French: "J'exercerai sur eux de grandes vengeances, En les châtiant avec fureur. Et ils sauront que je suis l'Eternel, Quand j'exercerai sur eux ma vengeance." Ha.

from the bathroom at Butch's apartment immediately after he flushes the toilet, still fastening his belt. You think I'm making too much of it. If so, then why do Jules and Vinnie have an argument about washing their hands in Jimmie's bathroom? And I quote:

> **JULES:** What the fuck did you just do to his towel?
> **VINCENT:** I was just dryin' my hands.
> **JULES:** You're supposed to wash 'em first.
> **VINCENT:** You watched me wash 'em.
> **JULES:** I watched you get 'em wet.
> **VINCENT:** I washed 'em. Blood's real hard to get off. Maybe if he had some Lava,[21] I coulda done a better job.
> **JULES:** I used the same soap you did and when I dried my hands, the towel didn't look like a fuckin' Maxipad.

Nothing happens by accident in a Tarantino movie. As Aristotle puts it, "that which makes no perceptible difference by its presence or absence is no real part of the whole."[22] Tarantino doesn't waste your time with "that which makes no perceptible difference." If Vinnie had the sense to wash his hands, thoroughly, he might still be with us—Butch would have had time to escape, and some noise to cover his exit. But no. Vinnie is lazy and careless and incontinent. Tarantino tells us what we need to know. It comes when Vinnie has taken Mia Wallace home after their "date" at Jack Rabbit Slim's. Mia has her own issues with incontinence (as Marsellus well knows, from the infamous "foot massage" episode—he is testing Vinnie's loyalty). Having excused himself to go to the bathroom after an "uncomfortable silence" with Mia, Vinnie has the following conversation with himself in the mirror:

> One drink and leave. Don't be rude, but drink your drink quickly, say goodbye, walk out the door, get in your car, and go down the road. . . . It's a moral test of yourself, whether or not you can maintain loyalty. Because when people are loyal to each other, that's very meaningful. So you're gonna go out there, drink your drink,

---

21 "Lava," from "laver," the French verb for "to wash." It's a French soap.
22 Aristotle, *Poetics*, lines 1451a–35.

say "Goodnight, I've had a very lovely evening," go home, and jack off. And that's all you're gonna do.

That's the password to Tarantino's tree house: "loyalty." It's very meaningful. I noted that the McGuffin for Butch is the watch and for Jules it's the briefcase. What is the McGuffin in Vinnie's story? Let me ask it another way. What does he truly want that he cannot get? I mean he has the drugs and the cars and the money and women if he wants them (he turns down a free tryst with Trudi, so we know this isn't his weakness). He tells us what he doesn't have that he wants: self-control and true loyalty. The McGuffin evades him.

We may not be able to understand a world filled with people none of whom is morally similar to us, except that Tarantino shows us that they *do* have loyalties. Jules will deliver that briefcase to Marsellus even after he has decided to leave the "business," and will risk his life to do so. Loyalty. Butch is loyal to the memory of his father, yes, but why, pray tell, does he turn around and save Marsellus Wallace when he could just as easily leave him to die at the hands of Zed and Maynard and The Gimp? If they kill Marsellus, all of Butch's problems are over. But Butch is a man of honor, a man's man, and he knows Marsellus is another man of honor, and to put it in his own words Marsellus at that moment is "very far from okay." A loyal man just can't let another loyal man meet such an end. Marsellus recognizes the deed for what it is when Butch saves him and also leaves him the privilege of taking care of Zed in "medieval" fashion.

The scene in the back of the pawn shop is a rerun of the rape of Ned Beatty from *Deliverance*. Butch's search for the right weapon is the key to the scene. He picks up a hammer, then a chainsaw, then a baseball bat, discarding each after a moment's thought, trying to decide what movie he's in. Is it *Friday the 13th*? No. Is it *The Texas Chainsaw Massacre*? No. Is he in *Walking Tall*? Is this about justice? No. This is about honor. It's the katana. Uma Thurman and Tarantino are already writing *Kill Bill* on the set of *Pulp Fiction*.

We never quite learn whether Vinnie is capable of genuine loyalty or not. We know he *wants* to be loyal. We know he is *trying* to be loyal. We know he *values* loyalty. We also know that he is weak-willed, careless, and incontinent; he knows that too, and doesn't like it. But in the end, there is something different about Vinnie that curbs our sympathy. He doesn't wash his hands when he goes to the bathroom. So the moral of the story? It's three morals, but they all amount to one: Be loyal. It's important. Don't be weak-willed. It will lead you to a bad end. And wash your hands when you go to the bathroom . . . thoroughly; it says more about your character than you may realize.

# 11

# Coke into Pepsi: The Miracle in *Pulp Fiction*

KEITH ALLEN KORCZ

> **JULES:** Don't do that! Don't you fuckin' do that! Don't blow this shit off! What just happened was a fuckin' miracle![1]
>
> —*Pulp Fiction*

So says Jules Winnfield shortly after a man fires six shots point blank from his hand cannon at Jules and his partner Vincent Vega, missing with every shot. But is this experience enough to conclude that, as Vincent puts it, "God came down from heaven and stopped the bullets"? True, it results in a sharp change in Jules's outlook, as he decides to give up his life as an enforcer for crime boss Marsellus Wallace and just walk the earth, "like Caine in *Kung Fu*," "tryin' real hard to be a shepherd." But there have been too many failed predictions from self-proclaimed prophets, too many pious frauds and too many cult suicides to accept just any report of a miracle at face value.[2] Those who *want* to believe find it all too easy. But what about those of us with a more philosophical bent who instead want to *know*? What sort of evidence should we demand before accepting a supposed miracle as a good enough reason, all on its own, to believe in the existence of a particular god?

---

[1] All dialogue quotes from *Pulp Fiction* are from Quentin Tarantino, *Pulp Fiction: A Quentin Tarantino Screenplay* (New York: Hyperion, 1994).

[2] For a fascinating look at some of these, I'd recommend Joe Nickell's *Looking for a Miracle* (Amherst: Prometheus, 1993).

# It's a Freak

By far the most famous philosophical attempt to answer this question was written by the great Scottish philosopher David Hume (1711–1776).[3] The main point of his reasoning is pretty straightforward. Suppose a generally reliable and trustworthy friend were to tell you that they left their DVD of *Pulp Fiction* in your living room. Would you believe them? Presumably, yes. This sort of thing happens all the time. Now suppose that your friend were to tell you that an aging boxer was in the process of punching out a leather-clad man named "The Gimp" in your living room. Would you believe him? Now, I don't know what goes on in *your* living room, but I am presuming that this sort of event would be pretty unusual, and that you would assume that your friend was just kidding (at best) or had been conversing a bit too much with Choco the madman (at worst). Finally, imagine what would happen if Mia were to tell her husband, crime boss Marsellus, that she was pregnant, but the baby is definitely not his or that of any other human, contrary to the laws of nature. Rather, she claims that the baby came from God. What would Marsellus do? I suspect that Marsellus would not believe her. In fact, I suspect that Mia and whoever he suspected of being Mia's partner would quickly become grease spots. "No marriage counselor, no trial separation—fuckin' divorced" as Jules's friend Jimmie says in another context. Tony Rocky Horror would have gotten off easy by comparison. If you were Marsellus, would you believe her?

It would be easier to believe that an aging boxer was punching out The Gimp in your living room. However unlikely this is, at least it wouldn't involve the suspension of a law of nature. And this is Hume's point: events contrary to what we take to be well-established laws of nature are about as unlikely as things get.

You are more likely to win two lotteries and then get struck by lightning and survive, all within the space of a few minutes, than you are to witness a suspension of a law of nature. Why is this? It's because of all the evidence we have that laws of nature

---

[3] David Hume, "Of Miracles," *An Enquiry Concerning Human Understanding*, edited by Tom L. Beauchamp (New York: Oxford University Press, 1999 [1772]).

do not get suspended. Even the U.S. Patent and Trademark Office will not patent a purported perpetual motion machine.[4] They won't do this because they know that a perpetual motion machine would violate a law of nature, hence that such a device can't possibly work. A lot of people have tried, and all of them have failed.

We generally take something to be a law of nature because (a) it has been very carefully and repeatedly tested in controlled conditions and found never to be violated and (b) claims that it has been violated have been found to rest on mistakes or outright fraud. On the basis of these repeated observations, we conclude that this is how nature operates. These are not legal laws which, when violated, may lead to a cold shower in a county jail. Rather, they are observed regularities with regard to how things work in nature. Unlike legal laws, one cannot choose to create or to violate them. The kind of scientific testing involved is far more than any one person could do in a lifetime. The evidence, both testimony and physical evidence,[5] supporting the claim that something is a law of nature is so overwhelming that we know that reports of its suspension are almost certainly mistaken.

Now, being shot at six times without being hit, as happened to Jules and Vincent, need not involve a suspension of a law of nature. Vincent realizes this when he says,

> Ever seen that show *Cops*? I was watchin' it once and this cop was on it who was talkin' about this time he got into this gun fight with this guy in a hallway. He unloads on this guy and he doesn't hit nothin'. And these guys were in a hallway. It's a freak, but it happens.

It's merely a lucky coincidence. Should lucky coincidences be good enough evidence to believe that a god exists? I don't think so. Suppose the odds are one in a billion that some lucky coincidence will happen to someone today. So, it's pretty unlikely

---

[4] United States Patent and Trademark Office, *Manual of Patent Examining Procedure (MPEP), Eighth Edition*, August 2001, Latest Revision August 2006, subsection706.03(a), http://www.uspto.gov/web/offices/pac/mpep/documents/0700_706_03_a.htm#sect706.03a, accessed 4/12/07.
[5] Hume's argument is limited to mere testimony, but can be extended to include physical evidence.

that it will happen to you. But given six billion people in the world, it should happen six times today. Is this good evidence that the gods of these six people exist? If a cat (or a Samoan) falls four stories, through a greenhouse, and survives, the news reports it as a miracle. If a cat falls four stories, through a greenhouse, and dies, the news doesn't report it at all. But if you drop enough cats out of enough windows, some are going to survive. A fortunate coincidence is not necessarily a miracle.

## Making the Impossible Possible

Hume recognizes, with Vincent, that you need more than a lucky coincidence to show that a god exists. Instead, you need something only a god could do, such as suspend a law of nature. If a law of nature gets suspended, you know you are more than just lucky. Thus, we can think of a miracle as a suspension of a law of nature brought about by some supernatural being.

Vincent seems to have a sense of this point when, in response to a question from Jules in the coffee shop, he says that an act of God is "when God makes the impossible possible. And I'm sorry, Jules, but I don't think what happened this morning qualifies." Jules replies:

> Don't you see, Vince, that shit don't matter. You're judging this thing the wrong way. It's not about *what*. It could be God stopped the bullets, he changed Coke into Pepsi, he found my fuckin' car keys. You don't judge shit like this based on merit. Whether or not what we experienced was an according-to-Hoyle miracle is insignificant. What is significant is I felt God's touch. God got involved.

Hume agrees with Jules on one point: the event does not need to be dramatic for it to be a miracle. As Hume puts it:

> A miracle may either be discoverable by men or not. This alters not its nature and essence. The raising of a house or a ship into the air is a visible miracle. The raising of a feather, when the wind wants ever so little of a force requisite for that purpose, is as real a miracle, though not so sensible with regard to us.[6]

---

[6] Hume, "On Miracles," p. 173n23.

But notice that Jules's argument now has shifted. The argument is not now that a miracle occurred, and that this is good evidence that God exists. Rather, the argument is that the apparent miracle has occasioned a feeling in Jules that God has touched him. But we won't pursue this issue here.[7] I mention it because it's not uncommon for a person to present one argument and, in response to objections to it, shift to another without realizing that they have done so.

## A Moment of Clarity?

Jules's experience doesn't seem to count as a miracle because it's apparently merely a coincidence that he was not shot. But what about Hume's argument? Hume claims that it's probably never going to be reasonable to believe that a genuine miracle has occurred because a genuine miracle involves a suspension of the laws of nature, and claims that laws of nature have been suspended have almost invariably been shown to be mistaken. As Hume says, when faced with a person claiming to have seen a miracle, "I immediately consider with myself, whether it be more probable, that this person should either deceive or be deceived, or that the fact, which he relates, should really have happened."[8] Hume thinks it's clear that it's always going to be more likely, based on our past experience with such claims, that the person was mistaken than that a law of nature was actually suspended.

Philosophers have disagreed about whether Hume is right. Here are some of the more common reasons given for thinking that Hume was mistaken.

There have been times when scientists thought that something was a law of nature but discovered that they were mistaken. If Hume is right, how could this be? How can we ever discover that we were mistaken about what we thought was a law of nature?

Well, there are a couple of ways we can imagine this happening. One way involves a wholesale rejection of a law of

---

[7] An argument for the existence of God along these lines has been defended by the contemporary philosopher Alvin Plantinga in Part Three of his book *Warranted Christian Belief* (New York: Oxford University Press, 2000).

[8] Hume, "On Miracles," p. 174.

nature and all, or virtually all, of the observations which support it. Someone, for example, might argue that there is nothing like a law of gravity, and all of our apparent experiences of things (including Samoans) falling down rather than up, let's say, were really hallucinations. Obviously, this is never going to happen. Mistakes about the laws of nature tend not to be this dramatic. But even if this did happen, one would have to be able to describe repeatable experiments showing that it were so for it to be reasonable to believe. For instance, perhaps one could show that it were true by explaining the mechanism that caused the hallucination, and then showing how anyone could come to see how things really are by being given an antidote to whatever is causing the hallucination. In this case, the quality of the evidence for the claim that we hallucinated might well outweigh the quantity of evidence we have that something like gravity is at work. I don't think this is at odds with the spirit of Hume's argument. After all, we are simply weighing the evidence, and taking into account its quantity and quality, as Hume suggests.[9]

But revisions to laws of nature don't usually work this way nowadays. What is more likely to happen is that we discover that what we thought was a regularity throughout nature is only a regularity in less than extreme conditions. Scientists do not reject a law of nature by discovering situations where the law ordinarily does hold, was suspended once or twice, but still holds. Rather, they discover new conditions under which what was thought to be a law never holds, and where this can be shown repeatedly.

Compare Jules's experiences with giving ladies foot massages. In Jules's view, "Foot massages don't mean shit." Vincent continues:

> **VINCENT:** Have you ever given a foot massage?
> **JULES:** Don't be tellin' me about foot massages. I'm the fuckin' foot master.
> **VINCENT:** Given a lot of 'em?
> **JULES:** Shit yeah. I got my technique down man, I don't tickle or nothin'.

---

[9] Hume makes the point with regard to the quality of testimony in "On Miracles," p. 171.

**VINCENT:** Have you ever given a guy a foot massage?
**JULES:** Fuck you.

Jules interprets his past experiences with foot massages to apply to *all* foot massages, and Vincent realizes that this isn't so. It won't be so whenever it is a man rather than a woman being given a foot massage.

As with Jules, sometimes our past experiences don't tell us what will be the case in very different circumstances. For example, prior to 1919, let's suppose, our experience with light did not suggest that gravity would bend it. In 1919, an experiment is done that indicates that the gravitational field of the sun bends the light of distant stars such that, during an eclipse, we can see the shift in the apparent position of the star. This test, actually performed in 1919, was taken to be an important step in confirming Einstein's General Theory of Relativity, which predicted such a shift. It also helped overthrow some very long-standing views about the nature of our universe. But we don't take our previous-to-1919 experience with light to undermine the claim that light can be bent by gravity because our previous experience with light did not involve viewing light as it passed through such a strong gravitational field. The testimony we have that light here on Earth does not appear to bend outside of a very strong gravitational field does not undermine the testimony that light bends as it passes through a very strong gravitational field. It's not as if it were discovered that light sometimes bends in a strong gravitational field and sometimes does not, as would be the case with a miracle. Rather, it's that light always bends in a gravitational field, and this can be shown repeatedly.

If someone does an experiment showing how Coke can be spontaneously turned into Pepsi, we can ask how the experiment was done and try it for ourselves as often as we like. With enough careful observation, we can, if needed, revise our understanding of the laws of nature to account for what we observe. There is not a lot we can do, however, to determine whether water was turned into wine by God two thousand years ago. There is no way to check repeatedly to see whether he really did, and asking him to do it again so we can check tends not to work. Hume's point is not that it is impossible that miracles occur, but rather that the evidence against their occurrence is always going to be overwhelming.

## Zed Is Dead

Sometimes it's argued that if we have good reasons to believe that a god who performs miracles exists, then we shouldn't be at all surprised when people report having seen one. Rather than thinking it's unlikely that they are correct, we should expect that there is a good chance that they witnessed the real thing.

The problem here is that the appeal to miracles, all by itself, was supposed to be sufficient evidence to believe that a god exists. If we already need good reasons to believe that a god exists for the appeal to miracles to work, then we don't need the appeal to miracles at all.

But what if two hundred atheistic scientists witnessed an apparently miraculous, non-repeatable event? Or you witness one yourself? Shouldn't you then accept that a miracle has occurred?[10]

In a famous line, Hume says that a wise man "proportions his belief to the evidence."[11] So, I think Hume's answer to these questions would be "No." After all, what if, fifty years ago, two hundred atheistic scientists saw the Empire State building disappear? Then they would likely have thought it a miracle. Now we know it's just David Copperfield. When our ability to collect or evaluate the evidence is very limited, it still seems more reasonable to withhold judgment as to whether a miracle occurred than to accept something that appears highly unlikely.

No doubt Jules was strongly affected by his experience. Perhaps it will even change his life. Is this evidence that it was a miracle? Well, whether it was a miracle or not does not seem relevant to the effect on Jules. His belief that it was a miracle is causing the change, and it would do so whether or not his belief is correct.

Hume, with characteristic wit, concluded his essay by writing that, "The Christian religion not only was at first attended with miracles, but even at this day cannot be believed by any reasonable person without one."[12] That's a bold statement, but I think he was on to something.

---

[10] Richard Swinburne, "For the Possibility of Miracles," *Philosophy of Religion: An Anthology, Fourth Edition*, edited by Louis P. Pojman (Belmont: Wadsworth, 2003), p. 272.

[11] Hume, "On Miracles," p. 170.

[12] Hume, "On Miracles," p. 186.

# 12

# Quentin Tarantino and the Ex-Convict's Dilemma

RICHARD GREENE

A common occurrence in most Quentin Tarantino films is what has come to be known as a "Mexican standoff." This refers to a situation in which two or more persons have weapons (usually firearms) pointed at one another, such that the persons are essentially paralyzed. They *can* act, but their doing so, no matter what they do, will likely result in either serious injury or death. I'm not going to use the term "Mexican standoff" in this chapter because (1) there is some question as to whether the term is racist in origin, and, more importantly for our purposes, (2) there may be a more apt description of the scenario as it appears in Tarantino's films. Instead, I'll use the term "ex-convict's dilemma."[1] I'll refer to any scenario involving an ex-convict's dilemma as an "ECDS."

In this chapter I'll argue that the ex-convict's dilemma is a special instance of what philosophers, economists, and decision theorists typically refer to as a "prisoner's dilemma." I'll further argue that the most popular solution to the prisoner's dilemma—the group rationality solution—cannot be applied to the ex-convict's dilemma. This, of course, shows that the solution under consideration is lacking; a good general solution to a philosophical puzzle or paradox ought to be applicable to all or nearly all instances of the phenomenon. Tarantino's frequent employment of the ex-convict's dilemma is interesting in that he

---

[1] I don't mean to suggest that only ex-convicts find themselves in these scenarios, but, at least in Tarantino films, ex-convicts tend to be involved.

manages (speaking very broadly) to show most or all of the different ways things can end up for a person who finds herself in just such a circumstance. While the results for persons in ex-convict dilemmas aren't always catastrophic, they usually are. When things turn out well in these cases, there is usually quite a bit of luck involved. This will turn out to have interesting implications for the prospect of a rationality-based general solution to the prisoner's dilemma.

## The Prisoner's Dilemma

So just what exactly is a prisoner's dilemma? Suppose hypothetically that Ordell Robbie and Louis Gara (a couple of despicable hoods from *Jackie Brown*) have been arrested for fencing stolen goods and are being interrogated by the police. Ordell is in one interrogation room and Louis is in another. Suppose further that the police don't have enough evidence to convict either of the more serious charge of fencing stolen goods, but have enough evidence to convict each of a less serious charge, such as possessing stolen stuff.[2] The police make the following offer to each. "If you rat on your partner and your partner remains silent, then you will go free and your partner will go to jail for seven years. If neither you nor your partner rat on the other (in other words, if each stays silent), then you will both go to jail for one year (on the minor charge). If both partners rat on the other, then each will go to jail for four years." Since both Ordell and Louis are in separate rooms, neither knows what the other one is doing. What should Ordell and Louis do?

The best thing from Ordell's perspective is to rat on Louis and have Louis remain silent. Under that scenario, Ordell would do no jail time. The best thing for Louis, of course, is to have just the opposite happen. The problem is that if each goes for the optimal solution—no jail time—each ends up doing four years. They would be better off if neither spoke. Then each would get just one year. To this point it seems that perhaps the rational thing for each to do would be to remain silent, since if they don't remain silent, they will both end up doing four years in the slammer as opposed to one year.

---

[2] These probably aren't the real names of these charges, but since I'm not involved with law enforcement nor am I a lawyer, I'll just continue to fake it.

Unfortunately, matters are not quite so simple. Notice that no matter what Ordell does, Louis is better off if he rats on Ordell. Consider the case in which Ordell remains silent. If Ordell doesn't rat and Louis does, then Louis goes free. If Ordell stays silent and Louis doesn't rat either, then each gets one year. So if Ordell stays silent, Louis should rat (assuming he's going only by his own self-interest).

Now consider the case in which Ordell rats on Louis. If both Ordell and Louis rat, then each gets four years. If Ordell rats and Louis doesn't, then Louis gets seven years. So if Ordell rats, Louis should too. So regardless of what Ordell does, Louis should rat on Ordell. The same holds for Ordell—he should rat regardless of what Louis does. Given this line of reasoning it seems like the rational thing for each to do is to rat on the other. But, again, if each does the rational thing, then each gets four years in the pokey and is worse off than if each had remained silent. The result of all this is a paradox—rationality is typically cashed out in terms of behavior that maximizes self-interest, but rational behavior in this case results in the persons involved being worse off than had they not done the rational thing.

## The Prisoner's Dilemma—Not Just for Prisoners Anymore

The term "prisoner's dilemma" is applicable to any number of situations, provided that the situation has the essential elements described above—that persons behaving "rationally" leads to everyone being worse off, and, paradoxically, that no matter what others do, one is better off doing the "rational" thing. It's not essential that a prisoner's dilemma involve only two decision makers (although there must be at least two), nor is it essential that a prisoner's dilemma actually involve prisoners.

While the term "prisoner's dilemma" was formulated only recently (in the 1950s by folks at the RAND Corporation), prisoner's-dilemma scenarios have played key roles in philosophical arguments for centuries. Perhaps the most famous instance of a prisoner's dilemma scenario occurs in Plato's *Republic*. The character Glaucon argues that the origin and nature of justice involves a situation where persons in a state of nature improve their lot by agreeing *not* to behave in rational and self-interested ways. The result is a contract state in which everyone (or almost everyone) is better off than they would be in the state of nature. William Forster Lloyd's *Tragedy of the Commons* is also an instance of the prisoner's dilemma (if everyone fully exploits commonly owned resources for their own individual benefit, the result is the over-exploitation of those resources, and every individual is worse off). Even certain day-to-day situations, such as traffic jam scenarios, can have the essential elements of a prisoner's dilemma.

Notice that the ex-convict's dilemma has the essential elements of a prisoner's dilemma, and thus is an instance of the prisoner's dilemma. Consider the first of two ECDS's that Tarantino treats his audience to in *Reservoir Dogs*. Two criminals, known only to each other by their codenames—Mr. White (Harvey Keitel) and Mr. Pink (Steve Buscemi)—have just been involved in a failed robbery attempt. To say things have gone terribly wrong would be a huge understatement. They are at the rendezvous point, which is an empty warehouse, along with an incapacitated Mr. Orange (Tim Roth). As tempers flare, they scuffle and eventually wind up in very close proximity with handguns pointed directly at each other's faces. As in a prisoner's dilemma scenario they have two actions available to them: lower their handgun or do nothing for the moment. If they both lower their guns, they both survive. If Pink lowers his gun but White does not, Pink could be shot and White can accomplish whatever goal he had hoped to accomplish by pointing his gun at Pink in the first place (in this particular case White desires to take Orange to a hospital against the protestations of Pink). Similarly, if White lowers his gun and Pink does not, then White could die and Pink would be able to accomplish his goal (Pink is trying to get White not to take Orange to the hospital, as doing so might endanger the group). Finally, if neither lowers their weapon, then both may well end up seriously injured or dead. In such cases people tend to become more rash or panicky as time goes on. Hence the likelihood of both persons being shot increases with each passing moment, although the greater likelihood is that the person who shoots second will end up in worse shape than the person who shoots first (being shot at tends to mess up one's aim and concentration).[3]

---

[3] This holds for two-person scenarios. In scenarios where there are more than

Given that if each person acts in a self-interested way, both could end up seriously injured or dead, it would *appear* (as was the case in our original prisoner's dilemma scenario) that the rational thing to do would be for each person to behave in the way that *doesn't* lead to the best-case scenario from his perspective: that is, each should put down his gun.

Once again, things are not so simple. Notice that no matter what White does, Pink is better off if he does not lower his weapon. Consider the case in which White doesn't lower his weapon. If White doesn't lower his weapon and Pink does, then Pink will likely get shot. If White doesn't lower his weapon and Pink doesn't either, then Pink will likely get shot (since both will likely get shot in that scenario) but may not end up as badly off (because Pink may be the first to shoot and as we've seen the first to shoot typically ends up better off than the second). Now consider the case in which White does lower his weapon. If White lowers his weapon and Pink does as well, then Pink survives the scenario (as does White). If White lowers his gun and Pink does not, then Pink survives the scenario and is in a position to have his desire (to get White to act in a more "professional" manner) satisfied. So regardless of what White does, Pink is better off not lowering his gun. The same goes for White. The same exact paradox has resulted—doing the "rational" thing leads to all parties being worse off.

## Solving the Prisoner's Dilemma

There have been a number of approaches to resolving the prisoner's dilemma. Most are designed (roughly) to show how the term "rational" can be applied to the co-operative course of action (such as neither Ordell nor Louis ratting on the other, or both Mr. Pink and Mr. White lowering their firearms) despite the fact that any participant in such a scenario will be better off not taking that co-operative course of action. Some strategies involve multiple iterations of the scenario. So, for example, persons put in these situations over and over will

---

two persons, the person who shoots first is virtually assured of being seriously injured or killed, because the person they shoot at is not the only person who has a gun pointed at them.

eventually co-operate. These solutions work well under controlled circumstances, such as in a game theorist's laboratory. They also work well in real life situations that tend to be recurrent, such as traffic-jam scenarios. Eventually people learn to co-operate (for example, by letting others merge in) so as to minimize the badness experienced by all. It should be obvious that these approaches to solving the prisoner's dilemma will not be applicable in a sufficiently wide variety of cases. Specifically, for our purposes, they won't be applicable to ECDS's, because such scenarios tend to not be recurrent (one would have to be extremely lucky to survive more than a few of these in one's lifetime).

A second class of solutions, which I'll call "group rationality solutions," appears a bit more promising. These tend to involve denying the claim that it is always rational for an agent not to co-operate in prisoner's dilemma scenarios. Proponents of this view argue that a rational person would take into consideration the rationality of others in the scenario. Ordell, for example, would think through things as follows: "I'm better off ratting on Louis, no matter what Louis does; but Louis will also realize that he'll be better off ratting on me, no matter what *I* do. Louis, in turn, will realize that I'm also aware of this. Since we are both rational, we'll both know to cooperate." So, in short, once someone in a prisoner's dilemma scenario takes into consideration the rationality of others, then it is rational to choose the co-operative course of action.

One virtue of this solution is that it shares the main advantage of the previous solution discussed—that it results in co-operation. Here, rather than eventually being a learned behavior, co-operation results from persons' abilities to reason in advance that co-operation in such circumstances is optimal. Given that the group rationality solution seems to have the virtues of the first solution and is wider in scope (in that it is not limited in application to recurring events), it is clearly the preferable solution to the prisoner's dilemma.

There's a drawback to the group rationality solution: it is overly optimistic about human behavior. One could easily imagine Ordell going through the thought process described above and then thinking, "Fuck it! I'm still better off if I screw Louis over, so that's what I'm gonna do." Once Ordell believes that Louis will choose co-operation, then it is no longer rational for him to do so as well. (We could complicate matters further by observing that Ordell is far more likely than Louis—who is as dumb as a brick—to be able to work all of this out rationally at all, and that Ordell would have to work this fact into his reasoning.)

This worry aside, there's a deeper problem with the group rationality solution. It's not applicable to the ex-convict's dilemma. The group rationality solution relies on the fact that the persons in the scenario have common goals. Neither prisoner wants to spend time in jail, so their goals of minimizing jail time dovetail nicely. Persons who find themselves in ECDS's typically are at odds with one another. Causing serious injury (or death) to the other may often be a desirable state of affairs from such persons' point of view. This is a huge impediment to group rationality leading to co-operation.

Moreover, persons sometimes put themselves in ex-convict's dilemma scenarios intentionally. Consider the ECDS in *Kill Bill Volume 1*. A couple of trained assassins, Beatrix Kiddo (Uma Thurman) and Vernita Green (Vivica A. Fox), are fighting to the death and wind up with knives directly in each other's face. The co-operative solution wouldn't satisfy either, given that each strongly desires to kill the other. If given the opportunity, each would willingly get back into the situation, if they thought that it would further their ultimate goal. So if there's a general solution to the prisoner's dilemma that covers cases of all types, it lies elsewhere.

## Tarantino's Treatment of ECDS's

I'm not optimistic that a satisfactory general solution to the prisoner's dilemma exists. It may well be the case that everybody behaving "rationally" ultimately makes things worse for all involved. One might hope that most persons would choose not to behave in obviously self-interested ways most of the time, but experience (at least the experience of someone who lived through the yuppie era, for example) indicates otherwise.

Despite my pessimism regarding a general solution to the prisoner's dilemma there is still much to be said about getting into and out of ECDS's. Here Tarantino's treatment of ECDS's should be of great help. I'll make use of a simple taxonomy: ECDS's in which people die and ECDS's in which people don't die.

Given that Tarantino makes frequent use of ECDS's in his films (we'll look at six!) and more often than not people come out of them unscathed, one might be tempted to conclude that he's a kind of optimist about the role reason plays in helping one negotiate one's way through such precarious situations. This, I'll argue, is not borne out. The further implication will be that rationality-based solutions to the prisoner's dilemma are unsuccessful.

Tarantino presents us with two ECDS's in which things go very badly for those involved and attempts to employ reason fail miserably. Consider the second ECDS from *Reservoir Dogs*. In this scene Mr. White, Joe Cabot (Lawrence Tierney), and Joe's son Nice Guy Eddie (Chris Penn) are arguing about what went wrong with the heist (and whether Mr. Orange tipped off the cops). Emotions are running high. Eventually, White points his gun at Joe, Joe points his gun at Orange (who is lying on the ground in a pool of blood), and Eddie has his gun pointed at White. Eddie suggests that they put their guns down and settle things with a conversation. White warns Joe that if he shoots Orange, he will be shot. Eddie's attempt at providing a rational way out of the situation has proven very short-lived: he then screams at White and all three fire their guns simultaneously. The "rational" solution in this case fails, at least in part, because the three participants have different goals. Eddie wants to protect his father, White wants to protect Orange, and Joe wants to exact revenge on Orange. If getting out of the situation were a priority for each, perhaps things would go differently.

Now consider the ECDS from *True Romance*.[4] This one is pretty much the mother of all ex-convict dilemmas. In this scene Clarence Worley (Christian Slater), Alabama Whitman (Patricia Arquette), and Dick Ritchie (Michael Rapaport) are involved in a drug deal with movie producer Lee Donowitz (Saul Rubinek) and his assistant Elliot Blitzer (Bronson Pinchot). Elliot is a police informant, and is wearing a wire. Once the transaction occurs the police bust in and point their guns at the producer and his bodyguards. The bodyguards have machine guns pointed at the police. Matters get complicated when four mob-

---

[4] Tarantino wrote, but did not direct *True Romance* (it was directed by Tony Scott in 1993).

sters who have been looking for Clarence (he stole the drugs from them earlier in the film) bust in and point their guns at the cops and bodyguards. The only attempt at reason—Lee pleads for everyone to calm down—falls on deaf ears. At this point there are six cops, four mobsters, and two armed guards with guns pointed at one another, all screaming "PUT IT DOWN, PUT YOUR FUCKING GUN DOWN." It's not difficult to see how this scenario plays out: everyone shoots at once and almost everyone gets killed.

This situation doesn't really lend itself to a rational solution in the first place; the people involved aren't really talking with one another. Given the conflicting interests and goals of the participants, however, a rational solution based on co-operation would be necessarily unattainable even if they were to engage in conversation.

Let's look at ECDS's in which persons don't die. In fact, these ECDS's are more pertinent than those just discussed. This is because in cases where people die, it follows, necessarily, that the optimal state of affairs—co-operation—doesn't obtain. Hence, such cases don't count as resolved ex-convict dilemmas. The category of ECDS's in which persons don't die can be broken down into two subcategories: ones in which fate or luck intervenes and ones in which reason plays a role in resolving the situation.

We've already discussed the two ECDS's in which persons don't die and fate or luck intervenes. The first is the one early in *Reservoir Dogs* involving Mr. White and Mr. Pink. The standoff ends when Mr. Blonde enters the room distracting each and causing them inadvertently to lower their guns. Here there is a co-operative solution, but it is not one that is chosen by either White or Pink—it just happens.

The second is the one in *Kill Bill Volume 1*. The standoff between Beatrix and Vernita ends—temporarily at least—when Vernita's young daughter, Nikki, comes home from school. Beatrix and Vernita both, almost instinctively, hide their weapons behind their backs in an effort to make it appear to Nikki that nothing bad is going on (despite the fact that Vernita's living room has been completely destroyed moments earlier during their fight). Again, the result is a co-operative solution (albeit a short-lived one, as Beatrix kills Vernita shortly thereafter). While this solution *is* chosen by the persons in the scenario, it is not chosen for its own sake; rather, it is chosen because each recognizes that getting out of the situation is what is best for Nikki. It would be disastrous for Nikki to see her mother kill someone or be killed by someone.

Although having good luck or having external events come into an ECDS may get one out of the situation, they certainly are not reliable means of doing so. Let's turn our attention to ECDS's in which people don't die and reason plays a role in resolving the situation.

Consider the ECDS in the final scene of *Pulp Fiction*. Here the situation is potentially ripe for a co-operative rational solution. The persons in the scenario, Pumpkin (Tim Roth), Honey Bunny (Amanda Plummer), Jules Winnfield (Samuel L. Jackson), and Vincent Vega (John Travolta) don't desire to be in the situation and don't have any particular animosity toward one another; rather they just end up in the situation when Pumpkin's and Honey Bunny's attempt to rob diners of a restaurant is thwarted by Jules' pulling a gun on Pumpkin. The situation mirrors the second ECDS in *Reservoir Dogs* almost perfectly. Jules has a gun pointed at Pumpkin, Honey Bunny has a gun pointed at Jules, and Vincent has a gun pointed at Honey Bunny. While the result is, for all intents and purposes, the co-operative solution—that is, each eventually puts down his or her gun—it's not in virtue of group rationality that the co-operative result obtains; rather, it's in virtue of Jules's willingness to buy off Pumpkin and Honey Bunny (he gives them $1,500). In an important sense, true co-operation doesn't actually occur: Pumpkin and Honey Bunny profit more from the situation than do Jules and Vincent.

Perhaps the best example of a co-operative solution to an ECDS occurs in *Kill Bill Volume 2*. Here the persons in the situation actually reason their way out, and neither has to buy the other out. Here's what happens. Karen Kim (Helen Kim) is an assassin sent to kill Beatrix. Karen shoots her way into Beatrix's hotel room and they end up with guns pointed at one another. Beatrix convinces Karen to put her gun down and walk away by informing Karen that she (Beatrix) is pregnant. Beatrix convinces Karen that in her pregnant state she doesn't desire to be in the ECDS nor does she desire to harm Karen.

While the co-operative solution is attained by means of reason and rationality, it, once again, isn't the sort of rationality employed in the group rationality solution to the prisoner's dilemma. Rather, it is the recognition that each person in the ECDS has a greater interest in something else: the well-being of Beatrix's unborn child.[5]

## Don't Get Into One

The most promising solution to the prisoner's dilemma—the group rationality solution—fails, as it doesn't apply to a wide enough range of instances of the prisoner's dilemma. Specifically, it doesn't apply to a considerable number (if not all) of ECDS's.

Tarantino's use of ECDS's nicely bears this out. While it would be too much to conclude on the basis of Tarantino's six cases that group rationality solutions never apply to ECDS's, the examples presented by Tarantino nicely illustrate why they tend not to apply. Every ECDS is different. The persons in such situations are not always motivated by the same things. Moreover, persons in ECDS's are not even always motivated to get out of them (except by maximizing their own interests or by having their goals satisfied). The upshot of this is that what constitutes rational behavior under such circumstances will vary from person to person. The group rationality solution, conversely, trades on the idea that what is rational to desire in a particular situation must be the same for all persons.

So, perhaps the only plausible solution to an ECDS is to avoid getting into one in the first place. I think Tarantino would agree with this.

---

[5] It seems clear that Karen must have an interest in the well-being of Beatrix's unborn child or she wouldn't give up her interest in assassinating Beatrix. Evidence for this lies in the claim that Beatrix has to convince Karen that she is in fact pregnant.

# PART IV

## "God Will Be Cut"

### Psychology, Spirituality, Identity

# 13

# *Kill Bill*: Tarantino's Oedipal Play

MARK T. CONARD

Quentin Tarantino burst onto the Hollywood scene with *Reservoir Dogs* in 1992, which, despite its multiple perspectives and non-chronological ordering of events, is as blatant an exercise in brutal realism as they come. He solidified his reputation as a filmmaking *Wunderkind* and further stretched his cinematic muscles with *Pulp Fiction* in 1994, a film that brings into play more of a postmodern cinematic sentiment than his earlier effort, but one which is still realistic in its portrayal of violence and which sticks or conforms largely to a single genre or story-telling mode. 1997's *Jackie Brown* was solid entertainment but lacked the spark and originality of his first two full-length feature films.

However, none of these earlier efforts could have quite prepared us for his next oeuvre, *Kill Bill.* Although he apparently conceived of the film as a single project, Tarantino released it in two segments, and those two parts are really quite different. While each is a blend of genres (unlike his earlier works), each likewise arguably has a primary genre: *Kill Bill Volume 1* is in large measure a Japanese martial arts film and is thus Eastern in its orientation, and *Kill Bill Volume 2* is mainly a Sergio Leone-inspired Western. Given these different generic orientations, the pacing of the two volumes is vastly different, the first segment being rather frenetic, and the second being much slower and more deliberate. In fact, the two parts are *so* different that it can be difficult to understand how they might fit together as one work.

## *Kill Bill Volume 1*: **Violence as Therapy, or:**
## **How to Be a Dick**

Like so many of us, Quentin Tarantino not only grew up with movies, he lived vicariously through them. They were an integral part of his childhood and adolescence, providing word and image to act as fodder for his imagination and his fantasy life.[1] Further, as we know, movies provide for children images of gender roles, expressions of value and meaning, and safe glimpses into a large and dangerous world. In *Kill Bill Volume 1*, more than in any of his other films, Tarantino revisits those movies and movie genres that he so loved as a kid, particularly the martial arts films and the spaghetti Westerns (with cartoons and "blaxploitation" films thrown in for good measure). He even includes the grainy "Our Feature Presentation" graphic from those good old days at the beginning of the movie, and thus we in the audience are instantly transported with Tarantino back to childhood or adolescence.

But he doesn't simply revisit or recreate the films or the film genres of his youth, he changes them in significant ways. First, he fuses the genres into a kind of postmodern collage, with a storybook fantasy feel to it, and with wildly exaggerated confrontation scenes and violence. Imagine if, as an adult, you took from your childhood and adolescent memories the images and sounds that had the greatest impact on you—a childhood and adolescence lived vicariously through movies, remember—and you condensed them into a two-hour experience, and all in the exaggerated and fantastic way in which adolescents and children view the world, but also in the somewhat confused manner in which the mind often recalls events, fusing disparate and distinct scenes or images into one picture or idea. The result would be something very like *Kill Bill Volume 1*. It's short on plot and character development, and is rather made up of a

---

[1] In a Sunday *New York Times Magazine* interview, for example, Tarantino admits to having fallen "hopelessly in love with Tatum O'Neal" when he saw *The Bad News Bears*. He then proceeded to write an ABC "Afterschool Special" about himself and Tatum O'Neal. "I called her Somerset in the script," he says, "and I did what I could never do in real life." After that, he says, "that's all I could do in school, just write new scripts." "Screenwriters are (Obsessive, Creative, Neurotic) People, Too," *New York Times Magazine*, November 9th, 2003, p. 82.

series of spectacular individual scenes—just like the conglomeration of your childhood memories probably would be.

## The Transition from Pussy to Cock

But the changes in these early memories go beyond simply fusing movies and movie genres; Tarantino changes them in other significant ways. The most important alteration is clearly the fact that he's put women in most of the lead roles. In *Kill Bill Volume 1*, women are now the heroes and villains. True enough, it's Bill (David Carradine) who pulls the strings, and more about that below, but every member of the Deadly Viper Assassination Squad (DiVAS—an acronym that obviously suggests femininity), save one, is a woman, and the man (Budd, played by Michael Madsen) hardly appears in the film at all. And not only are the main roles filled by women, but Tarantino also plays with traditional gender expectations and stereotypes. O-Ren Ishii (Lucy Liu) is the head of Tokyo organized crime, in a reversal of traditional Japanese sex roles. Further, and perhaps more interestingly, Gogo (Chiaki Kuriyama) is the hot young Japanese schoolgirl, the object of our fantasies and our porn, the epitome of passivity and little-girlish taboo sexuality. Only here she's empowered, strong, aggressive. Elle Driver (Daryl Hannah) dresses in a nurse's uniform—again, a typical male porn fantasy, except that she's an assassin. Vernita Green (Vivica A. Fox) plays the traditional housewife and mother role, but is likewise strong and self-assertive, protecting her home and family in the way that a husband might—with physical strength and violence.

However, despite these reversals, there is perhaps an underlying conservatism about gender and sex roles at work in the film. Note that, at the time of her wedding, The Bride (Uma Thurman) is pregnant and is thus poised to take on the traditional roles of wife and mother, and it's when she's prevented from doing so, by her attack, that she becomes enraged and without pity ("It's mercy, compassion, and forgiveness I lack, not rationality,"[2] she says to Vernita), as if taking on those traditional roles is what

---

[2] Quotes from the film are taken from the *Kill Bill* script: http://tarantino .webds.de/tarantino/movie/killbill/script/killbill-script.htm. Alternate spellings and poor use of punctuation are to be found in the original.

would have made her happy and complete. Further, yes, Gogo is strong and self-assertive, but she's also psychotic. She asks the Japanese businessman if he wants to penetrate her—of course knowing the answer already—and then she penetrates him with her sword, suggesting that when a woman is empowered, becomes too much like a man, there's something terribly deforming about it, that it goes hand in hand with psychosis.

Further, playing the lead doesn't necessarily imply wielding power, or at least ultimate power, here. This latter is symbolized by the pussy-cock distinction. When she awakens from her coma, The Bride, as she attempts to regain the use of her legs, says, "I could see the faces of the cunts who did this to me, and the dick responsible: members all of Bill's brainchild, 'The Deadly Viper Assassination Squad.'" So in other words, though deadly, the DiVAS are underlings—they're pussies, while Bill wields the real power—he's the cock. In order, therefore, for The Bride to be able to reap her revenge, in order to overcome the DiVAS, and ultimately Bill, she must transform herself from pussy to cock.

Let's consider how this transformation takes place, how it is that The Bride becomes empowered in the film. This is symbolized in a sequence of events and images, beginning with the "Pussy Wagon." In the opening scene, after the lead-in and the credits, The Bride shows up at Vernita's suburban home, in order to confront her. Having dealt with Vernita, she leaves, peeling out in her truck, and we get a glimpse of the truck's emblem, announcing that it's a Pussy Wagon. We're thus led to believe at first that this is The Bride's vehicle. In other words, we're led to believe that she is still a pussy, and is in fact the pussy in question. She is, perhaps, offering herself up as receptacle, albeit in a dramatic, self-conscious way.

We then learn through flashback that while she was in a coma, after her attack, she was in fact pure receptacle. The hospital orderly, Buck (who's "here to fuck"), was selling her as a catatonic fuck doll for seventy-five dollars a pop. Further, he mentions that she's barren, and this inability to produce a child is further evidence of her status as a simple receptacle ("Her plumbin' down there don't work no more, so feel free to

---

[3] Recall too that, as she lies on the floor of the chapel, having been beaten and shot in the head, she spits at the Sheriff, and he refers to her as a "tall drink

cum in her all ya want," he says).[3] When The Bride awakens from her coma, she dispenses with Buck, and then steals his truck, the Pussy Wagon. In other words, "Pussy Wagon" refers not to the pussy offering itself as receptacle. Rather, it refers to the cock ("here to fuck"), ready to take all comers. It refers to the fucker rather than the fuckee. So by killing Buck (or at least smashing his head in), and stealing his truck, The Bride begins to transform herself from pussy, the receptacle, to cock, the one in charge and in power. She's now out to fuck someone else.

Next, The Bride goes to Okinawa to procure a sword from Hattori Hanzo, played—significantly—by Sonny Chiba. That is, Sonny Chiba, once Tarantino's martial arts hero (he's referenced both in *True Romance* and in *Pulp Fiction*[4]), is reduced to a supporting role. Further, and importantly, we see him working in a Japanese café/sushi house, and in a relationship that has definite homosexual overtones. He and his male partner (in business, at least) squabble like an old married couple. When Hattori Hanzo calls to his partner in the next room to bring the tea, the latter calls out that he's watching his soap operas. And when he finally comes into the room, the two of them have a spat over their respective roles in their thirty-year relationship. In other words, not only have the women been thrust into the leads and the men reduced to supporting roles in the film, the latter have been emasculated as well. Hattori Hanzo hands over his sword—symbolically, his penis—to The Bride. She is now fully empowered and ready to reap her revenge. She's been completely transformed from pussy to cock, from fuckee to fucker. And it's only then that she seeks out O-Ren Ishii, the first target on her revenge list. (The confrontation with Vernita actually occurs later in the narrative, but appears earlier in the film, because of the way the film is chopped into stories and rearranged. This non-chronological ordering seems at first gratuitous, but seen in the light of this process of empowerment, the move from pussy to cock, it makes perfect sense.)

---

of cocksucker." Again, as a "cocksucker," she's a receptacle, but that she spits (as opposed to swallowing) might be indicative of her resistance to being one, even in that early, comatose state.

[4] The Biblical passage that Jules quotes is from a Sonny Chiba movie.

## Therapy

But why? Why has Tarantino done all this, recreated his past but inverted these male-female roles? Because *Kill Bill Volume 1* is in a sense his own therapy session. We all realize that our childhoods are formative, that we develop our neuroses due to those unhealthy childhood relationships, neuroses that we have to deal with in our adult lives, and that if we're going to understand ourselves as adults, we have to address those childhood issues. Tarantino is here not only confronting his past, in good psychoanalytic fashion, but remaking it at the same time.

As kids, we saw our fathers as heroes. My dad *was* Clint Eastwood to me. (When I was too little to know better, he used to tell me stories of having fought at the Battle of Little Bighorn—*sorry, dad*—and I believed him and was enthralled by the tales, just as I was enthralled by Sergio Leone's westerns.) Our mothers, on the other hand, played supporting roles. They were passive, loving (if we were lucky), trying to make up for our fathers' short-comings. Now, as adults, we realize that (for most of us) our fathers were simply absent, removed, distant (if there at all), and a threat. *Just like Bill.* In the film, we don't see Bill. He's in the background, removed, but ever-present as an ominous threat. Bill is the father—our father, Tarantino's father, and, significantly and symbolically, the father to The Bride's unborn child.

In *Kill Bill Volume 1*, Tarantino is reliving his childhood as a pastiche, a postmodern fusion of the different styles that he loved and that gave his life meaning, all with an air of unreality—of the fantastic so characteristic of a child's imagination—and at the same time he's recreating his past in a more honest way. He's depicting his father as the removed, distant, danger that he was. And he's recognizing his mother as the central figure that she was. For so many of us, our mothers were the heroes and villains of our lives. They were the leading players, the ones who held everything together in our fathers' absences. What's more, Tarantino not only remakes this past according to this more mature perspective, but also according to his desires. Uma Thurman is not only his substitute mother and ideal actress, but also his dream lover. Who didn't fall in love—or at least lust—with her, watching, say, *Henry and June*? I know I did. So, interestingly, despite its unreality, and its storybook character, the film is a truer-to-life version of our childhoods than what most of us remember. The fathers are out as heroes; mothers have taken their place, as the central figures struggling for power we now recognize them as. And it's all tinged with an air of blood and violence, symbolic of the unhealthy, neurotic character of the entire history.

Consequently, the film's apparent conservatism about gender may in fact represent the very enlightened view that, in those leading roles, the women in our lives were psychically (if not physically) deformed in their struggle to gain the power that they needed to perform those roles and that was due to them.

This all may be more a confession about my own neuroses than about Tarantino and his film, but if this interpretation holds any water, then in *Kill Bill Volume 2* we would expect Tarantino to perform the Oedipal act by having The Bride kill Bill, the father. And this is in fact exactly what happens, as if Oedipus, directing the play himself, had Jocasta (mother and lover simultaneously) kill Laius in his stead.

## *Kill Bill Volume 2*: Mommy Kills Daddy

As we saw, in *Kill Bill Volume 1*, the Bride acquired the power necessary to reap her revenge on Bill and the DiVAS, but she acquired it in a way that alienated her from her true, feminine nature. She took up a Hattori Hanzo sword, a masculine symbol of power, indicating that the way a woman gains power is to become like a man, but in being so empowered, in becoming like a man, she is apparently psychically deformed, alienated from her true nature as a woman. Thus all the women in *Kill Bill Volume 1* are powerful, but they're also all psychotic.

In *Kill Bill Volume 2*, Tarantino fulfills the Oedipal promise by having The Bride kill Bill, the father. But before she can complete the act, two things have to happen: First, The Bride has to reject the masculine notion of power and become empowered as a woman, thus reconnecting herself to her true nature. Second, Bill, the father, godlike in *Kill Bill Volume 1*, must be humanized, must be turned into a man, in order to be killed.

## The Bride and Budd

In *Kill Bill Vol. 2*, we return to the Bride as we left her. She's still a Samurai, and she's coming after Budd. As it turns out, Budd is

Bill's brother, and like the other men in *Kill Bill Volume 1* (except Bill), he's emasculated. He's given up his Hanzo sword (his symbolic penis), is a drunk, and we see him taken down a notch by his boss at the "titty bar" where he works.

As The Bride hunts down Budd in his trailer, music from Sergio Leone's *A Fistful of Dollars* plays, indicating that what she doesn't yet realize is that this (unlike *Kill Bill Volume 1*) is primarily a Western and the rules have changed. Her sword is no good here, and so Budd gets the best of her with a shotgun blast of rock salt. He then takes the sword from her, divesting her of the earlier symbol of power, and offers to sell it to Elle. On the phone to Elle, Budd refers to The Bride as a cowgirl. So if she's a cowgirl, and this is a Western—a Sergio Leone inspired Western—then The Bride is the hero, she's playing Clint Eastwood's character, the Man with No Name. That is, she's the Woman with No Name. Thus, while she had many aliases— Black Mamba, The Bride, Arlene—up to this point she's had no real name of her own, no real identity.

In this new milieu, and without her sword, The Bride is powerless, and Budd proceeds to bury her alive. At the grave site, Budd asks the gravedigger if she, The Bride, isn't the "sweetest little piece of blond pussy" he's ever seen, indicating that she's once again returned to pussy, receptacle, that without her symbol of masculine power she's helpless. About to be nailed into the coffin, The Bride struggles, and Budd threatens to burn her eyes out with mace. He gives her the option of the mace in the eyes, or a flashlight, but either way, he tells her, she's going into the ground. She chooses the flashlight, light being a traditional symbol of enlightenment, wisdom, and knowledge, and refuses to be blinded.

## A Mystical Journey

Budd buries the Bride in the grave of Paula Schultz, a reference to *The Wicked Dreams of Paula Schultz*, a 1968 comedy starring Elke Sommer and the cast of *Hogan's Heroes*. The heroine is an East German athlete who dares to wear miniskirts and ultimately escapes to West Germany. Thus the reference brings into play the East-West dichotomy that so important in *Kill Bill*, as well as questions and symbols of masculinity and femininity (there's also cross-dressing in the movie), which are also crucial to the film.

Inside the coffin, and under the ground, The Bride goes on a mystical journey, in the form of a flashback for us, to visit the Kung Fu master, Pai Mei (Gordon Liu). In front of a campfire, during former happier times, Bill plays the flute and tells the Bride a story about how the mythical Pai Mei received an insult from a Shaolin monk, and how Pai Mei repaid the insult by killing the entire order of monks. This is all nicely self-referential, given that David Carradine's character on the TV show *Kung Fu* was himself a Shaolin monk (and of course played the flute). This foreshadows the fact that the Bride will ultimately use the skills and techniques she acquires from Pai Mei to kill Bill. Then we see Bill take the Bride to Pai Mei's temple. The master has agreed to give her training, despite the fact that he despises Americans, Caucasians, and especially women.

Upon first meeting her, Pai Mei mocks The Bride's ability with the sword. He then forces her to learn to smash her hand through a thick piece of wood from just a few inches away. The process is painful, and her hand is bruised, bloody and nearly useless for everyday tasks like using chop sticks. But under his cruel tutelage, what the master teaches her is that her power and strength lie not in the sword, but rather in her own hands. In other words, she learns that she doesn't have to take up the sword—the symbol of masculinity—in order to be empowered. She can have strength and power without denying her true nature; she doesn't have to reject her femininity, and thus doesn't have to be psychically deformed.

## Resurrection

Having made this mystical journey and learned this lesson, The Bride uses her hands, her own natural power, to break out of the coffin and escape the grave, as blatant a metaphor for death and resurrection as they come. The Bride has been reborn or resurrected and can now both wield power *and* be a woman and a mother, something she previously thought impossible. Because of this transformation, because she realizes and connects to her true nature, she now gains her identity and can be named.

Back at Budd's trailer, Elle has arrived with a suitcase full of money to purchase The Bride's Hanzo sword. Budd tells her of the Bride's fate and hands over the sword, but when he goes to count the money a black mamba snake (which is The Bride's codename, remember) appears from within the suitcase and bites him on the face. Elle collects the money and phones Bill to tell him that his brother is dead.

During that phone call, Elle uses The Bride's name for the first time. Previously, whenever anyone tried to name her, to use her name, the sound was bleeped out. Now, after the Bride's resurrection and transformation, Elle speaks her name: Beatrix Kiddo. The joke (and surprise) is that "Kiddo" was what Bill had been calling her all along. In other words, what we thought was an endearment turns out to be (or becomes) her real name. It's as if Bill, like God, has the power of *logos*, the word, and the ability to name things.

When Beatrix returns to Budd's trailer, she and Elle fight, and during the battle, Beatrix spots Budd's own Hanzo sword sitting idle in a golf bag. The two women then face off, swords drawn, as if this will be another epic clash of Samurais, of the sort that we witnessed in *Kill Bill Volume 1*. Staring each other down, Elle reveals to Beatrix how it is that she lost her eye. It turns out that she, too, trained with Pai Mei and had the temerity to insult him, so he plucked it out. She then reveals that for that injury, she killed Pai Mei by poisoning him.

The two of them cross swords, but, again, this isn't the Orient any longer, so there is no sword fight. Rather, Beatrix plucks out Elle's other eye, drops it on the floor and squishes it with her foot. Elle is now completely blind, symbolic of her blindness to her servitude to a masculine conception of power, and to Bill, her master.

When the Bride first encountered Pai Mei, Bill was her master as well (she was enslaved to him) and then Pai Mei became her master. He, however, gave her the tools to escape her servitude, and now, especially since he is dead, she has no master. She serves no one but herself, having reconnected to her femininity and her true nature. She is now ready to confront Bill.

## Killing Bill

*Kill Bill Volume 2* erases any doubt that Bill is indeed the father that Tarantino is symbolically killing in his Oedipal play. He's the father of Beatrix's child, and at the wedding rehearsal

Beatrix tells her fiancé that Bill is her father as well. But in *Kill Bill Volume 1*, we're presented with a child's view of the father—he's godlike, removed, an ever-present threat; and as Tyler Durden so astutely reminds us, if our fathers were our model for God, and our fathers abandoned us, then we have to accept the possibility that God hates us.[5]

But, remember, when Nietzsche said that God is dead,[6] he didn't mean that an actual being, the Almighty, the First Cause, an omniscient, omnipotent creator, had actually been killed. Rather, he meant that the idea, the institution of God ceased to have any meaning or relevance for us, because we simply couldn't believe the fiction any longer. Similarly, killing the father means killing the father's power over us, and that means that we have to stop viewing him as God, we have to reject that fiction, that misinterpretation.

And this is *exactly* what Tarantino does to the father in *Kill Bill Volume 2*. Bill, the father, God, is completely humanized. He's turned into a mortal. Whereas in the earlier film, we barely saw him, and never saw his face, he just existed as an omnipresent threat, and a kind of puppet-master, pulling the strings of his DiVAS; now he's locally and physically present as a man, a mortal. Now he has a brother; he plays the flute; he tells stories; he gets beaten up by his master, Pai Mei; he plays games with his daughter; his heart can be broken (and this is literally what kills him); he even makes sandwiches, going so far as to cut off the crust.

In fact, Bill becomes *so* human in *Kill Bill Volume 2* that we start to sympathize with him, almost to the point where we don't want to see him die. He no longer seems worthy of killing, no longer seems to deserve to die. We know now that he never knew his real father, and that his own father figure— Esteban Vihaio (Michael Parks)—is a pimp who cuts women's faces when they're disobedient. In other words, we see that his father is as big a prick as he (our father) is, and thus that his childhood was no doubt as perverse and dysfunctional as our own. This is that transforming moment when, as an adult, you recognize your old man's frailties and his shortcomings. You

---

[5] See *Fight Club* (David Fincher, 1999).
[6] See Section 125, "The Madman" in *The Gay Science*, translated by Walter Kaufmann (New York: Random House, 1974).

see him having trouble getting out of the chair, or see him drunk and acting stupid. You overcome your hatred and resentment and start feeling sorry for him. This is part of what it means to mature, to become an adult, and to see your father for what and who he is. It's then that he loses his power over you. Symbolically, as the godlike threat, he's dead. And now that Bill, the father, has been humanized, de-mythologized, he's vulnerable and can be killed.

## Mommy's Five-Point Palm Trick

When Beatrix finally tracks down Bill, she discovers that her now four-year-old daughter is alive and that Bill has been raising her, playing daddy to her. Beatrix tells Bill that she ran away from him when she found out she was pregnant, believing that she had to choose between being an assassin (that is, powerful, which is part of her essential nature—Bill says she's a natural born killer) and being a mother. But now, since her resurrection, since she's found her identity, she's realized that she can be strong and powerful as a woman; she doesn't have to be empowered as a man. This is nicely symbolized by the fact that she now wears a skirt, and by the fact that she doesn't need the sword to kill Bill.

Indeed, their final clash begins with sword play, but Beatrix's sword is quickly flung away in the fight, and as Bill jabs his sword towards her, she sheaths it in the case she's still holding. If the sword has all along symbolized the penis and the power it represents, then the sheath is symbolically the vagina, and consequently the pussy overcomes the cock in this fight, the woman, *as woman*, defeats the man.

Beatrix then uses the "Five Point Palm Exploding Heart Technique" on Bill, a move which Pai Mei taught her, but didn't teach Bill. She touches him at five pressure points on his body, and as soon as he takes five steps his heart explodes, and he dies. She can now reclaim her daughter, and become a mother, as herself, as the strong, powerful woman that she always was.

So Tarantino succeeds in killing the father, but not, like Oedipus, unknowingly and tragically. Rather, by remaking his childhood and cleverly empowering his wife-mother to do the job for him—and thus recognizing her as the powerful, central figure that she is—he escapes the unhealthy, self-destructive consequences. There's no need to blind himself. His therapy session has succeeded.[7]

---

[7] This chapter originally appeared on Metaphilm.com in two parts: "*Kill Bill: Volume 1*, Violence as Therapy," November 12th, 2003; and "*Kill Bill: Volume 2*, Mommy Kills Daddy," April 26th, 2004.

# 14

# Travolta's Elvis Man and the Nietzschean Superman

BENCE NANAY and IAN SCHNEE

One might easily think that Nietzsche—a philosopher constantly at odds with religion who urged his readers to transcend value judgments of good and evil—would be right at home in the morally ambiguous universe of Quentin Tarantino. Aren't Tarantino's films full of the violence and moral-suspending motivations that an everything-is-permitted Nietzschean would rush to the Cineplex for? *Reservoir Dogs* is a film about violence for personal gain. *Kill Bill Volume 1* and *Kill Bill Volume 2* are films about violence for revenge. *Natural Born Killers* and *True Romance* are films about violence and love-redemption. If one looks back at all the reviews of *Pulp Fiction* from 1994 and 1995, "violent" is the one word they are all compelled to use in characterizing the film—even though, as Tarantino likes to point out, most of the violence occurs offscreen.

But if violence is the in-your-face feature of all of Tarantino films that's impossible not to notice, it's also one of the most complex features that's easily misunderstood—especially in *Pulp Fiction*. To think that *Pulp Fiction* is an amoral film that celebrates violence for its own sake (or for the sake of our goonish entertainment), and that it thereby reflects the hard-nosed outlook of Nietzsche's anti-religion philosophy, would be to misunderstand both Tarantino and Nietzsche. In fact *Pulp Fiction* is a film etched with Nietzschean themes, but not for the reason commonly supposed.

Consider the celebration-of-violence charge. This criticism overlooks the anomaly of Jules, Samuel L. Jackson's character, the hit man who has a mystical experience and gives up "the life." Jules's religious experience helps him refrain from blasting Pumpkin and Honey Bunny in the final moments of the film—in contrast to Vincent, the John Travolta character, who is caught off guard on his return trip from the toilet and finds the idea of not shooting them inconceivable. The fact that Jules's conversion was chosen to be the climax of the film should make us think twice about how the film portrays violence.

And the fact that religion plays a key role in Jules's motivations should make us think twice about how we should use Nietzsche to shed light on the film. At first blush, Jules as the hero of the film might make us think it's a deeply anti-Nietzschean movie. But Nietzsche himself didn't just celebrate violence and denigrate religion. Nietzsche was aware that religion can no longer provide the locus of meaning in our lives. In that negative sense he was a nihilist: he denied life has any meaning, if what we mean by "meaning" is the ultimate, get-your-rewards-in-Heaven kind. But he was anti-nihilistic in another sense: just because life doesn't have any ultimate, religious meaning does not mean that it has no meaning at all.

Nietzsche's concept of the superman helps illustrate this point. The superman is able to create new values, and see the meaning in life, in the face of the "ultimate irrationality" of it all. As we will argue, this is in fact just what Jules does, when he has his mystical experience, and it is just what Vincent is incapable of doing. Which is why the real hero of the film is not Vincent Vega the "Elvis man" (as Mia repeatedly calls him), but Jules, the Nietzschean superman.

## Chance Governs Everything

"Chance governs everything; necessity, which is far from having the same purity, comes only later," writes Luis Buñuel, Spanish film director, whom Tarantino acknowledges as one of the most important influences on his films.[1]

Indeed, chance governs everything in *Pulp Fiction*. Each subplot of the movie has a critical unlikely event: Vincent has to take a dump on stakeout just at the moment that Butch sneaks

---

[1] The idea that we never see what's in the briefcase that is central to much of the film comes from one of Buñuel's films, *Belle de Jour*. The Buñuel quote is from *My Last Sigh* (New York: Knopf, 1983), p. 171.

back home; a kid, one of Marvin's buddies, jumps out of the bathroom blasting six rounds at Jules and Vincent at pointblank range, the bullets missing everything but the wall; Butch and Marsellus run into each other on the street; Mia comes back to life after OD-ing on Vincent's smack; Vincent accidentally blows off Marvin's head; Pumpkin and Honey Bunny rob a diner which happens to contain (1) Jules with a portmanteau full of untold riches, and (2) a man with a gun (Vincent) popping out of the toilet.

One tempting way to find meaning in these seemingly chaotic events would be to attribute them to some divine plan. Whether you think that God has a hand in every event, or that some divine clockmaker wound up the universe and now lets it run its course, this way of thinking about these events gives them meaning and purpose. It also gives the universe a set of values, or moral code—a distinction between good and evil.

One of Nietzsche's key insights is that value systems shouldn't be taken at face value. Instead of asking straightforward questions, like what's the value of a certain action (is it morally wrong?), Nietzsche asked once-removed value questions: what's the value of certain systems of value, like the religious distinction between good and evil?[2] In the end he argued that the religious system of values is a bad one because it denigrates life—but we will return to that issue below.

The world of *Pulp Fiction* is certainly not this traditional religious one full of divine purpose. Events of the universe are not part of some divine plan but are just "freak occurrences," in the words of Vincent. A consequence of this is that traditional values have no force. Killing isn't morally wrong. Consider, for example, Vincent and Jules's reaction when Vincent accidentally blows off Marvin's head. They're not in trouble because they killed someone—the moral issue is a non-factor, not even worth bringing up. They're in trouble because they have bits of brain scatter-shot in the back of the car which might get noticed by Joe Blue. The Wolf, not the priest, comes to the rescue.

---

[2] This theme runs throughout Nietzsche's work, but it is especially important to *Beyond Good and Evil* and *On The Genealogy of Morals*. See, for example, *Genealogy* Preface, p. 6: "We need a *critique* of moral values, *the value of these values themselves must first be called into question.*"

Of course, this doesn't mean the characters in *Pulp Fiction* have no values. They are actually obsessed with values, but they are the values of cool rather than religious morality. Here's a short list of values characters espouse or act upon.

> **VINCENT:** "You don't be giving Marsellus Wallace's new bride a foot massage."
>
> **LANCE:** (the dope dealer) People who key cars should be killed: "no trial, no jury, straight to execution."
>
> **VINCENT:** "Don't fuck with another man's vehicle; it's against the rules."
>
> **JULES:** "Jimmie's a friend; you don't come into your friend's house and start telling him what's what."
>
> **VINCENT:** You don't sleep with your boss's wife (at least, not if your boss is Marsellus Wallace).
>
> **BUTCH:** You don't abandon anyone, even your mortal enemy, to the S&M fate of two rednecks with a gimp.

The Nietzschean question would be to ask, what approach to life do these values signify? Value judgments themselves are just the starting point. Those judgments are treated like symptoms of underlying motivations that give rise to them.[3] It is those underlying motivations that Nietzsche wants to expose and evaluate. As a matter of empirical fact, Nietzsche thought that secularization was destroying the traditional role of religion as the ultimate source of meaning in human life. To use a common metaphor, religion provided a mythical "narrative" that structured life's events and gave life meaning. The world of *Pulp Fiction* precisely is this modern world of fractured "narratives"— a theme nicely illustrated by the formal factors of Tarantino's filmmaking, the fractured temporal sequence and plotting devices—and we can get insight into the film's characters by seeing how they react to this crisis of meaning.

## Elvis Man versus Superman

Nietzsche famously proclaimed that God is dead—but he wasn't claiming that religious beliefs are false and therefore we should

---

[3] Talk of "symptoms" is one of Nietzsche's favorite metaphors. See, for example, *Twilight of the Idols* II, p. 2.

believe science instead. He wasn't trying to be provocative at the expense of the faithful. In *The Gay Science*, Section 125, it actually isn't Nietzsche himself who says "God is dead." He puts the line in the mouth of a "madman," who's shouting it not in the face of churchgoers but to modern, seemingly sophisticated unbelievers. Their reaction: laughter at the madman's earnestness.

They find it ridiculous that religion should even be taken seriously—as the madman does, and as Nietzsche himself does, because he realizes the monumental role religion has played in giving meaning to our lives. In *Pulp Fiction* Vincent is the sophisticated unbeliever fresh off the plane from Amsterdam. And Vincent has nothing but scorn for Jules when the errant bullets lead Jules to have a mystical experience and to start taking religion seriously.

We can see this aspect of Vincent's character elsewhere in the film too. He spouts a bit of cultural relativism when he tells Jules that in Paris they call a quarter-pounder with cheese a "Royale with cheese." At the same time, the film doesn't portray Vincent as a broad-minded cosmopolitan. He's not even a broad-minded cosmopolitan with regard to the fast-food in Europe he pontificates about. We immediately see his limitations when he doesn't know what they call a Whopper: "I didn't go into Burger King."

The deeper implications of different systems of measure, like the English pound versus the metric kilo, are a surprise to Jules. He's further surprised (and disappointed, because he can't be the know-it-all) when Brett, one of the kids soon to be executed by Jules, guesses why the French don't use the name "quarter-pounder with cheese" ("Check out the big brain on Brett").

At the beginning of the film, then, both Vincent and Jules are unaware of any deeper meaning to events. At this point Jules thinks the Ezekiel 25:17 line is just a meaningless vehicle of intimidation. But once Jules sees the light, he and Vincent embody different interpretations of the unlikely events that they keep encountering. Jules says we should see the six bullets, and chance itself, as a sign. Vincent says it's just a low-probability event.

Their banter isn't just hipster philosophical reflection; it embodies two fundamentally different reactions to the existential crisis heralded by the demise of religion. To see this, let's return to the religious mode of thinking about the world and values. Religious thinking relies on a kind of duality. On the one hand, there is the created world: the transient, physical world in which we live, full of evil in need of redemption. On the other hand, there is the eternal, all-good heavenly realm. Nietzsche noted that once we posit a second realm, the heavenly, as the source of infinite value, then worldly events by themselves can have no value at all.[4] Whatever value some worldly event has is given entirely by its relation to the divine.

As we noted before, this isn't a picture that anyone in *Pulp Fiction* buys. But, as Nietzsche argues, modern "rationalists" like Vincent do buy some of its metaphysical presuppositions, for they endorse the dualist idea that either the meaning of events in our world is imposed from without, or those events lack all meaning. The rejection of religion, in Vincent's case, means that he is a nihilist: there's no meaning to the world whatsoever. A second aspect of this point of view is its "dogmatism." By this Nietzsche means that, for someone like Vincent, his own viewpoint, and system of value, is universally binding.[5] If the bullets are just a freak occurrence and have no meaning to Vincent, they have no meaning, period. They don't have any meaning to anyone—and if Jules believes otherwise then he's just wrong. For Vincent, his interpretation is *the* interpretation. It just so happens that the universally right valuation is vacuous—events have no meaning—but Vincent's view is dogmatic, just like the religious one, because it purports to universal validity.

Nietzsche himself wasn't fond of either the religious or the rationalist view of values. He thought that both their dualist assumption about meaning and their dogmatic claim to universality were expressions of "sickness": symptoms of an "unhealthy" view of life, which in turn he thinks is an expression of a certain kind of "weakness."[6] Not weakness in the sense of lacking physical strength, but a sort of weakness that may be called existential: those who are weak in this sense can't face the chaotic facts of life. Vincent Vega, in spite of his macho image, is extremely weak in this sense.

---

[4] See, for example, *Genealogy* III, especially Section 11.
[5] See *Beyond Good and Evil*, Section 43.
[6] See, for example, all of *Genealogy* III, and *Twilight of the Idols* V, p. 1.

In contrast to these expressions of weakness, Nietzsche advocated a form of life that has a kind of existential "strength": this is embodied by someone who can face the fact that the universe has no ultimate, universally binding meaning and value, but who can nevertheless advocate perspective-relative (that is, non-dogmatic) systems of value that are creative and life-affirming. The person capable of doing this becomes a creator of meaning—someone who sees the significance of events and thereby *gives* the events that significance. This new meaning then is not some kind of heavenly meaning coming from a postulated "other" domain; it is immanent, coming from within our world—from the person who creates it. Nietzsche has a lot of names for this form of life; most commonly he calls it the "free spirit" or the "superman."

And Jules is just such a free spirit. In Tarantino's world of violence, strength is all-important: not only (and not primarily) physical strength, but also strength in the existential sense. It is discovering meaning in seemingly meaningless and random events that makes one strong. This strength gives Jules the ability to stand up to Pumpkin and Honey Bunny in a way he wouldn't have been capable of in the beginning of the film, and in a way that Vincent is still incapable of. Recall Vincent's obstinacy: "Jules, you give that fucking nimrod fifteen hundred dollars and I'll shoot him on general principle."

Jules and Vincent have always had physical strength: Pumpkin and Honey Bunny are just small-time heisters looking for an easy score. Jules, by contrast, is one "bad motherfucker." But once he has his mystical experience he is able to resolve the situation without recourse to violence. Still, the reason why his action is "good" is not because it is the morally right thing to do. That would be simply reverting to the religious system of value. It's good because it's an essentially life-affirming and creative act on Jules's part. It's an act that breaks free from the hyper-cool and might-makes-right gangster values of the underworld that Vincent is still stuck in. It's an act that makes Jules a free spirit.

## The Significance of Toilets

Vincent cannot see the significance of chance events. He's the one person best placed to see some connection between the seemingly chaotic events of the movie, because his character is connected to almost every subplot. But, in one of the funniest running gags of the film, he is metaphorically "out of touch" because all the important things that happen to him happen while he (or someone else) is in the bathroom.

Marvin's buddy is sweating it out in the bathroom with a .357 Magnum before attacking Jules and Vincent. Vincent is in the toilet giving himself a pep talk about loyalty during Mia's OD and near-death. And he's in the diner restroom during Pumpkin and Honey Bunny's robbery. One would think all these eye-openers would make Vincent chary of using the john. But he (unlike Jules) sees them only as low-probability events, and the next time he's in the bathroom he gets axed by Butch.

There are also more mundane events in the film full of significance that Vincent can't see. For example, when his Chevy Malibu is keyed in the parking lot, he thinks it's just bad luck. He complains to Lance: "I had it in storage three years. I was out five days and some dickless piece of shit fucked with it." In fact, his car was keyed by Butch. This fact is hard to catch in the final cut of the film, but in both the script and a scene filmed but eventually deleted we see Vincent parking his car next to Butch's while Butch is at Marsellus's bar. Butch, then, is getting back at Vincent for calling him a "palooka."

But this fact, like everything else, blows by Vincent. Vincent does exactly the opposite of what the Nietzschean superman is supposed to do. He is blind to the significance of the seemingly random events and doesn't attend to the danger signs around him. As Nietzsche would say, he fails to become the creator of meaning.

In an unpublished note, Nietzsche calls this condition "passive nihilism."[7] Vincent passively assumes the values of others. He gets his style from imitating Elvis. He wants other people to lavish him with respect without earning it: "A 'please' would be nice," he whiningly complains to the Wolf. And he inherits the values of the gangster underworld without ever questioning them. The Nietzschean free spirit, by contrast, is spontaneous, creative, and continuously questions any values—her own and others. She continually outgrows old values, just as Jules outgrows the gangster values of Vincent.

---

[7] *The Will to Power*, Section 22.

Nietzsche is often put down as a moral relativist, as someone who thinks that any system of value is just as good as any other because there is no way to adjudicate between them. But this way of thinking about Nietzsche is both a simplification and wrong. While he might think that Vincent's nihilistic view of life is as bad as a dogmatic or religious one, he also claims that there is a way of going through life that is better than either of them: we can refuse to take any moral system (religious or nihilist) for granted and become the creators of meaning ourselves. Just like Jules does.

## The Cycle of Violence

All of Tarantino's films are concerned with ways to end violence, but the theme of the cycle of violence, and of breaking out of the cycle of violence, is perhaps strongest in *Pulp Fiction*. This theme is responsible for the causal structure of the film's subplots: a violent event in one subplot is the catalyst for another subplot and the violence in it (witness how the killing of Brett sets up Marvin's death, and how Butch's killing of his boxing opponent leads to the events with the rednecks).

This theme is also reflected in the film's cyclical narrative structure: it begins and ends with the same robbery, the rest of the film, in a sense, providing a background and contrast to it so that the audience can understand the significance of the diner-scene climax. In this scene, which stands out from the rest of the film in as much as it is the only sequence in the film that does not end in violence (in spite of the fact that it has the largest potential head-count of all), Jules halts the cycle of violence by giving an interpretation to, by finding meaning in, the chance events of the movie.

In Nietzschean terms, it is discovering meaning in seemingly meaningless and random events that makes one strong, and only the strong can escape the cycle of violence. If you can't be a meaning-creator, the film tells us, you'll get killed.[8] The reason you get killed is not because you kill: everyone kills. There is no ethical punishment; Tarantino's is not a religious moral

---

[8] Or you could escape on "Grace" like Butch, gaining redemption by returning to free Marsellus. We don't mean to claim that the Nietzschean redemption of Jules is the only theme in the film.

universe. Rather, you get killed because you take the world at face value and hubristically fail to attend to the danger signs around you. You're blind to the significance of seemingly random events. Jules does see the signs, and he is strong enough to stop. Vincent is blind, and ends up dead.

## Like Caine in *Kung Fu*

We don't want to suggest that there's a perfect fit between Nietzsche and *Pulp Fiction*. If there were, the film would probably not be as enjoyable as it is. It would be a dry illustration of some abstract philosophical theses, which rarely makes for good drama.

There are several aspects of Jules's mystical experience, for example, that might not fit the superman model. For one thing, Jules calls his experience religious, and says it was the "hand of God" that came down and stopped the bullets. That doesn't sound very Nietzschean at all. Furthermore, his new interpretation of the Ezekiel 25:17 passage still seems to be religiously inspired—he says he's "trying real hard to be the shepherd." How does that square with our claim that Jules is a Nietzschean superman?

Firstly, the fact that Jules uses religious imagery and concepts shouldn't surprise us. He doesn't have any other way to express the deep existential realization he's just had. We shouldn't expect him to start spouting Nietzschean terminology when he has no inkling of it at all. After all, Jules is a real, three-dimensional character rather than a cardboard-cutout philosophical mouthpiece.

Nietzsche himself was well aware that there is no creation in a vacuum; one can create new values only by using the broken materials of the old values one is familiar with. For example, Nietzsche himself often uses Christian imagery in discussing the superman or free spirit. In his work *Thus Spoke Zarathustra* Nietzsche created the fictional character Zarathustra, which is the closest Nietzsche comes to giving us of an extended illustration of what the superman is like. And in that work Nietzsche actually calls Zarathustra a shepherd.[9] He also continually uses

---

[9] Though note that being a shepherd is not a final state that Zarathustra stays in. It is one of the stages he passes through in his continual state of over-coming.

redemption language to characterize Zarathustra and the super-man.[10] So the fact that Jules uses religious concepts and imagery should not bar us from seeing him as embodying a Nietzschean free spirit.

As Nietzsche urges, what we need to do is look beneath the surface-level imagery Jules employs and try to figure out the sig-nificance of the values he is espousing. When discussing the sig-nificance of the "miracle" with Vincent in the diner, Jules says it actually doesn't matter whether it was an "according-to-Hoyle" miracle. What matters is the significance of the experience as he felt it: it was "a moment of clarity." Jules's experience was inher-ently personal, rather than dogmatic: he is not tempted to think that, through his "miracle," he discovered some kind of univer-sal meaning everyone should live by. This fits nicely with Nietzsche's claim that meaning is always perspective-relative: what Jules is saying is, relative to his perspective and experi-ence, it was a miracle. The "objective" question that Vincent is obsessed with is irrelevant.

What this experience lets Jules do is question the value sys-tem that has structured his life, and the process of re-evaluating the importance of values is a very Nietzschean reaction. But, critically, Jules does not do this by lapsing into a religious meta-physics—he doesn't claim that meaning is provided by an infi-nitely important heavenly realm. And there's no hint that he is now dogmatic, thinking that everyone has to see the world his way.

Rather, what is Jules's new plan for his life? "I'm just going to walk the earth. You know, like Caine in *Kung Fu*." Walking the earth and seeking new adventures is actually just what Nietzsche's fictional hero Zarathustra does. Vincent, of course, would be just as negative about Zarathustra as he is about Jules: "They got a name for that, Jules; it's called a bum." But Jules is strong enough to shrug off Vincent's negativity. Jules no longer relies on others' approval or values in deciding how to live his life. In effect, his experience has given him a new kind of free-dom, precisely of the kind that Nietzsche would be proud:

---

But the point is that Nietzsche was not afraid of re-appropriating religious con-cepts. The name "Zarathustra" itself is a reference to another religion, Zoroastrianism.

[10] For example, see *Zarathustra* II, p. 20, and *The Antichrist*, Section 33.

"Whoever has attained intellectual freedom even to a small extent cannot feel but as a wanderer upon the face of the earth—and not as a traveler toward some final destination; for that does not exist."[11]

---

[11] *Human All-Too-Human* I, p. 638.

# 15

# Could Beatrix Kiddo Reach Enlightenment? Traces of Buddhist Philosophy in *Kill Bill*

LUKE CUDDY and MICHAEL BRUCE

If you've ever studied Buddhism, we know what you're thinking. How could we even dream of associating a movie series by the infamously violent director Quentin Tarantino with such a peaceful, spiritual, and joyful practice? How can the pitiful, bloody mess Beatrix Kiddo makes of the Crazy 88 be explained in any Buddhist system?

We admit, you might have a point. But we want to bring a couple of things to your attention. First, take note of the "could" in our title. The word implies that Beatrix is not yet enlightened. As we will see, in Buddhism there is never a reason to dwell on the past, since the world and everything in it is impermanent. So if it's possible for Beatrix to put her murderous past behind her, who's to say she can't one day reach enlightenment? Second, the Dalai Lama himself tells us that the Buddha forbade killing, but he indicated that under certain circumstances it could be justified. Is the revenge story of Beatrix Kiddo one of those circumstances?

## Buddhism for the Desert-Ridden Texan

There are several schools of Buddhism. Some schools are detailed, like Tibetan Buddhism, while others, like Zen Buddhism, don't have grueling, laundry-list-like instructions. Luckily for us, there are core concepts underlying every school.

What does it mean to be enlightened? Enlightenment (also known as "Nirvana") is, normally, the culmination of the entire Buddhist practice. Enlightenment is a sublime bliss, the end to

189

all suffering, the highest spiritual attainment. What we mean in English by the word "happiness" is not enlightenment. In fact, Western reviewers of Eastern thought often miss this point.[1] The theatrical joy of a nineteen-year-old whose father just bought her a 2007 Mustang is not happiness in the Buddhist sense. Enlightenment is a higher experience of existence, the climax of a lifetime of practice in most Buddhist systems. It's not the fulfillment of a desire but the release from desire, the un-learning of attachment and deluded ideas about the world.

The path out of suffering is the path to enlightenment. Buddhism tells us that human beings seek an escape from suffering. Suffering can be psychological or physical. In the psychological case, you might lose your copy of *Kill Bill Volume 2* and feel sorrow as a result. Physical suffering is the pain of being whipped, burned, hit, or, of course, having your arm chopped off by a Hattori Hanzo sword. The psychological can impact the physical: when you are depressed or stressed, you feel it in your gut, shoulders, and forehead. Your psychological state has a bearing on your actions. Depending on this state you treat people differently. And other people, depending on their respective states, treat you differently. Beatrix's state of anger, for example, makes her a more hostile person in general, despite the fact that the object of her anger is only Bill's assassination squad.

To a Buddhist, all aspects of existence are *interconnected*. In the interconnected world, causes and results are linked and therefore interdependent. Think of an ecosystem. Every part of the ecosystem plays a specific and interdependent role. If there is a change in one aspect of the system, then every other facet changes in a causal response. The river is the home of the fish, crawdads, water spiders, and beavers. The river is cut into the bank of the surface of the earth. Plants and shrubs grow in the top soil and their roots grow down to drink from the river and water below. Deer and other animals consume the vegetation, fruit, and river water, and there is a whole life-dependent cycle of predator and prey which seeks a balance of sustainability. If one aspect of the system is off, then all other aspects are

---

[1] See for example the review of the Dalai Lama's *The Art of Happiness* by Richard Bernstein (*New York Times*, October 7th, 1999).

affected. In other words, an ecosystem is a collection of interdependent causes and results, existing in an interconnected world.

## Karma and the Butterfly Effect

Another way to understand interconnectedness is through the principle of Karma. To a Buddhist, Karma is the law of causation and is dependent on the interconnectedness of phenomena. Karma does not deal with any notion of justice. It deals with what is, with what causes what. Simply stated, all the actions a person undertakes have consequences.

Think of the "Butterfly Effect." The Butterfly Effect goes back to nineteenth-century mathematicians and chaos theory, but some of us remember it from the movie with Ashton Kutcher.[2] Like Karma, the Butterfly Effect is based on the idea that all causes are interconnected. The Butterfly Effect typically deals with time travel, and the idea that changing something of seemingly miniscule import (like killing a butterfly) can have drastic consequences in the future (like a completely altered world). While the Buddhist does not advocate building a time machine, the principle of a single event having future consequences is the essence of Karma. But a Buddhist's understanding of Karma and suffering is deeper than any notion of time travel, so while a fictional Sci-Fi character goes back in time to keep the butterfly from being killed, the Buddhist never kills the butterfly to begin with.

A Buddhist recognizes the cause of suffering and puts an end to it. She recognizes that causes and results are interdependent and to stop a result, she must stop its cause. Let's say you are getting ready to watch your DVD of *Kill Bill Volume 2*. You put the DVD in the player, turn on the TV, and hit *play*. But you see static rather than the *Kill Bill* menu. What is the cause? Eventually you realize you forgot to hit "*TV/Video*" so the TV is not reading from the proper input. You hit the appropriate button, and, *voilà*, you can watch *Kill Bill* in peace! You have also just understood and utilized the Buddhist principle of Karma:

---

[2] *The Butterfly Effect*, directed by Bress and Gruber, 2004. Alternately, one could have recognized the concept in the Ray Bradbury story "A Sound of Thunder," in *The Golden Apples of the Sun* (New York: Bantam, 1970), pp. 88–100.

you recognized the cause (your failure to hit the *TV/Video* button) of a specific result (a screen of static instead of the *Kill Bill* Menu). And you changed the result at the cause.

This is a microcosmic example that reflects the macrocosm. You might notice that the method of investigation in assessing causality is very scientific—testing a hypothesis and evaluating the evidence—and includes the assumptions of psychological as well as physical reality. Have you ever felt like you had static in your head? A constant buzzing confusion that drove you crazy? Buddhism wants to show you the way to reduce the suffering caused by this static, to calm it down, to channel it and to transform it into happiness and enlightenment. Buddhists hold that negative emotions like anger, sorrow, pride, and annoyance are the cause of psychological suffering, mental static. Such emotions can potentially lead to physical suffering: anger commonly leads to violence, for example. A Buddhist, understanding suffering as an unwanted result, stops it at the cause, and is therefore on the road to enlightenment since (remember) the path to enlightenment is the path out of suffering.

## The Impermanent Emptiness of Pai-Mei

Life for the Buddhist is impermanent, always in flux and never static. Not only is everything interconnected and related to everything else, but the "things" that make up the interconnected whole are fleeting, which is why when you try to obtain them, you suffer. You cannot grasp, strangle, or lock up the world. If you're attached to something—an idea, a time in your life, a reality—you will experience suffering.

Are you the same person you were ten years ago? It's safe to say that you're much different, since your physical appearance, likes, and dislikes have changed. Are you the same person you were one week ago? Your life has changed since then too. And what about yesterday? Or one second ago? To a Buddhist, you're continually changing. Buddhism does not posit a soul like the Judeo-Christian tradition; there is no concrete essence that makes you you. This is part of the Buddhist concept of *emptiness*, which is deeply related to interconnection. The world we experience is the connection and complement of "things" that are themselves relations of the whole. There is no stable thing "chair." A chair is a certain relationship between yourself and the material it's built out of. This chair is made out of wood, but there are chairs made out of plastic and metal. This chair is brown, but there are black and red chairs too. This chair is tall and rocks, while other chairs are short and stiff. The chair is the relationship of properties and not a template that is filled by a catalogue of features.

Take Beatrix Kiddo. Who is she? What is she? Is she a mother? Is she a cute blonde? Is she a sword fighter? An American? Tall? Smart? To a Buddhist, Beatrix is not any one of these things. We can take away the characteristics, but we will not get to the one thing that defines Beatrix. Like the chair, she is impermanent, constantly changing. And, yes, even the object of our envy and admiration, the wise master Pai-Mei, is impermanent. There are two perceptions of reality for a Buddhist, known as the two-fold truth. There is the *partial*, material, independent reality where we find chairs, Kiddos, and Pai-Meis. Then there is emptiness, the *complete* level of reality where all things are, in fact, interconnected.

There are consequences to understanding reality only on the superficial level: when Beatrix finds out that she's pregnant, Bill suffers as a result of her desire to change her life. Beatrix leaves him, and this brings great sorrow and anger to Bill. Trying to imprison Beatrix, to keep her in a changeless box—an impossible feat—Bill suffers immensely. His violent actions—shooting Beatrix in the face, among other things—continue the cycle of suffering, and in the end do not lead to Bill's enlightenment (or even happiness in the Western sense of the word) but to his ultimate demise.

## The Origin of Beatrix's Suffering

The Buddhist recognizes that she is suffering. She recognizes that she is in an interconnected world. She recognizes Karma. Part of her understanding of these things involves emptiness, the idea that everything in the world—her personality, the chair, Pai-Mei—is impermanent. With these understandings she can begin her path to enlightenment by cutting off the cause of her suffering.

What about Beatrix? Does she recognize her suffering? Is she part of an interconnected world? Does she understand Karma? Emptiness? Impermanence?

Beatrix is no stranger to suffering. From the first scene in *Kill Bill Volume 1*, the viewer hears her unsteady breathing, sees her bruised and bloody face: confined to a hospital bed in a darkened room, she's like a goldfish out of water, desperately trying to breathe. She suffers physically—she was shot in the face by Bill, after all. And this causes her to suffer psychologically; it causes her to seek revenge. If she did not undergo psychological suffering, we would expect her to wake up in the hospital four years after the Massacre at Two Pines and simply get on with her life. But the first thing she does is cry at her memories, at the loss of her baby. What is causing her to suffer? She sees the cause of her suffering as Bill's assassination squad. They're the ones that killed her baby, massacred her wedding, and put her in a coma for four years. How will she alleviate her suffering? Like a good Buddhist, she will eliminate her perception of the cause. Namely, eliminate Bill and the assassination squad.

## Beatrix's Interconnected World

So Beatrix recognizes her suffering. But is the world of *Kill Bill* interconnected? Surely it is. Any fan of Quentin Tarantino knows and appreciates his use of nonlinear plotlines in the movies he directs,[3] and the *Kill Bill* series is no exception. Although the plotline is nonlinear, it is by no means disconnected.

This doesn't mean that the viewer will necessarily see the connectedness of the plot on the first viewing; it might take several. In fact, there are times when the plotline *appears* disconnected. For example, the viewer might wonder why Beatrix is in the hospital *after* killing Vernita in the kitchen. Has something happened to land her in the hospital since Vernita's death?

But as the movie progresses, a seemingly disconnected plotline is shown to be connected, and the viewer is aware of being shown a connected plot in a disconnected fashion. The observant viewer will see that when Beatrix crosses Vernita off of her list, O-Ren *is already crossed off*. O-Ren's death, of course, doesn't occur until the very end of the movie.

---

[3] Directs, as opposed to writes or produces. He wrote *From Dusk Till Dawn* (directed by Robert Rodriguez, 1996) and executive-produced *Hostel* and *Hostel: Part II* (both directed by Eli Roth, 2005 and 2007) each of which were linear.

Someone might ask how a nonlinear plotline even relates to interconnectedness. Is nonlinearity alone evidence for inter-connectedness? The answer is no, not necessarily. But nonlin-earity can be more conducive to revealing interconnectedness than linearity. By showing events out of a linear sequence, the relation between two events can sometimes be seen more clearly.

Budd captures Beatrix and gives her a "Texas Funeral" in which she is shot with rock salt and buried alive in a nailed-down coffin. We fear for Beatrix's life until, in a flashback, we learn of the close-punch technique taught to her by Pai-Mei. Beatrix's ability to escape Budd's grave reverts back to her learning of the technique. That is, the result (Beatrix's escape from the grave) is dependent on the cause (Pai-Mei's teaching her the technique). Now, had these two interconnected events been shown in a linear order, they would have been separated by so much time as to make the connection between them less conspicuous.

One of the more memorable things about *Kill Bill Volume 2* is the Five Point Palm Exploding Heart Technique. Besides being a cool-sounding phrase, the Five Point Palm Exploding Heart Technique gives us another example of the intercon-nected world of *Kill Bill*. What allows Beatrix to dispose of Bill and complete her gruesome cycle of revenge is her knowledge of the Five Point Palm Exploding Heart Technique. The result (killing Bill) is dependent on the cause (her learning of the tech-nique from Pai-Mei). Again, would the connection between these two events be as obvious without Tarantino's use of non-linear plotting?

Karma, too (being related to interconnectedness), is signifi-cant. The movie's story is a telling example of Karma. Beatrix suffers because she has been beaten and shot by Bill and his gang. How does she stop this suffering? She eliminates the cause. She eliminates those people who caused her to suffer. The actions of Bill and his gang have consequences: being hunted down by Beatrix.

Although Budd is on Beatrix's list of people to kill, he is already the recipient of Karma in *Kill Bill Volume 2*. He was a murderous killer, part of Bill's infamous gang. And where is he now? He's a low-life living in a trailer park, working as a would-be bouncer in a less than auspicious titty bar. His boss, who snorts coke and resides in a filthy office, barely treats Budd like a human being and is all over his case for being a few minutes late. Even the strippers disrespect Budd, one of whom tells him, "Hey Budd, honey, the toilet's at it again. There's shitty water all over the floor," to which he can only respond, "I'll take care of it, Suzy-Pie." There are causes and results in the world of *Kill Bill*: Budd killed people; now he's a low-life. His actions—since actions have consequences—led his life to its shameful conclusion.

Budd acknowledges both his and Beatrix's place in an interconnected world. "That woman deserves her revenge. We deserve to die," he says while talking to Bill outside his trailer. Curiously, he follows this up with, "Then again, so does she." Budd makes it easy for us by pointing out the Karma. Sure Beatrix has been wronged, but she has killed so many people (she *was* a trained killer) that she is as likely to be hunted down and killed as is Bill.

## Beatrix's Knowledge of the Interconnected World

So the world of the *Kill Bill*s is interconnected, so what? What does this say about Beatrix's enlightenment? Well, part of being a Buddhist is having an understanding of the interconnectedness of the world, an understanding of Karma. There is evidence that Beatrix has such an understanding.

Beatrix kills Vernita in her own kitchen after Vernita's daughter, Nikki, comes home from school. Afterwards Beatrix notices Nikki in the doorway—she has evidently watched the murder of her mother. While cleaning off her bloody knife, Beatrix says, "It was not my intention to do this in front of you. . . . When you grow up, if you still feel raw about it, I'll be waiting." Beatrix's words here imply an understanding of Karma and interconnectedness. In the same way that the cause of Beatrix's suffering lies with Bill and the assassination squad, the cause of Nikki's suffering lies with Beatrix. Thus Beatrix declares that she will be waiting.

Beatrix seems to indicate that there is no right action, only causes and results. We would expect Nikki to seek satisfaction in killing Beatrix. Beatrix acknowledges her place in an interconnected world of cause and result, even if she is the cause of another's pain. We can see how two cycles of revenge interconnect: Beatrix's plot for revenge could cause the lust for revenge to grow in Nikki. (Will there be a movie called *Kill Kiddo* in which Nikki is the protagonist, relentlessly hunting down Beatrix?) This scene shows Beatrix's acknowledgement of her status as a possible recipient of Karma, but she is nonetheless driven to end her suffering, to kill Bill.

## Beatrix's "Nature"

Bill discusses Beatrix's status as a killer in one of the last scenes of *Kill Bill Volume 2*. He tells a story of Superman and Clark Kent. Clark Kent, he says, was Superman's disguise, and not the other way around. Superman was superhuman and so he felt awkward, out of place, a stranger as Clark Kent. In the same way, Bill continues, Beatrix is a natural born killer (Tarantino patting himself on the back for writing *Natural Born Killers?*)[4]. He points out all the people she's killed to get to Bill; he points out the sadistic nature of her past.

Bill is saying that people have a nature that cannot be changed. One is reminded of the nature-nurture debate that— when it does show up in philosophy—typically surfaces in the Philosophy of Science. The nature side says what Bill does: our genes and biological factors primarily determine our complex range of behaviors. The nurture side says our behaviors are determined, largely by our environment. It's possible that the environment alone made Beatrix a killer, but Bill says "natural born," clearly positioning him on the nature side.

As we said, to a Buddhist everything is impermanent, so Beatrix as a natural born (nature) killer does not make sense, nor would it make sense to characterize her as a naturally conditioned (nurture) killer.[5] What Beatrix is is constantly changing, as the Buddhist world is constantly changing. So Bill is wrong here. Much as Clark Kent and Superman (or Peter Parker and Spiderman) are aspects of a single reality, Buddhism, as we said, posits the two-fold truth: the partial perception of superficial reality and the ultimate perception of emptiness. Beatrix

---

[4] Directed by Oliver Stone, 1994.

[5] On the superficial perception of reality Buddhism recognizes nature and nurture as significant factors that can be overcome by a deeper perception of reality.

and Bill perceive the world only at the conventional level, that of stable and concrete independent things. They are ignorant of the great power they possess to transform themselves and their karma.

   To illustrate, imagine that your mind is a plot of land or a garden which has been planted with positive and negative seeds. It is up to you to water the right seeds in order to convert anger, fear, and jealously into compassion and right actions. If you understand this, when your roommate yells at you for eating the last microwave burrito, you know she is acting that way because she is suffering. You can relate to her suffering, and instantly, you are closer and have compassion for the person. The knowledge of why someone is suffering—divorce, disease, attachment—creates empathy in you for that person, and you don't return with negative actions. If Beatrix adopted this perspective, then she would water those positive seeds and not seek revenge.

## Show Some Compassion for Buddha's Sake

In order to be enlightened, a person must be compassionate. Compassion is a natural growth of the understanding of interdependence. Buddhist compassion is not selective; a Buddhist must show compassion towards all living creatures from ants to aunts to elephants. She must also minimize the amount of suffering she causes to any sentient creature.

   Clearly, cutting off Sophie's arm of in front of O-Ren is no sign of compassion. Beatrix herself, before killing Vernita in the kitchen, says, "It's mercy, and compassion, and forgiveness I lack." To follow the Buddhist path Beatrix has to be compassionate and she just isn't. She doesn't have a genuine concern for living creatures. At the beginning of this chapter we mentioned the Dalai Lama, who said that the Buddha permitted killing under certain circumstances. Unfortunately for Beatrix's enlightenment, killing for revenge is not one of those circumstances. Conditions that might merit killing in Buddhism are typically ones in which the only way to avert the death of a certain number of sentient beings is to kill a lesser number. Beatrix was not faced with such a situation and under no Buddhist system is her relentless bloodbath acceptable.

## You're Kidding Yourself, Kiddo—or Is She?

Beatrix lives in the interconnected, interdependent world of *Kill Bill* where the law of causation (Karma) is in full effect. On one level she understands *her* interconnectedness with the world and her place in it. Unfortunately, she doesn't see the extent of interconnectedness. Her understanding is limited. She sees Bill and the assassination squad as the cause of her suffering, so she kills Bill and the assassination squad. What she doesn't see is that this is only a band-aid and that more suffering will occur.

What if someone else massacres her next wedding? Will she go on another rampage? Is she completely free from suffering now? A Buddhist would answer "No" since a Buddhist can see deeper than superficial causes and results to emptiness. To truly end suffering, Beatrix has to look inside and begin to eliminate that internal static. Now we understand her lack of compassion: her lack of a true understanding of interdependence does not allow compassion to grow.

But Beatrix can be enlightened yet. In Buddhism, when an organism dies, it is reincarnated as another organism. It's common to present this idea through the metaphor of a candle: the dull, flickering flame of an old candle (the dying organism) is transferred to the flame of a new candle (the reincarnation of the dead organism). Buddhists believe that the impermanence of life continues beyond death. There is no self; a person is not the same person he was a year ago or ten minutes ago. Each moment gives rise to another, and another, and another—and in this there is a momentum that carries beyond death. It is this momentum that is reborn. There is an ordering principle (your mind) that gives you your identity and perspective. It is birthless and deathless, continually manifesting itself in sentient beings. So if Beatrix can't be enlightened in this life, then maybe she can in the next. Or the one after that. If Beatrix is able to cultivate the right wisdom and compassion—if she can water the right seeds—then she can be enlightened in some future rebirth.

Another concept we haven't mentioned yet is Buddha Nature.[6] Because all creatures possess Buddha Nature (the potential to be enlightened), all creatures can, of course, potentially be enlightened. So, yes, Beatrix can be enlightened, but so can Charles Manson, and so can Buddy. Over many rebirths, Beatrix can possibly attain enlightenment as she comes to understand the ultimate nature of reality and follows the Buddhist path.

## Sudden Enlightenment

But there's yet another route for Beatrix. In Zen Buddhism, there are two roads to enlightenment: a sudden or instant one and a gradual trajectory towards enlightenment.[7] The idea in sudden enlightenment is that a person reaches Nirvana instantly without rebirths, without a lifetime of practice, and with little cultivation of Buddhist principles. The problem is that it's very, very, very difficult. Sudden enlightenment is the realization of your own Buddha Nature, that peace and enlightenment are dormant within you. It is not something "over there" that you work towards but an actualization of the joy that has been covered by the deluded mind and attachment. It's also easy for people to claim that they're enlightened when they're clearly not. Monks, in fact, are examined by their teachers to verify claims of enlightenment and levels of understanding.

Beatrix's possible case for sudden enlightenment is in the last scene in *Kill Bill Volume 2*. She's just killed Bill, and she's in a hotel with her daughter, with whom she's been reunited after four years. As her daughter watches TV, Beatrix rolls around on the bathroom floor in ecstasy with the door closed. She's laughing. She's crying with joy. She's in a new world of emotion. There is an old Zen saying: "If you're not laughing, you're not getting it." So is Beatrix enlightened?

We decline to give a definitive answer as there may not be one. We leave the decision to the reader. But we leave the

---

[6] Buddha Nature is a complicated concept in Buddhism. For further reading see B. King Sallie, *Buddha Nature* (New York: State University of New York Press, 2007).

[7] These divergent paths are a source of tension in Buddhism. See for example Sam Van Schaik, *Approaching the Great Perfection* (Somerville: Wisdom, 2004).

reader who answers in the affirmative with the following thoughts: how will Beatrix respond to Vernita's daughter, Nikki, if she seeks revenge in the future? If Beatrix does anything but extend a compassionate hand to Nikki, she is not enlightened.[8]

---

[8] There's a story in Buddhism of Angulimala, a killer turned Buddhist monk. When the relatives of his victims attacked and eventually killed him, he did not fight back, having undergone an inner transformation. For a modern account see Satish Kumar, *The Buddhist and the Terrorist: The Story of Angulimala* (Totnes: Green Books, 2005).

# Our Names Don't Mean Shit!

**AARON C. ANDERSON** is a Ph.D. student in Literature at the University of California, San Diego. In between consuming tasty meals at Big Kahuna Burger and debating the esoteric meanings of obscure song lyrics to K-Billy's Super Sounds of the 1970s, he studies hip-hop and reggae culture, theoretical and applied Marxism, and psychoanalysis with an eye to contemporary U.S. and Japanese film studies.

**TRAVIS ANDERSON** is Associate Professor of Philosophy and former Director of International Cinema at Brigham Young University. He generally publishes on topics involving the phenomenology of art, film, and architecture. His response to grumbling students is to paraphrase Mr. White: "You complain to me in a dream, you'd better wake up and apologize."

**RANDALL AUXIER** lives in the French Quarter of "Illinois," which is a corruption of a Native American word for "boring, endless fields of maize." There are two notable features of his hometown of Carbondale, a university at which he teaches, and a small cinema which shows only French films and Tarantino movies. He may be found in attendance at one of the two, but not both.

**MICHAEL BRUCE** holds multiple degrees in philosophy and hopes to make it as a professional Ninja. If that does not work out, he plans to fall back on his safety occupation—acting.

**MARK T. CONARD** is Assistant Professor of Philosophy at Marymount Manhattan College in New York City. He's the co-editor of *The Simpsons and Philosophy* (2001) and *Woody Allen and Philosophy* (2004), and editor of *The Philosophy of Film Noir* (2005), *The Philosophy of Neo-Noir* (2006), *The Philosophy of Martin Scorsese* (2007), and *The Philosophy of the Coen Brothers* (2008). He is also the author of the novel, *Dark as Night* (2004). Though he has no cool reptilian codename, in his spare time Mark likes to play the wooden flute and practice the Five Point Palm Exploding Heart Technique.

**LUKE CUDDY** is a graduate student at San Diego State University. He is currently editing *The Legend of Zelda and Philosophy*, due for publication in 2008. Nerd that he is, reading philosophy and playing video games take up most of his time. Of course, since he experiences time nonlinearly he often loses track of what activity he's engaged in.

**RICHARD GREENE** is Associate Professor of Philosophy at Weber State University. He received his Ph.D. in Philosophy from the University of California, Santa Barbara. He has published papers in epistemology, metaphysics, and ethics. Richard would eventually like to learn the Five Point Palm Exploding Heart Technique, because his Hattori Hanzo butterknife doesn't quite do the trick.

**DAVID KYLE JOHNSON** received his PhD in Philosophy from the University of Oklahoma and is currently an Assistant Professor of Philosophy at King's College in Wilkes-Barre Pennsylvania. His philosophical specializations include philosophy of religion, logic, and metaphysics. He also co-authored a chapter in *Johnny Cash and Philosophy*. Additionally he has done work on *South Park*, *Family Guy*, *The Matrix* and *The Office*. He has taught many classes that focus on the relevance of philosophy to pop culture, including a course devoted to *South Park*. (One that incorporates Tarantino is in the works.) Lastly, Kyle doesn't tip—he says he don't believe in it.

**KEITH ALLEN KORCZ** is Assistant Professor of Philosophy at the University of Louisiana at Lafayette. He has published in *The Canadian Journal of Philosophy*, *The Journal of Social Philosophy* and *The American Philosophical Quarterly*. If he's curt with you, it's because time is a factor. However, he is utterly convinced that any time of the day is a good time for pie.

**K. SILEM MOHAMMAD** is the author of three books of poetry: *Deer Head Nation* (Tougher Disguises, 2003), *A Thousand Devils* (Combo Books, 2004), and *Breathalyzer* (Edge Books, 2007). He is co-editor (also with Richard Greene) of *The Undead and Philosophy: Chicken Soup for the Soulless* (2006). He teaches literature and creative writing at Southern Oregon University—his office is the one that says "Bad Motherfucker."

**BENCE NANAY** is Assistant Professor of Philosophy at Syracuse University and Visiting Assistant Professor at the University of British Columbia, Vancouver every spring. There is an uncanny resemblance between Bence and Fabienne from *Pulp Fiction* in that both are European and both adore blueberry pancakes. Bence, however, unlike Fabienne, knows what Choppers are.

**RACHEL ROBISON** (DiVAS codename: Gopher Snake) is a graduate student in the philosophy department at UMass Amherst. She does research in metaphysics and epistemology, and has published papers in epistemology. She drives a tricked-out sedan known as "The Scaredy-Cat Wagon."

**TIMOTHY DEAN ROTH** is a Philosopher and Life Artist from the scenic town of Ridgefield, Washington. As a Farmer on the Field of Consciousness, he believes he majored in epistemology at Wheaton College but is not one hundred percent certain about that. He received his BMF in Theology at Duke University. Occasionally Tim has been mistaken for Mr. Orange, or Pumpkin, or even Ringo. As a cab driver for the Washington State DSHS, Tim would much rather "continue this theological discussion in the car" than "in the jailhouse with the cops."

**BRUCE RUSSELL** is Professor of Philosophy at Wayne State University, home of Edmund Gettier in 1963 (there are pictures of him on the wall in the Commons Room, though some say it's just a picture of a double with Gettier hiding behind him). Russell writes on the philosophical limits of film, the problem of evil, *a priori* justification, epistemic and moral duty, contextualism, the killing/letting-die distinction, and other topics in ethics and epistemology. He has heard his colleagues talk about some other philosopher named B. Russell who is obviously trying to steal his reputation. If the real B. Russell ever meets up with the imposter, he will ask him to massage his feet and then will throw him off a balcony if he does.

**IAN SCHNEE** is a graduate student in the philosophy department at UC Berkeley, as well as a wannabe screenwriter. His most prized possession is his father's gold ashtray.

**JAMES H. SPENCE** is Assistant Professor of Philosophy at Adrian College in Michigan, though his students know him only as "Mr. Shades of Grey". He is interested in moral and political philosophy, and is the author of "What Nietzsche Could Teach You" in *Movies and the Meaning of Life: Philosophers Take on Hollywood* (2005). When he isn't philosophizing, arguing about tipping, or watching Tarantino movies he travels and goes camping with his daughter, Daphne. He likes to believe that he tips well, acts like a professional, and don't want to kill anybody.

**JOSEPH ULATOWSKI** is Visiting Assistant Professor of Philosophy at Weber State University. He did a six-year stretch at the U (that's the University of Utah) for impersonating a philosopher, a two-year stretch before that at Ole Miss for a crime he didn't commit, and a five-year stretch before that at Methodist College for aiding and abetting a professional golfer. He's unsure of his future, but what his current P.O. doesn't know about Joe won't hurt him (unless he finds out).

# Any of You Fucking Pricks Move, I'll Index Every Motherfucking Last One of You!

advice, practical, 6
Alabama (character from *True Romance*), 57, 70
    ECDS of, 156
Alcibiades, 3
Alighieri, Dante, 87, 92
    *on contrapasso*, 87
    on God's nature, 87
    Hell of, 86
    on Lukewarm, 88
*America* (Baudrillard), 15
Angel Eyes (character from *The Good, the Bad, and the Ugly*), 133
Angulimala, 201n8
Antwan Rockamore (character from *Jackie Brown*), 71
*Apocalypse Now!*, 35
Apollonian power, 23, 31
    dismemberment of, 32
    Nietzsche on, 33
aporia, 112
    in *Jackie Brown*, 116
Aquinas, Thomas, 87
    on God's nature, 87
    on self-defense, 93
Aristotle, 22, 82
    on accidents, 138
    on action, 124
    on audience, 128
    on "global mean," 82

    on incontinence, 134
    on "poetic art," 123
    on revenge, 90
    on "Uncaused Cause," 87
Arquette, Patricia. *See* Alabama
Asian Philosophy, xi, 63–65
aspect-change, 114
    duck-rabbit as, 113
    in *Jackie Brown*, 114, 116
aspect perception, 112

Baudrillard, Jean
    on America, 15, 18
    on "historical centrality," 17
    on hyperreality, 14
    on simulation, 16
BB (character from *Kill Bill*), 94
Beatrix Kiddo (character from *Kill Bill*), 5, 61
    as agent of God, 90
    Bill and, duel between, 94
    break from Bushido by, 65
    Buddhism and, 193–201
    Budd on revenge of, 80
    as child, 89
    as cowgirl, 170
    "death list" of, 85
    discovery of BB, 94, 174
    as Eastwood, 170
    ECDS of, 155, 157

in *Reservoir Dogs,* 152–53, 156,
157
Tarantino's treatment of,
155–59
in *True Romance,* 156–57
of Vernita Green, 155, 157
of Vincent Vega, 158
exploitation cinema, 15
expression, 126
"Ezekiel 25:17," 55, 60, 63, 91,
137$n$20
as meaningless vehicle of
intimidation, 181
new interpretation of, 186

family honor, 134
*Faster, Pussycat! Kill! Kill!,* 17
father
Bill as, 168
as God, 173
as hero, 168
killing, 173
*Fistful of Dollars,* 39
"Five Point Palm Exploding Heart
Technique," 95, 174
interconnectedness and, 195
Fonda, Bridget. *See* Melanie
*For a Few Dollars More,* 39
Formula of Humanity, 78, 80
Formula of Universal Law, 78–79
*Forrest Gump,* 26
Forster, Robert. *See* Max Cherry
Fox, Vivica A. *See* Vernita Green

*Game of Death,* 59
*The Gay Science* (Nietzsche), 181
Gerstad, Harry, 35
Gibbard, Allan, 9
Gibson, Mel, 125, 126, 127
Gladstein, Richard, 25
Glaucon (character from *Republic*),
151
Glover, Jonathan, 45
Go-Go (character from *Kill Bill*), 76,
77
qualities of, 165, 166

utilitarian perspective on, 77
"golden rule," 86, 92–93
*Gone in 60 Seconds,* 16
*The Good, the Bad, and the Ugly,*
135$n$15
Mexican Stand-off in, 133
Gordon Liu. *See* Pai Mei
gravity, law of, 146
Grier, Pam. *See* Jackie Brown
*Grindhouse,* 14
*Grosse Pointe Blank,* 25

Hammurabi's law code, 86
Hannah, Daryl, 5. *See also* Driver,
Elle
Hare, R.M.
on morality, 10, 11
on universal prescriptivism,
10
harm principle, 102, 103
Hart, H.L.A., 104
Hattori Hanzo (character from *Kill
Bill*), 65, 70
homosexual overtones of, 167
as moral conscience, 90
on punishment, 71
on revenge, 90
*Henry and June,* 168
*High Noon,* 35
Hitchcock, Alfred, 37, 130
Hobbes, Thomas, 67$n$10
on mercy, 67
on vengeance, 66–67
*Hogan's Heroes,* 170
"Hollywood ending," 135
Honey Bunny (character in *Pulp
Fiction*), 62, 183
ECDS of, 158
hostages/hostage takers, 106
human nature, 5, 154
Hume, David, 142
on existence of God, 144
on miracles, 144, 145, 148
on morality, 11, 53
on virtues, 44
hyperreality, 15–17
Baudrillard on, 14

as truth-telling, 88

Vernita Green (character from *Kill Bill*), 5, 165
death of, 76, 89
ECDS of, 155, 157

Vincent Vega (character from *Pulp Fiction*), 5, 62
bathroom and, 137–38, 184
chance events and, 183
character flaws in, 136
ECDS of, 158
on facts, 111–12
failure to become creator of meaning by, 184
on foot massages, 147
on "freak occurrences," 179
McGuffin of, 139
morality of, 9–10, 11
negativity of, 187
nihilism of, 182
on philosophy, 65
on punishment, 71
as "sophisticated unbeliever," 181
values of, xii, 180
weakness of, 182

Vinnie Barbarino (character from *Welcome Back Kotter*), 131n8

violence, 177
cycle in *Pulp Fiction,* 185–86
music and, 34

Virtue Ethical theory, 82

virtues
artificial, 44, 45
of Beatrix Kiddo, 81
Hume on, 44
natural, 44

Wagner, Richard, 35
Weinberger, Stephen, 37
Weinstein, Harvey, 34
*Welcome Back Kotter*, 131
*The Wicked Dreams of Paula Schultz*, 170
Williams, Elmo, 35
Willis, Bruce. *See* Butch
Winston Wolf (character from *Pulp Fiction*), 134
Wittgenstein, Ludwig, 113, 121
on aspect perception, 112
thought-experiments of, 113
World War I, 46
wrongness
Gibbard on, 9
Mill on, 8–9

Yolanda. *See* Honey Bunny

Zemeckis, Robert, 26
Zinneman, Fred, 35